THE ILLUSTRATED GUIDE TO THE COLLECTIBLES OF Coca-Cola

Trade-mark ®

ALSO BY CECIL MUNSEY

The Illustrated Guide to Collecting Bottles

THE ILLUSTRATED GUIDE TO THE COLLECTIBLES OF

by Cecil Munsey

HAWTHORN BOOKS, INC.
PUBLISHERS / *New York*

This book was manufactured in the United States of America and published simultaneously in Canada by Prentice-Hall of Canada, Limited, 1870 Birchmount Road, Scarborough, Ontario.
Library of Congress Catalog Card Number: 71-39276.

3 4 5 6 7 8 9 10

To Wilbur G. Kurtz, Jr., archivist of The Coca-Cola Company, who has devoted his entire working life to the collecting and preserving of the history and memorabilia of Coca-Cola

ACKNOWLEDGMENTS

It takes more than an author to make a book such as this a reality.

To my wife Dolores and my son Cecil III, who not only continue to love and honor a husband and father but also help in many ways to make my creative attempts possible, I wish to express my deepest love and gratitude.

To Paul F. Evans, former publisher and editor, who encouraged me, in 1967, to write about the great firm that produces Coca-Cola, I am especially grateful.

To Louis A. Fournier, my friend and the person who patiently reads my work and offers the severe criticism necessary to ensure an accurate, consistent, and logical development, I express deep gratitude.

Wilbur G. Kurtz, Jr., archivist of The Coca-Cola Company and his able and willing assistants, Margaret Hopper and Mary Jane Thompson, have contributed many hours helping me assemble much of the material presented in this book. Their patience, help, and encouragement are most gratefully acknowledged.

Joseph W. Jones, William Bass, and William Pruett, all executives of The Coca-Cola Company, deserve special thanks for their assistance.

To the people who operate The Coca-Cola Bottling Company of San Diego, California, I offer my gratitude. Without the cooperation of Jeannie Rivkin, who created and maintains this firm's fine museum, and the cooperation of the chief executives of the firm, A. B. Polinsky and Art Rivkin, many of the photographs in this book would not have been possible.

To Bruce Aschenbrenner, of San Diego, California, and Tauni Brustin, of Los Angeles, California, who have both allowed me to photograph much of their impressive collections, I am especially grateful.

It is with pleasure that I acknowledge a special debt of gratitude to Carmen Roenker, of Santee, California, for her assistance in preparing my final manuscript.

I am also indebted to the following publications: *The Coca-Cola Bottler, The Refresher Magazine, Soft Drinks Magazine* (formerly the *National Bottlers' Gazette*), and *Whistl'n Dixie.*

I am especially obliged to Harold J. Terhune, of East Point, Georgia, for photography. All photographs credited "Archives, The Coca-Cola Company, Atlanta, Georgia," are the work of Mr. Terhune. Other professionals who have contributed and deserve thanks are: Chris's Studio of Photography, Roseburg, Oregon;

Nostalgia Photos, Inc., Los Angeles, California; Herman "Bill" Berner, San Diego, California; Richard P. Daley, Rochester, New York; and Lou Alvarado, San Diego, California.

I owe special thanks to Photic of San Diego for turning my photographs into acceptable prints.

The following people also deserve thanks for their contributions to this work: Jack K. Rimalover, Stonybrook Associates, Princeton Junction, New Jersey; Sidney Voice, Consolidated Lithographing Company, Long Island, New York; Robert Gelink, Otento Collector's Shop, San Diego, California; Harald J. Torgesen, Savannah, Georgia; E. M. Smith, Smith's Antiques, San Diego, California; LeRoy S. Hanna, Coca-Cola Bottling Company, Roseburg, Oregon; Byron and Ann Underhill, Desert Coca-Cola Bottling Company, Las Vegas, Nevada; Roselyn Grosholz, Tole House Antiques, Erie, Pennsylvania; and Thurman Maness, Maness House, Inc., Valatie, New York.

Finally, I am especially grateful to the following people for their various contributions to the book: Harry L. Branchaud, San Leandro, California; Jim Cope, Orange, Texas; Harry W. Copleston, Kettering, Ohio; Dorothy Cutts, Huntsville, Alabama; A. "Ed" Degler, Poway, California; Gordon G. Esslinger, Huntsville, Alabama; William J. Forbes, Washington, D.C.; Jani Gardner, Cincinnati, Ohio; Susan Imhoff, San Diego, California; Edward Kilcline, Detroit, Michigan; Ray Klug, Akron, Ohio; Russ Leadabrand, Pasadena, California; David L. Pyne, Orlando, Florida; A. N. Shpil, Castro Valley, California; Thomas Sommerville, Orchard Park, New York; Dr. Burton Spiller, Rochester, New York; and Dr. Julian H. Toulouse, Hemet, California.

C. M.

CONTENTS

PART III. Production and Merchandising Items

PART IV. Advertising Items

INTRODUCTION

Coca-Cola has proved to be the most popular of all the cola beverages. The success of The Coca-Cola Company in marketing Coca-Cola has not only provided students of history with an interesting subject to study, but it has also provided collectors of Americana with a challenging hobby.

Beginning in the early 1930's a few collectors began to gather the interesting relics of The Coca-Cola Company; it is because of these early efforts that we can today enjoy many of the oldest objects used to produce and promote Coca-Cola. The 1940's and 1950's produced more collectors of Coca-Cola memorabilia, but the number was small compared to that of other collecting hobbyists.

Today there has been a surge of interest in collecting early advertising artifacts of many firms. Of all the collecting specialists those who specialize in memorabilia produced by The Coca-Cola Company are by far the most numerous.

The great variety of objects used by The Coca-Cola Company and its bottlers over the years number in the thousands because Coca-Cola is one of the most heavily advertised single products in the United States, and probably in the world. The giant beverage firm has, since its inception, been a leader in advertising; today its annual advertising budget approaches one hundred million dollars. Collectors therefore can be assured of constant activity because, in addition to the collectibles of the past, collectibles will be produced in the future.

Along with a recent interest in "nostalgia," the trend in collecting has moved toward the "new" antiques of the 1900-to-1950 period. Those interested in the history of The Coca-Cola Company and its artifacts will become one of the most important forces in collecting. Those people who are alert enough to participate in the initial stages of a relatively new specialty will be rewarded with extensive and sophisticated collections at bargain prices—even though some of the earliest and rarest items have risen in value as much as 1,200 percent in the last five years.

This book is extensive in its coverage of the history and collectibles of The Coca-Cola Company, but it is not a definitive or authorized history of that giant firm. Although assistance was provided by officials of The Coca-Cola Company, it was of a technical, *not* a philosophical, nature.

It is hoped that this book will satisfy the tremendous interest in the history of The Coca-Cola Company and its collectibles in recent years. This work is not exhaustive. It does, however, present many of the historic facts (and fancy) about The Coca-Cola Company, and it does picture a large variety of items with collecting possibilities.

The book was written for the collector/historian. It is divided into four parts and, in addition, contains an abundance of reference material in its four appendixes and the Selected Bibliography.

In Part I of the book an attempt has been made to answer the inevitable question: "What is Coca-Cola?" In addition to the answers provided in the initial section, the reader will find other answers sprinkled throughout the book.

Part II deals mostly with the chronological history of The Coca-Cola Company and Coca-Cola. Five of the chapters trace the history of Coca-Cola through discussions of the pioneers who started, developed, and otherwise built the business. Another chapter traces the history and discusses the trademarks of The Coca-Cola Company. The final chapter in Part II focuses on the early years of Coca-Cola, when it could have been considered a proprietary medicine as well as a soft drink.

In Part III seven chapters are devoted to the collectible items of The Coca-Cola Company that have to do with the actual production and merchandising of the product. An additional chapter is included which discusses the Standardization Committee and its effects on collecting.

Part IV, the largest section, deals with the advertising items of The Coca-Cola Company and its bottlers. It begins with a chapter devoted to the advertising history of the giant firm. The remaining twenty-five chapters discuss and picture the various items used to advertise Coca-Cola over the years. Each chapter presents items falling into an admittedly arbitrary category.

The book concludes with (1) four appendixes that will guide collectors and historians in numerous ways, including the important dating of artifacts; (2) a selected bibliography—all the references included were examined and felt to be of special interest to the reader; and (3) a comprehensive index.

It should be noted that the items pictured throughout the book represent only a portion of the collecting possibilities. In certain chapters the coverage in pictures is intentionally extensive, because the items represented are of particularly current interest. On the other hand, several chapters were given an extensive coverage in photography because these items have great collecting potential but have seldom, if ever, been presented as a total package.

Special attention is given in this book to *both* the beginning and the advanced collector. Both, it is hoped, will find the material comprehensive, clear, accurate, and logically developed. In addition, it is hoped that both groups will discover that for the first time they have an extensive coverage of the history and collectibles of The Coca-Cola Company.

I truly hope that this work will contribute to the continued growth and development of a fine hobby as well as bring pleasure to its readers. If such turns out to be the case, the five years of research and one year of writing involved have been worth the effort.

Part I

THE QUESTION

CHAPTER 1

WHAT IS COCA-COLA?

The above question is not an easy one to answer. According to a booklet produced by The Coca-Cola Company in 1916, *The Romance of Coca-Cola*, Coca-Cola is "Pure water sterilized by boiling. Sugar, granulated, best quality. Flavoring extracts and caramel. Caffein—the active principle of tea. Citric and phosphoric acids."

Company letterheads of around the turn of the century stated that Coca-Cola is a beverage based on "the tonic properties of the wonderful COCA PLANT and the famous COLA NUT."

Fortune magazine (July, 1931) claimed that Coca-Cola is 99 percent sugar and water. The other 1 percent, it maintained, is caramel; fruit flavors (lavender, fluid extract of guarana, lime juice, and various citrus oils); phosphoric acid; caffeine from tea, coffee, or chocolate; "Merchandise No. 5": three parts coca leaves (decocainized) and one part cola nut; and a secret ingredient, "7X." E. J. Kahn, Jr., in *The Big Drink*, adds, "Among the other ingredients that outsiders have claimed to have found in Coca-Cola are cinnamon, nutmeg, vanilla, and glycerin."

It could be stated, along the same lines, that Coca-Cola is a syrup generally made in 5,000-gallon batches, with each batch containing 28,000 pounds of sugar, or Coca-Cola is 1 ounce of syrup and $6^{1}/_{2}$ ounces of carbonated water mixed together and served chilled.

Coca-Cola is a carbonated beverage produced by a company that sells more soft drinks annually than its next six competitors combined. In

1971 Coca-Cola was the soft-drink leader, with a record of 1,634,700,000 cases sold, as compared to 662,500,000 cases of Pepsi-Cola, 271,400,000 cases of Seven-Up, 165,000,000 cases of Royal Crown Cola, and 164,100,000 cases of Dr. Pepper sold during the same period (Maxwell survey figures, in *Beverage Industry* magazine).

There are other answers to the question. Coca-Cola is the soft drink of which New York City alone consumes 14,000,000 cases every year, and of which Cairo, Egypt, consumes 1,000,000 cases every ten months.

Coca-Cola is the carbonated soft drink that inspired a Carrollton, Georgia, Coca-Cola route salesman to be married in his uniform, and another route salesman in Joplin, Missouri, to be buried in his.

Coca-Cola is, according to a doctor writing in the *Journal of Pediatrics*, a beverage containing xanthine, which is a substance found in caffeine that reduces intestinal contractions and, as a result, "soothes colicky infants."

Coca-Cola is a beverage that was provided to millions of servicemen during World War II by sixty-four overseas bottling plants—fifty-nine of them carried abroad at government expense.

Coca-Cola is a drink that was considered so valuable by servicemen during World War II that in the Solomon Islands a bottle sold for five dollars; in Casablanca a bottle sold for ten dollars; in Alaska a bottle sold for forty dollars; and in Italy in 1944 a bottle was raffled off for a charitable cause for four thousand dollars, with the winner so overcome with emotion that he couldn't drink it.

Coca-Cola is a drink so important to Americans that during World War II the Japanese radio tortured American servicemen by frequently describing the pleasure of drinking Coca-Cola.

Coca-Cola is the soft drink that Emperor Haile Selassie of Ethiopia used to import on the imperial plane from Cairo, Egypt, for palace use until a bottling plant was erected in Addis Ababa.

Coca-Cola is a drink so much favored by King Farouk of Egypt that he ordered it kept beside the table he had reserved in every night club in Cairo each evening.

Coca-Cola is a beverage that a sixty-five-year-old used-car salesman in Memphis, Tennessee, claimed he had drunk on the average of twenty-five times a day for fifty years.

Coca-Cola is a beverage consumed by a ninety-seven-year-old Alabama woman at exactly ten o'clock in the morning every day since it first appeared on the market in 1886. She attributed her longevity to the unusual habit.

Coca-Cola is the carbonated drink that, according to a survey, accounts for more transactions at service stations in the United States than motor oil.

Innovative people have used Coca-Cola as a furniture polish, chrome cleaner, fire extinguisher, and even as part of a hypo solution in developing photographs. While currently The Coca-Cola Company does not suggest auxiliary uses for Coca-Cola out of fear that such uses might tend to compromise its trademark, in past years several cookbooks have been produced promoting the beverage as something that could be blended with solid foodstuffs. Such publications are collectible today.

So it can be truly said in answer to the question, "What is Coca-Cola?," that it is, indeed, many things.

Part II

THE HISTORY OF THE COCA-COLA COMPANY

CHAPTER 2

JOHN S. PEMBERTON: INVENTOR OF COCA-COLA

Coca-Cola, a beverage that is consumed more than 150,000,000 times each day in well over 130 countries, can trace its roots back to 1886, the year that the world was introduced to A. Conan Doyle's master detective, Sherlock Holmes, and the Statue of Liberty was unveiled in New York harbor. The Coca-Cola Company, the largest single user of pure granulated sugar in the world and a company that spends well in excess of $75,000,000 annually advertising its products, actually began in the backyard of a two-story red-brick house at 107 Marietta Street in Atlanta, Georgia. The man responsible was John Styth Pemberton.

John Styth Pemberton was born in Knoxville, Georgia, in 1833 and early in life moved to Columbus, Georgia. In Columbus Pemberton grew up and received his basic education. Later, it is claimed, he obtained a degree in pharmacy at Macon, Georgia. Records do not substantiate this, and it is quite possible that Pemberton learned his trade as an apprentice. In 1853, at the age of twenty, he married Miss Clifford Lewis, also of Columbus.

Until the latter part of the Civil War, Pemberton worked in Columbus as a pharmacist. In June of 1864 he laid aside his mortar and pestle and organized Pemberton's Cavalry. He served as a captain under General Joe Wheeler for the remaining months of the war.

In 1869 Pemberton moved to Atlanta from Columbus and established himself as a wholesale druggist and pharmaceutical chemist. He began to manufacture and market his own original compounds. A year later, in 1870, he became associated with P. Wilson, Taylor & Company, druggists in Atlanta. Shortly thereafter, the firm became known as Pemberton, Wilson, Taylor & Company. By 1873 the firm had become the Pemberton Pulliam Drug Company, and early 1883 records reveal John Pemberton's next affiliation to be with the firm called Pemberton, Iverson & Denison. In 1885 he established the J. S. Pemberton Company, and shortly thereafter Pemberton established The Pemberton Chemical Company.

"Dr." Pemberton (as he became known among his associates) continued to develop, manufacture, and market the various compounds which he advertised as panaceas for a multitude of human frailties. His list of compounds, which were well known throughout the South, included Extract of Styllinger (a blood medicine), Gingerine, Globe of Flower Cough Syrup, Indian Queen Hair Dye, and Triplex Liver Pills.

While it has been speculated that the original idea for the mixture that would eventually become the drink known as Coca-Cola was planted in Pemberton's mind around 1880, the actual syrup was not created until 1886. It should be noted that much of what is known about the early years of Coca-Cola is a mixture of fact and fancy resulting from years of word-of-mouth narration. The first batch of what was to become Coca-Cola was mixed in a three-legged iron kettle in Pemberton's backyard in the spring of 1886. According to one historian, E. J. Kahn, Jr., in *The Big Drink*, the new syrup was a modification of a mixture which Pemberton had patented in 1885 as French Wine Coca, an "ideal nerve and tonic stimulant." Pemberton, according to this same writer, had taken out the wine and substituted a "pinch of caffeine," some extract of cola, and other oils.

If the atmosphere and measurements described above sound crude, it must be remembered that science during the nineteenth century had not progressed to the point it has today. Pemberton's equipment was simple; it is reported to have been merely a brass kettle, a percolator, measuring cups, ladles, apothecary scales, and the means for heating mixtures.

Again, according to the story, John Pemberton was trying to produce a headache cure. This seems to be verified by some of the early advertisements and advertising items pictured throughout this book. It will be readily noted that among other claims is one which states that Coca-Cola "relieves headaches immediately."

In 1885, when Pemberton was putting the final touches on his new discovery, his business had become known as the J. S. Pemberton Company. Pemberton had only one partner, a man named Edward W. Holland. On January 1, 1886, a new company was formed. The new firm was called the Pemberton Chemical Company, Inc. Holland was listed as president and J. S. Pemberton as secretary. Frank M. Robinson, who was later to play a vital role in the early development of the new product, came into this newly organized firm as bookkeeper.

It was on Saturday, May 8, 1886, that Pemberton took a jug of his new reddish-brown syrup to Willis E. Venable, the manager of the soda fountain at Jacobs' Pharmacy. Venable's soda fountain was the leading one in Atlanta in those days; it was an impressive twenty-five feet long and ranged along one side of the store. The space for the soda fountain was leased to Venable by Joseph Jacobs, who owned the drugstore. Pemberton had Venable mix the then unnamed syrup with water and taste it. Venable liked the taste and agreed to dispense it at his soda fountain.

A persistent but as yet unverifiable story of this early period is that Pemberton's new syrup was sold mixed with plain water until the morning of November 15, 1886. On that morning John G. Wilkes came to Jacobs' Pharmacy complaining of a terrible headache, the result of too much imbibing the night before. The story continues that a new clerk at the soda fountain mixed the Coca-Cola syrup with carbonated water by mistake and sold it to a surprised but pleased Wilkes. Apparently the mistake, if indeed it did happen, was a fortunate one because it thereafter became standard practice to mix Coca-Cola syrup with carbonated water, a practice continued to this day.

Venable's agreeing to sell the new product necessitated naming it. Within a few days "Coca-Cola" was chosen. The name was the result of a discussion between Pemberton, David D. Doe, Edward Holland, and Frank Mason Robinson, all associated with the Pemberton Chemical Company. It was Robinson, bookkeeper of the firm, who suggested the name "Coca-Cola Syrup and Extract." Robinson reasoned that choosing an alliterative compounding of the names "Coca" and "Cola" was good because they were two of the constituents of the new product. Robinson went even further and suggested the name be written in Spencerian script, a form of penmanship popular at the time. Pemberton liked both ideas, and after modifying the name to simply "Coca-Cola," adopted them.

Coca-Cola was first advertised on Saturday, May 29, 1886 in *The* (Atlanta) *Daily Journal.* While the name was used in the advertisement, the Spencerian script was not. It was a simple presentation stating: "Coca-Cola, Delicious! Refreshing! Exhilarating! Invigorating! The New and Popular Soda Fountain Drink, containing the properties of the wonderful Coca plant and the famous Cola nuts. For sale by Willis Venable *and Nunnally & Rawson*" (italics added). From the advertisement it can be seen that Venable was not the only one selling Coca-Cola at that time—approximately three weeks after the first drink had been mixed at Venable's soda fountain. On the same page of *The Daily Journal,* one column to the left, there are two advertisements for another famous soda water. One advertisement reads, "The marvelous Moxie Nerve Food on draught at H. C. Beerman's Soda Water Palace." The other reads, "Now is your chance to test the virtue of Moxie Nerve Food, on draught at H. C. Beerman's Soda Water Palace."

Coca-Cola was not an overnight success. During the first year only 25 gallons of the syrup, or enough for 3,200 drinks, were sold. That first year Pemberton spent on advertising more than the total earnings from the sales of his new product. He earned approximately $50 from sales, but according to the record, he invested exactly $73.96 in advertising. This unfortunate ratio of earnings and advertising costs was soon reversed.

For the first two years Coca-Cola did not enjoy much success, although sales had jumped from 25 gallons in 1886 to 1,049 gallons in 1887. Lack of money for promotion and failing health prevented Pemberton from aggressively marketing his new product. In July, 1887, Pemberton, because of illness and an accompanying need of money, offered to sell two-thirds interest in the Coca-Cola formula and accompanying rights to George S. Lowndes, a friend and former boarding-house roommate. Lowndes, although impressed with the offer, did not wish to become actively involved in the marketing of Coca-Cola. Lowndes went to Willis Venable, the manager of the soda fountain at Jacobs' Pharmacy who first dispensed Coca-Cola, and offered to go into partnership with him. Since Venable did not have the necessary money, Lowndes agreed to put up the required $1,200 for the two-thirds interest in Coca-Cola, and Venable agreed to conduct the business and pay his half of the $1,200 from the resulting profits. The document consummating the deal was signed on July 8, 1887, and stated that the $1,200 was a loan to John Pemberton. The loan, it stipulated, was to be repaid out of Pemberton's one-third of the profits. For some unknown reason the document was revised on July 15, 1887, to read that the loan to Pemberton was to be repaid out of the total profits rather than from Pemberton's share alone. Another stipulation of the contract was that the new partners were to assume ownership of all material and fixtures used by Pemberton in the manufacture of Coca-Cola, "paying the said Pemberton therefor [sic] the original cost." An inventory drawn up on July 21, 1887, indicated the physical assets associated with Coca-Cola were worth $283.39. Collectors and historians will find it interesting that the inventory mentioned a stencil plate and woodcut of the original Coca-Cola script designed by Frank Robinson and a considerable amount of advertising material, including posters, signs, and cards.

After the inventory was drawn up and Pemberton was paid the $283.39, Venable and Lowndes loaded the purchased equipment into a wagon and hauled it to Jacobs' Pharmacy, where Venable was to begin the manufacture of Coca-Cola.

According to Lowndes nothing much was done after that about the manufacture of the syrup. When Lowndes discovered a month or so later that there were a number of orders for the syrup unfilled because Venable was apparently unable to find the time to produce it, he proposed to Venable that one of them buy the other out.

As a result of the proposal, Lowndes became the sole owner of the two-thirds share he and Venable had owned together. Later records reveal that on December 14, 1887, Lowndes sold his entire interest in Coca-Cola to Woolfolk Walker, a salesman for the Pemberton Chemical Company, and Walker's sister, Mrs. M. C. Dozier, for exactly what he paid for it—$1,200.

In the next few months Walker, realizing he needed capital to get the business moving, contacted Joseph Jacobs, owner of Jacobs' Pharmacy, where the equipment to manufacture Coca-Cola was stored. He also contacted Asa Griggs Candler, owner of Asa G. Candler & Company, a wholesale and retail drug business.

The three men decided to form a company and to attempt to buy out the remaining one-third interest still held by Pemberton. The resulting firm was called Walker, Candler & Company. On April 14, 1888, this company purchased for $550 the remaining one-third of the rights to Coca-Cola from Pemberton. The deal was not what it appeared to be, however, because it was Candler who actually advanced the entire $550 for the Pemberton share and it was understood that the purchase was being made for him, individually. As of April 14, 1888, Candler theoretically owned one-third of Coca-Cola, and he is the man history credits with the founding of The Coca-Cola Company. In the words of his son, Charles Howard Candler, his father bought, on April 14, 1888, "a one-third interest in the formula of an almost completely unknown *proprietary elixir* [italics added] known as Coca-Cola." On April 17, 1888, only three days after Walker, Candler & Company had obtained the Pemberton share, Candler bought half of the interest owned by Woolfolk Walker and his sister for $750. This purchase gave Candler a legal one-third interest in Coca-Cola.

Pemberton, whose health worsened, died during the night of August 16, 1888. *The* (Atlanta) *Constitution* of August 18, 1888, reported that all the druggists in Atlanta paid tribute to Pemberton by closing their stores during the hour of the funeral. Upon word of Pemberton's death Candler called a meeting of the Atlanta druggists at his drugstore. Candler was appointed chairman of the committee that decided to close the drugstores during the funeral as a gesture of respect for the passing of their colleague.

Pemberton was survived by one son, Charles M. Pemberton, and his wife, Clifford. Charles was never active in his father's business. Charles died in 1894, and Clifford died in 1909.

Pemberton's death at the age of fifty-five robbed him of the pleasure of seeing Coca-Cola grow into a successful and popular soft drink.

John Styth Pemberton, who created the drink that was later to be called Coca-Cola (*Archives, The Coca-Cola Company, Atlanta, Georgia*)

Frank Mason Robinson. While working as bookkeeper for the Pemberton Chemical Company in 1886, he suggested the name Coca-Cola for Pemberton's new syrup and that the name be written in Spencerian script. (*Archives, The Coca-Cola Company, Atlanta, Georgia*)

John S. Pemberton's Marietta Street home in Atlanta. In 1886, after months of experimentation, Pemberton created the syrup later named Coca-Cola in the backyard of this house. (*Archives, The Coca-Cola Company, Atlanta, Georgia*)

Jacobs' Pharmacy in Atlanta as it appeared May 8, 1886, when Pemberton convinced the soda-fountain manager, Willis E. Venable, to stock his new syrup, which was named Coca-Cola a few days later (*Archives, The Coca-Cola Company, Atlanta, Georgia*)

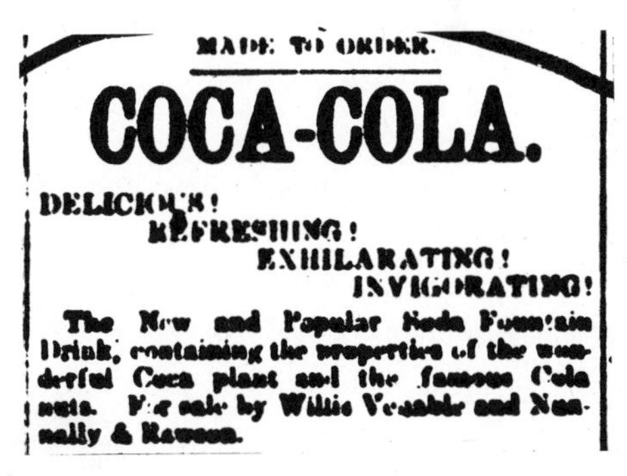

MADE TO ORDER.

COCA-COLA.

DELICIOUS!
REFRESHING!
EXHILARATING!
INVIGORATING!

The New and Popular Soda Fountain Drink, containing the properties of the wonderful Coca plant and the famous Cola nuts. For sale by Willis Venable and Nunnally & Rawson.

The first known newspaper advertisement for Coca-Cola (*Archives, The Coca-Cola Company, Atlanta, Georgia*)

CHAPTER 3

ASA G. CANDLER: FOUNDER OF THE COCA-COLA COMPANY

On August 30, 1888, just fourteen days after John S. Pemberton's death, Asa Griggs Candler acquired, for one thousand dollars, the remaining one-third of Coca-Cola still held by Woolfolk Walker and his sister, Mrs. M. C. Dozier. As stated on letterheads, invoice blanks, and advertising copy, Candler was now sole proprietor of Coca-Cola. The total amount Candler had spent to acquire the rights to Coca-Cola was $2,300. Candler's sole proprietorship was not made legal until a year and a half later when, on April 22, 1891, Walker, Candler & Company made the transaction a matter of record.

Asa Griggs Candler, the man who was destined to guide Coca-Cola from obscurity to national prominence, was born on December 30, 1851, near Villa Rica, Georgia. He was the eighth child and fifth son of Samuel Charles and Martha Beall Candler. In addition to Asa's fame as leader of The Coca-Cola Company, several of his eight brothers attained eminence in the South: Warren became a Methodist bishop and a college president; Milton became a congressman from Georgia; Ezekiel became a congressman from Mississippi; and John, in addition to being a lawyer for Coca-Cola, became a justice of the Georgia Supreme Court. Allen Candler, a cousin, became a distinguished historian and was a governor of Georgia.

Candler attended elementary school for five years. At the age of ten he was compelled to continue his education at home because the Civil War forced the closing of his school. Early in 1867 Candler went to Huntsville, Alabama, to live with his married sister, Florence, and attend high school. He attended high school for one year. When his sister moved to Cartersville, Alabama, he dropped out and returned home to Villa Rica. Again he entered school, one conducted by John H. Featherstone, but after one year of study the building burned and the school was closed. So, with seven years of formal education, Asa Candler faced the world.

On July 1, 1870, nineteen-year-old Candler made his way to Cartersville, Georgia, and apprenticed himself to two physicians, Dr. Best and Dr. Kirkpatrick, with the hope of becoming a doctor. The two doctors owned a drugstore, and it was in their store that Candler worked all day and slept at night. During the evenings he studied Latin and Greek and read medical books, still dreaming that one day he would become a doctor. After two and a half years in Cartersville, Candler gave up his dream and decided to move to Atlanta, Georgia, and become a druggist.

In 1873, when he arrived in Atlanta, Candler was wearing homemade clothes and had exactly $1.75 in his pocket. Beginning with the morning of the day he arrived, Candler walked the streets of Atlanta asking for work at each drugstore. One of the stores he visited was called the Pemberton-Pulliam Drug Company. He had no way of knowing then that the senior partner of this firm, John S. Pemberton, was to play an important part in his future. At any rate, around nine o'clock that evening he was hired by George Jefferson Howard, who owned a popular drugstore. He began work immediately and worked until midnight, when the store closed. Candler worked hard learning the wholesale/retail drug business, and he was soon promoted to chief clerk.

In April of 1877, when he was twenty-five years old, Candler went into partnership with Marcellus B. Hallman. They called their firm Hallman and Candler, Wholesale and Retail Druggists. The business went so well that Candler decided he could afford the responsibilities of a wife and family. The young lady he selected to become Mrs. Asa Candler was Lucy Elizabeth Howard, daughter of his former employer George Howard. The flaw in this romantic story is that Howard bitterly opposed the marriage and refused to cooperate in any way. On January 15, 1878, without the blessings of Howard, Asa and Lucy were married in the First Baptist Church of Atlanta. The young married couple lived under the shadow of Howard's disapproval for almost a year, but on November 24, 1878, George Howard finally capitulated and sent a curt note of reconciliation. The marriage and the business went well for Candler. He bought his first house shortly after the reconciliation and eventually filled it with five children: Charles Howard, Asa G., Jr., Lucy Beall, Walter Turner, and William.

By 1881 Candler bought Marcellus Hallman's half of the business and Hallman retired. The firm's name was changed to Asa G. Candler & Company. In April of 1882 Candler took in another partner; ironically it was George Howard, his former employer and father-in-law. They called their new organization Howard & Candler.

The firm of Howard & Candler was growing rapidly when, on October 13, 1883, a fire swept through the store and destroyed or damaged most of it. Candler and his father-in-law stayed in business by buying out another drug firm and merging the accounts and merchandise of that firm with their own. The firm that they purchased was Pemberton, Iverson & Denison. John Pemberton, who at this time was yet to create Coca-Cola, went on and established another firm, the Pemberton Chemical Company.

In 1886 Asa Candler bought out his father-in-law, and the firm once again became Asa G. Candler & Company.

Business flourished. In addition to Coca-Cola, which Candler acquired on April 30, 1888, he marketed several other proprietary products. Most famous of his mixtures were Botanic Blood Balm, Delectalave (a liquid dentifrice), and Everlasting Cologne.

During the period between 1888 and 1890 Candler brought Frank Robinson into the business as general superintendent. Dr. W. H. Ingram, professor of pharmacy at the Atlanta Medical College, was hired to run the retail portion of the business, P. M. Christian was hired as prescriptionist, and Charles T. Come as bookkeeper. Dr. H. S. Wright, a chemist, was in charge of manufacturing and wholesale activities. G. W. Little, J. W. Phillips, and Daniel Bevill Candler were salesmen and represented the firm on the road. The shipping department was run by Samuel Candler Dobbs, the son of Candler's sister, Elizabeth, while Samuel L. Willard was hired to run production. Asa Candler believed that it was good policy to involve relatives and close friends in his business activities.

During the 1888-to-1890 period Candler's business was grossing over $100,000 annually, a worthy sum in those days.

In 1890, at the age of thirty-eight, Candler decided to sell all of his other business interests and devote his entire efforts to developing Coca-Cola. He closed out his entire stock of drugs, perfumery, proprietary medicines, paints, oils, glass, varnishes, and so forth and invested the resulting fifty thousand dollars in the manufacturing and marketing of Coca-Cola.

In the latter part of 1891 Candler moved his operations from 47 Peachtree Street to the second and third floors of a building at 42 1/2 Decatur Street, over a pawnshop, a second-hand clothing store (the New York Clothing Store), and Ned Parrish's Saloon. The second-floor space was devoted to the manufacturing of Coca-Cola, and the third floor was used for storage, office space, and packing facilities for advertising matter. Shortly after the move Candler filed with the court a petition for charter of The Coca-Cola Company.

On January 29, 1892, the charter was granted, and an incorporators' meeting was held on February 22, 1892. At this meeting the charter was accepted, bylaws were adopted, and five directors were elected (Asa G. Candler, F. W. Prescott, J. M. Berry, John S. Candler, and Frank M. Robinson). Immediately the directors held another meeting and went through the formalities of electing Asa G. Candler, president; John S. Candler, vice-president; and F. M. Robinson, secretary. After officially being elected president, Candler transferred all his rights, the title, and the interest in the trademark and all other related assets, to The Coca-Cola Company, now a Georgia corporation, for five hundred shares of the capital stock which had a par value of one hundred dollars per share.

Just a year later, in 1893, the rapidly growing firm was moved again. The new home was a converted three-story residence at the southwest corner of Ivy Street and Auburn Avenue. The basement, which had a concrete floor, was used for manufacturing. Here were contained a fifteen-hundred-gallon wooden tank and a hundred-gallon copper kettle, among other things. The ground floor was used for sugar storage and shipping. The top floor housed the offices and provided storage for advertising materials. In March, 1894, Asa Candler sent his nephew Daniel B. Candler to Dallas, Texas, to open the first branch office. Business continued to be good, and the next year, in 1895, Candler opened two more branch offices—one in Chicago, the other in Los Angeles. Two years later, in 1897, a warehouse was established in Philadelphia. This was so successful that in 1898 a factory was added to the Philadelphia operation.

In Atlanta, on December 13, 1898, the first building built specifically for The Coca-Cola Company was opened. It was located at 179 Edgewood Avenue, on the corner of College Avenue (renamed Coca-Cola Place in 1899).

In 1909, owing to tremendous growth, the Atlanta company was forced to move its operations. The new factory, the last one constructed with Asa Candler at the company's helm, was erected at the corner of Marietta and Magnolia Streets at a cost of about $250,000. The building, constructed of reinforced concrete with concrete floors, was an architectural masterpiece.

In 1916, at the age of sixty-five, Asa Griggs Candler decided to resign as president of the large beverage firm. During his presidency The Coca-Cola Company had become one of the most successful businesses in the country.

It will be recalled that when The Coca-Cola Company was formed in 1892, there were five hundred shares of capital stock involved, with each share having a par value of one hundred dollars. From such beginnings the firm rapidly appreciated. At the company's first annual stockholders' meeting the report showed $61,700 in capital stock. Gross sales for the first ten months were $49,676.50, and 35,360 gallons of Coca-Cola syrup had been sold. The five stockholders decided not to declare a dividend for the year of 1892 but rather to plow the profits back into the business.

On December 6, 1893, the second annual stockholders' meeting was held. Seven stockholders were present. The minutes of the meeting reveal that by 1893 there were 534 shares of stock outstanding, and that Candler had sold 85 of his shares to the company, which left him with 400 shares. Candler's report to the stockholders reveals the condition of the company quite graphically:

> I address myself to the task of writing my second annual report to the stockholders of this company with feelings of profoundest gratitude. I would be grateful if we could claim solvency. More than once during the twelve months just past, it looked like we would be embarrassed by obligations which, though small, could promptly be met. We rejoice in being able to report a prosperous business year, taken as a whole. We have been able to do about twenty-five percent more business this year than last. I deem it safe and proper that a dividend of not more than twenty dollars per share, payable within, say sixty days from date as the Company's interests and safety will admit, to stockholders. This will leave us a very liberal surplus.

The mathematically oriented reader will quickly realize that the declared dividend amounted to 20 percent on the par value of the stock. The business-oriented reader will just as quickly realize that such a dividend from a two-year-old company is a little short of phenomenal. The history-oriented reader will be further amazed at such growth because during 1893 there was a severe business depression.

Each year Candler was able to report the increasing success of the firm. After 1896 the dividends increased substantially, and in several years the dividends were as much as three thousand dollars per share, which is thirty times the par value of the stock.

At the 1896 meeting Candler reported that for the first time Coca-Cola was being sold outside the continental limits of the United States: Coca-Cola was being regularly shipped to Canada and Hawaii. He also indicated that the company's product was about to be introduced into the Republic of Mexico.

By 1898 Candler could report the sale of 214,000 gallons of Coca-Cola syrup; by 1899 the total was 281,055 gallons; by 1901 the total had risen another 32 percent to 370,877; and by 1902 he reported a further increase of 26 percent and still another by 1903 of 45 percent.

The growth continued at a similar pace, and by the end of 1913 Candler reported that the annual sales of Coca-Cola syrup amounted to 6,767,822 gallons. Compared to the 25 gallons sold by Pemberton in 1886, the 1913 sales record is astounding. In 1914, it was estimated that Coca-Cola stock, which still had a par value of $100 per share, was worth approximately $17,000 per share.

Asa Candler's retirement at the age of sixty-five in 1916 ended his domination of the great firm he had started and headed for twenty-four years. He did remain as a director, but did not interfere with the business. However, his active years were far from over; he successfully campaigned for the mayoralty of Atlanta in 1916 and served for one two-year term.

As early as 1914 Candler began to feel the burden of the tremendous wealth he had accumulated (a fortune of about fifty million dollars). He began to lessen the pressure by giving some of his money away. By 1918, two years after his retirement, he had given the major portion of his wealth to his wife and children. Still, he retained enough so that throughout the remainder of his life he was able to continue to donate money to what he considered worthy causes. Preserved among his writings is at least one statement which clearly presents his feeling regarding the use of his accumulated wealth: "While I do not possess by a vast deal what some extravagantly imagine and confidently affirm, God has blessed me far beyond my just desserts by giving me such a measure of this world's goods as to constitute a sacred trust that I must administer with conscientious fidelity. . . ." Perhaps the most spectacular of his philanthropical activities was his periodic gifts to Emory University in Atlanta, which eventually totaled about eight million dollars. Much of the money was given secretly and only publicly acknowledged after his death.

By the time Asa G. Candler died, the wealth generated by his company had penetrated the whole of Southern life and industry. Practically every estate of substantial wealth in Georgia and its adjoining states has included large blocks of Coca-Cola stock that had been acquired early in the company's life at a relatively small cost. As a creator of wealth in a region, The Coca-Cola Company has had few if any equals. No one person can accurately estimate the extent to which Coca-Cola has boosted the economy of the South.

On March 12, 1929, at the age of seventy-eight, Asa G. Candler died at Emory Hospital. Reminiscent of the day the inventor of Coca-Cola, John S. Pemberton, was buried, the day of Candler's funeral was declared an official day of mourning in Atlanta. City offices were closed and flags were flown at half-mast in memory of one of the city's greatest citizens. Candler's name was immortalized in Atlanta on a hotel, park, street, and airport, as well as on the city's first skyscraper.

Above: Asa G. Candler & Co., at 47 Peachtree Street in Atlanta, as it appeared from 1886 to 1891. While at this location Candler gradually purchased the entire rights to Coca-Cola and manufactured it exclusively at this address for the first half of 1891. (*Archives, The Coca-Cola Company, Atlanta, Georgia*)

Left: Asa Griggs Candler, founder of The Coca-Cola Company, who made Coca-Cola a national beverage (*Archives, The Coca-Cola Company, Atlanta, Georgia*)

CHAPTER 4

JOSEPH A. BIEDENHARN: FIRST BOTTLER OF COCA-COLA

As unbelievable as it may seem today, between 1886 and 1894 Coca-Cola was dispensed only at soda fountains. In the summer of 1894 Coca-Cola was bottled for the first time. The man responsible for first bottling the beverage that has since become the world's most famous bottled soft drink was Joseph August Biedenharn, of Vicksburg, Mississippi.

Biedenharn was a native of Vicksburg, born on December 13, 1866. In his early teens Joseph joined his father's firm which, at the time, sold wholesale fruits, nuts, and raisins, in addition to a wide variety of candy and other specialties. Gradually Joseph began to assume more of the firm's responsibility, while his father, Herman Henry Biedenharn, moved into a shoe business which he had started on the side.

When Joseph was only twenty-four years old, the Biedenharn Candy Company and the shoe store were making so much money that he and his father built a two-story brick building which they divided equally between the candy and shoe business. It was in that building at 218–220 Washington Street in Vicksburg that Coca-Cola was first put into ready-to-drink bottles.

The Biedenharn Candy Company was truly a family business. In addition to Joseph A., six of his brothers were involved in the business: William G., Harry, Lawrence C., Herman H., Ollie Lee, and Albert M. Biedenharn. In 1888 Joseph married Annie Schlottman. They had four children. The three boys—Henry Alvin, Malcolm Stout, and Bernard William—also became involved in the family business. The one daughter,

Emma Louise, studied voice and eventually achieved a distinguished career as a Wagnerian contralto both in the United States and in Europe.

Ironically, Joseph Biedenharn entered the bottling business, which eventually included Coca-Cola, only in self-defense. As part of his confectionery business Biedenharn sold a variety of syrups with which soda water was mixed. Late in June of 1891, three customers approached Biedenharn with orders for a Fourth of July picnic they were planning for their plantation hands. The orders included ten cases of soda water each. Joseph placed the orders with the local soda-water plant but was informed that the thirty-case order could not be filled because of the excessive holiday business. Biedenharn was forced to give each of his customers a box of lemons, a sack of sugar, and some coloring and suggest that they serve pink lemonade at their parties instead of the soda water they ordered. The whole incident irritated him to the point that he decided to go into the soda-water bottling business himself. Within thirty days the Biedenharn Candy Company was bottling lemon, strawberry, and sarsparilla.

J. A. Biedenharn's experience with Coca-Cola actually began a year before he got into the soda-water bottling business. In 1890, shortly after the new Washington Street building was opened, Samuel Candler Dobbs, a Coca-Cola salesman, convinced Biedenharn to try a five-gallon keg of Coca-Cola syrup. Biedenharn dispensed the syrup at the fountain he maintained in the small retail section of the store. The experiment was successful, and the Biedenharn Candy Company began to order Coca-Cola syrup regularly.

Apparently Asa G. Candler was impressed with the success of the sales of Coca-Cola in Vicksburg, because in 1891 he personally visited Joseph Biedenharn and asked him to job Coca-Cola syrup to the soda fountains in the Vicksburg area. The resulting agreement was that the candy company would purchase not less than two thousand gallons of Coca-Cola syrup during a twelve-month period and that at the end of the period Biedenharn would receive a rebate of twenty-five cents a gallon. Such a deal, of course, encouraged Biedenharn to enthusiastically promote the syrup. In later years Joseph Biedenharn reported that he always more than made the quota, and consequently profits from his sales of Coca-Cola were good.

In 1894, three years after Biedenharn had started bottling soda water and four years after he began wholesaling Coca-Cola syrup, the Biedenharn Candy Company began to bottle Coca-Cola. The basic idea behind bottling Coca-Cola was to make it available to country people who did not live near soda fountains. Biedenharn further reasoned that many city people did not find Coca-Cola easily available and that they too would purchase the drink in bottles if it could be made available.

The original Coca-Cola bottles had a six-ounce capacity as do some of the bottles today. These were short-necked, Hutchinson-type bottles with a wire hook protruding from the mouth and were embossed "REGISTERED" across the shoulder and "BIEDENHARN CANDY CO. VICKSBURG MISS." in a circle on the body. Initially these bottles were packed upside down in wooden cases. The cases, with holes bored into false bottoms, were tall enough to encase entire bottles. The holes were just large enough for the neck of the bottle to pass through. The cases were made of one-inch dressed lumber and had no partitions. The price for a case of Coca-Cola was seventy cents as opposed to sixty cents for a case of regular soda water.

As a courtesy, Biedenharn sent the first two-dozen cases of bottled Coca-Cola to Candler in Atlanta. Candler, who was convinced that his product was a soda-fountain beverage to be sold by the glass, courteously acknowledged the gift with: ". . . it was fine." Such a response did not discourage Joseph Biedenharn, and soon he was delivering Coca-Cola throughout the Vicksburg area in a dray. To out-of-town customers he shipped by boat up and down the Mississippi River. Biedenharn was alone in the Coca-Cola bottling business for three years. The second to bottle Coca-Cola was the Valdosta Bottling Works in Valdosta, Georgia. This firm, headed by R. H. Holmes and E. R. Barber, attempted a limited program in 1897.

Joseph A. Biedenharn died on October 9, 1952, after having been a Coca-Cola bottler for fifty-eight years. It has been succinctly stated that "no one preceded him in the business, though many have come after him and followed in his footsteps."

Joseph A. Biedenharn, proprietor of the Biedenharn Candy Company in Vicksburg, Mississippi. First bottler of Coca-Cola. (*Archives, The Coca-Cola Company, Atlanta, Georgia*)

CHAPTER 5

THOMAS, WHITEHEAD, AND LUPTON: FOUNDERS OF THE COCA-COLA BOTTLING INDUSTRY

Although Joseph Biedenharn, of Vicksburg, Mississippi, in 1894, and R. H. Holmes and E. R. Barber, of Valdosta, Georgia, in 1897, can be credited with the earliest attempts at bottling Coca-Cola, three other men are generally thought of as the founders of the Coca-Cola bottling industry.

The man who thought of bottling Coca-Cola was Benjamin Franklin Thomas. Thomas was born the son of a Mayesville, Kentucky, wholesale grocer in 1861. Little is known about his parents, Oliver Hazard Perry Thomas and Sally Metcalf Bruce Thomas. After attending the University of Virginia, Benjamin worked in a bank, operated a stone quarry, and ran a hosiery mill in Mayesville. At the age of twenty-four, with a great deal of business experience behind him, Thomas enrolled in Cincinnati Law School. In 1887, shortly after his graduation, he moved to Chattanooga, Tennessee, and helped form the law firm of Wiltse, Thomas & Chapin. In 1889 he withdrew from that firm and joined the firm that became Pritchard, Sizer & Thomas. His next venture, in 1893, was to form the Tennessee Paving Brick Company with W. M. and T. H. Lasley. Later Thomas started a company that manufactured a proprietary product known as "Sofas," a baking powder.

Benjamin Thomas spent 1898 in Cuba, serving as chief clerk in the office of the Assistant Army Quartermaster, Major H. P. Young. It was during his short stay in Manzanilla, Cuba, that Thomas purchased a Cuban-bottled soft drink called Pina Fria (cold pineapple). He liked this carbonated pineapple drink and remembered how he used to drink carbonated Coca-Cola at the soda fountain back home in Chattanooga. When Thomas returned home in 1899, he took his idea to the second man who was to play an important role in establishing the business of bottling Coca-Cola. The man was his friend and fellow lawyer, Joseph Brown Whitehead.

Joseph Brown Whitehead was born in Oxford, Mississippi, on February 29, 1864, the son of the Reverend Richard H. and Mary A. Conkey Whitehead. Joseph took his law degree from the University of Mississippi. In 1888 he opened his own office in Chattanooga. Whitehead spent twelve years as an attorney-at-law and for a time was back-tax attorney for the city. During that period he met and married Miss Lettie Pate of Thaxton, Virginia. They were married on October 18, 1894, and had two children. Joseph Brown, Jr., was born in 1895 and Conkey Pate was born in 1898.

When Benjamin Thomas explained to Whitehead his idea of bottling Coca-Cola and further explained how brisk were the sales of bottled Pina Fria in Cuba, Whitehead agreed that it was a good idea. Whitehead, who was an enthusiastic baseball fan, had long pondered the lack of liquid refreshment at the ball park. Thomas' theory and Whitehead's ideas meshed very nicely.

The two young lawyers decided that they would go to Atlanta and try to get Asa Candler to give them exclusive rights to bottle Coca-Cola. Since neither of the men knew Mr. Candler, they decided that it would be easier to get someone who did to arrange the meeting. It happened that one Sam Erwin, who was a first cousin to Mr. Candler, lived in Chattanooga. Erwin was an ex-haberdasher who had operated a clothing store called Erwin & Goodpasture. In 1899, when he was approached by Thomas and Whitehead, he was manager of the East Tennessee Telephone Company and chairman of the Chattanooga Public Works Commission. Several years later, in 1902, he became clerk and master of the Chancery Court in Chattanooga—a position he held until his retirement in 1947. Thomas and Whitehead convinced Erwin to accompany them to Atlanta and arrange the desired meeting with Asa Candler.

The first meeting took place on July 19, 1899. Candler was not very much interested in Thomas' and Whitehead's idea, any more than he had been with Beidenharn's in 1894, and he tried to discourage them. The two lawyers from Chattanooga did not give up easily, and finally, after repeated assurances that they would assume full responsibility for bottling and that Candler would not be bothered by their venture, Candler reluctantly worked out an agreement with the two men. The agreement gave Thomas and Whitehead the exclusive rights to bottle Coca-Cola everywhere in the United States *except* New England, Mississippi (Biedenharn's territory), and part of Texas. The New England area was not included in the contract because Seth W. Fowle & Sons, of Boston, had already been given exclusive distribution rights, which technically included bottling rights, for twenty years in 1892. Texas was omitted because a similar agreement was under negotiation with a Corsicana, Texas, businessman; the deal was never consummated. To make the contract legal and binding, one dollar was to be paid to Candler (Candler never bothered to collect the token payment). It has often been said that the trip to Atlanta and the several meetings which concluded on July 21, 1899, netted Thomas and Whitehead one of the most valuable contracts in the annals of American business.

Many stories have grown up around the moment when Candler deeded to Thomas and Whitehead the almost exclusive rights to bottle Coca-Cola. One claims that Candler was suffering from one of his frequent, severe headaches and that the contract was written on the back of an envelope. Although it is true that the contract is rather terse, comprising approximately six hundred words, it is most probable that it was drawn up on regular stationery and that Candler did not have a headache on that historic day. It should be realized that the contract did not take anything from Candler but rather augmented his business in many ways. The fact that the contract called for Candler to supply the necessary Coca-Cola syrup at a fixed price per gallon and to furnish all necessary labels and advertising matter would alone prove its worth to Candler and The Coca-Cola Company in money and control.

With the contract in their possession the two lawyers returned to Chattanooga and faced their next problem: how to put into action their dream of franchised bottlers all over the country. Their first step was to form a firm called The Coca-Cola Bottling Company. They opened offices at 17 Market Square in Chattanooga. The officers of the new firm were Joseph B. Whitehead, president; John T. Lupton, vice-president; and Benjamin F. Thomas, secretary/treasurer.

In 1899 it took about five thousand dollars to equip the average soda-water bottling plant. Benjamin Thomas had enough money to start one plant, but Joseph Whitehead did not. Thomas immediately opened a Coca-Cola bottling plant in Chattanooga. His plant was on the first floor of a three-story building at 23 Patten Parkway.

Whitehead turned for financial assistance to John Thomas Lupton. For approximately $2,500 Whitehead sold Lupton a half-interest in his half of the recently acquired Coca-Cola bottling contract and made Lupton vice-president of The Coca-Cola Bottling Company.

John Thomas Lupton, the son of Jonah J. and Rebecca Catherine Lee Lupton, was born on March 6, 1862, in Winchester, Virginia. Lupton attended Roanoke College in Salem and was graduated in 1882, with both an A.B. and an M.A. For a while he studied law at the University of Virginia and later received his LL.B. degree. In 1886 he was admitted to the Tennessee bar, and the following year he set up practice in Chattanooga. On November 14, 1889, John T. Lupton married Miss Elizabeth Olive Patten, the daughter of one of Chattanooga's leading industrialists. Shortly after the marriage he gave up law and went to work for his wealthy father-in-law. Together they ran the Chattanooga Medicine Company. Before Lupton was thirty years old, he was made vice-president/treasurer of the firm, a job he held until 1906. This firm, incidentally, produced and marketed the famous female disorder patent medicine, "Cardui," and another equally famous proprietary medicine called "Black Draught."

With Lupton's $2,500 Whitehead moved to Atlanta, added his own $2,500, and opened a bottling plant in April, 1900. The new Whitehead-Lupton plant in Atlanta was located at the southeast corner of Edgewood Avenue and Courtland Street.

Almost immediately Thomas and Whitehead discovered they differed in their opinions about the newly acquired contract. Thomas preferred amber bottles for Coca-Cola, and Whitehead thought that clear-glass bottles were the best. More importantly, Thomas thought that the franchise they intended to offer individual bottlers should be given for only a two-year period. Whitehead, on the other hand, believed the contracts should be permanent. In addition Thomas favored selling franchises to inexperienced men, whereas Whitehead preferred to sell to experienced bottlers.

As a result the two men decided to divide the country into two regions and to run each region as each man saw fit. The men agreed that Whitehead would be the one to make the actual division and that Thomas would then have his choice of the resulting divisions. Thomas selected the heavily populated eastern and Middle Atlantic states and the Pacific coast. That left Whitehead with the warmer Southeast and Southwest and the Middle West.

Benjamin Thomas remained in Chattanooga and ran what was to become The Coca-Cola Bottling Company (Thomas), Inc. Joseph Whitehead moved to Atlanta and established the Dixie Coca-Cola Bottling Company. John Lupton remained in Chattanooga as the equal partner of Whitehead.

In 1901 Thomas sold the Coca-Cola Bottling Works of Chattanooga to James F. Johnston and William H. Hardin. The sale took Thomas out of the role of bottler and gave Johnston and Hardin the distinction of being the first to receive a franchise under the 1899 contract. Later in the year contracts were awarded in Chicago, Cincinnati, Louisville, Norfolk, and Rome, Georgia.

During 1902 bottling plants were opened in Augusta, Columbus, Macon, and Savannah, Georgia; Birmingham, Huntsville, Mobile, and Opelika, Alabama; Beckley, Parkersburg, and Wheeling, West Virginia; Charlotte, Greensboro, Hamlet, and Wilmington, North Carolina; Charleston, Columbia, and Greenville, South Carolina; Clifton Forge and Roanoke, Virginia; Knoxville, Memphis, and Nashville, Tennessee; Jacksonville and Tampa, Florida; Dallas and Houston, Texas; Meridian, Mississippi; Buffalo, New York; Kansas City and St. Louis, Missouri; New Orleans, Louisiana; Shawnee, Oklahoma; and Los Angeles, California.

During the first nine years of the twentieth century the number of bottling plants grew rapidly. In 1903, 32 were added; in 1904, 47; in 1905, 80; in 1906, 42; in 1907, 47; in 1908, 40; and in 1909, 43. By 1909 there were 379 Coca-Cola bottling plants in the United States.

Thomas, Whitehead, and Lupton, as the owners of the 1899 contract, were parent bottlers to the mushrooming individual bottlers. The three men derived their income from the differential in the price at which they were entitled to buy the Coca-Cola syrup from (Candler's) The Coca-Cola Company and the price at which they contracted to sell the syrup to their individual bottlers.

The history of Benjamin Franklin Thomas' Company, The Coca-Cola Bottling Company (Thomas), Inc., is rather brief, because the firm has essentially remained intact throughout the years. For twenty-five years the Thomas Company, as it is commonly called, issued individual bottling contracts for the states of California, Oregon, and Washington from the main office in Chattanooga. On November 19, 1924, George T. Hunter, then the president of the parent bottling company and nephew of Thomas, formed the Pacific Coast Coca-Cola Bottling Company. The newly formed firm remained under the control of the Thomas Company until January 2, 1942, at which time the subsidiary company was purchased by The Coca-Cola Company in Atlanta. Subsequently the states of Idaho, Nevada, and Arizona were added, and the name became the Pacific Coast Region of the Bottler Sales Development Department of The Coca-Cola Company.

The history of Joseph Brown Whitehead and John Thomas Lupton's Dixie Coca-Cola Bottling Company is a bit more complicated. On February 13, 1901, Whitehead and Lupton changed their firm's name to The Coca-Cola Bottling Company. Subsequently, to achieve better administration and contract supervision, Whitehead and Lupton decided to divide their territory into three separate companies. One of these companies, called the Southeastern Parent Bottler, was eventually acquired by The Coca-Cola Company on March 31, 1933. The Southeastern Parent Bottler embraced all of South Carolina and Florida and most of North Carolina, Georgia, Alabama, Mississippi, Louisiana, and Arkansas. Another of Whitehead and Lupton's companies, called the 1903 Company, was sold to The Coca-Cola Company in September, 1943. The 1903 Company comprised the states of Texas and Oklahoma as well as fractional parts of New Mexico, Kansas, and Arkansas. The third of Whitehead and Lupton's companies, and the largest in acreage, was the Western Coca-Cola Bottling Company. The original territory of the company included the states of Michigan, Wisconsin, Minnesota,

Iowa, Missouri, North and South Dakota, Nebraska, Montana, Idaho, Wyoming, Utah, Colorado, Nevada, Arizona, and most of Illinois, Kansas, and New Mexico. The Western Coca-Cola Bottling Company was purchased by The Coca-Cola Company on December 12, 1935.

The New England states—Massachusetts, Connecticut, Rhode Island, Maine, New Hampshire, and Vermont—were the last in the country to have Coca-Cola in bottles. Seth W. Fowle & Sons, of Boston, had been given exclusive distribution rights for twenty years in 1892. In January of 1912, when the agreement ran out, The Coca-Cola Company began granting individual bottling contracts in New England. On August 16, 1916, the New England Coca-Cola Bottling Company was formed. In 1923 The Coca-Cola Company purchased the New England Company.

In 1954 the five company-owned parent bottling companies banded together and became a division of The Coca-Cola Company. This was, of course, only a legal technicality. That left only the oldest of the parent bottler companies, The Coca-Cola Bottling Company (Thomas), Inc., as an independently owned and managed firm; all of the others (all of Whitehead and Lupton's and a portion of Thomas' territory) were owned by Asa G. Candler's original company, The Coca-Cola Company.

What happened to Biedenharn's Mississippi territory and Texas, both of which were not included in the 1899 contract? On March 31, 1907, The Coca-Cola Company granted Whitehead and Lupton approximately three-fourths of Mississippi and the remaining one-fourth to Thomas. (J. A. Biedenharn became an official Coca-Cola bottler under Thomas on December 31, 1907.) Texas became part of the Whitehead-Lupton territory on March 11, 1903.

Benjamin Franklin Thomas died on June 25, 1914, at the age of fifty-two. Thomas, at the time of his death, was a multimillionaire, and in addition to his Coca-Cola interests he owned a great deal of real estate and industry in Chattanooga. During his active career he was one of the organizers of the American Trust and Banking Company and vice-president of the Administration and Trust Company, which he also helped found. He was also school commissioner for a time, the only public office he ever held.

Joseph Brown Whitehead died on August 27, 1906, at the age of forty-two. At the time of his death he was president of The Coca-Cola Bottling Company and of the Bowden Lithia Springs Water Company, and treasurer of the Ponce de Leon Amusement Park Company.

John Thomas Lupton died on July 31, 1933, at the ripe old age of seventy-one. Lupton had many financial interests in addition to his investment in Coca-Cola. He was owner of the Chattanooga Medicine Company, an organizer of the Volunteer State Life Insurance Company, chairman of the board of the Dixie Mercerizing Company, and vice-president/treasurer of the Stone Fort Land Company. Lupton, through the latter interest, was instrumental in building the Hotel Patten, which was Chattanooga's first modern skyscraper hotel. He also built the Elizabeth Apartments, which were the first of such modern structures in Chattanooga. Lupton was one of the men involved in the development of Baylor School and for some time served as president of the Baylor School Corporation. He was also a member of the National Economy League, the Royal Society of Arts (London), the Phi Gamma Delta fraternity, Mountain City Club, Chattanooga Golf and Country Club, the Chattanooga Chapter of the University of Virginia Alumni Association, and the Congressional Country Club of Washington City. As if summarizing not only his own secret of success but also that of his partners, Benjamin Thomas and Joseph Whitehead, John Lupton often said that "work should be man's only vehicle of worthy accomplishment."

Benjamin Franklin Thomas, of Chattanooga, Tennessee, one of the three founders of the Coca-Cola bottling business. He conceived the original idea. (*Archives, The Coca-Cola Company, Atlanta, Georgia*)

Joseph Brown Whitehead, of Chattanooga, Tennessee, one of the three founders of the Coca-Cola bottling business. Whitehead and Thomas got the bottling franchise for most of the entire country from Asa Candler on July 21, 1899. (*Archives, The Coca-Cola Company, Atlanta, Georgia*)

John Thomas Lupton, of Chattanooga, Tennessee, one of the three founders of the Coca-Cola bottling business. Lupton purchased one half of Whitehead's share of the bottling franchise acquired by Thomas and Whitehead from Asa Candler. (*Archives, The Coca-Cola Company, Atlanta, Georgia*)

The Atlanta Coca-Cola Bottling Company, started in 1900 by Joseph B. Whitehead. This was the second Coca-Cola bottling plant. The first was opened in Chattanooga in 1899 by Benjamin F. Thomas. (*Archives, The Coca-Cola Company, Atlanta, Georgia; artist: Wilbur G. Kurtz, Sr.*)

CHAPTER 6

ROBERT W. WOODRUFF: COCA-COLA BECOMES AN INTERNATIONAL BEVERAGE

On September 13, 1919, Charles Howard Candler, who succeeded his father to the presidency of The Coca-Cola Company in 1916, and the other major stockholders of The Coca-Cola Company became involved in the largest financial transaction that had ever taken place in the South: They sold The Coca-Cola Company for twenty-five million dollars. The buyer was a syndicate of three banks. Two of the banks, the Chase National and the Guaranty Trust, were northern institutions (New York), and the third—and the one most involved—was a small Atlanta bank called the Trust Company of Georgia. At the time of the transaction the Trust Company of Georgia had a capitalization of only one million dollars; the president was a man named Ernest Woodruff.

Ernest Woodruff was a shrewd and wealthy man who not only ran the Trust Company but also headed the Atlantic Ice and Coal Company, Atlantic Steel, and Continental Gin. Ernest was born with money; his father, George Waldo Woodruff, was the millionaire owner of the Empire Flour Mills. Ernest further enhanced his fortune when he took Emily Winship for his bride. Emily's father, Joe Winship, made his money by founding and successfully operating a factory that produced cotton gins (Continental Gin).

However, it was Ernest Woodruff's son, Robert Winship Woodruff, who became involved with Coca-Cola. Robert was born on December 6, 1889. He graduated from the exclusive Georgia Military Academy and was enrolled in Emory College in Oxford, Georgia. Young Robert did not care for college and dropped out after one year. As a result, his father made him responsible for his college debts. Robert went to work in a foundry for sixty cents a day. His next job was as a salesman for the General Fire Extinguisher Company. After proving himself to his father, he next became an employee of his father's Atlantic Ice and Coal Company.

In 1912 Robert married Miss Nell Hodgson, of Athens, Georgia. In the same year he met Walter White, the president of the White Motor Company, of Cleveland, Ohio. After conducting a study that proved to his own satisfaction that trucks would serve the Atlantic Ice and Coal Company routes better than the horses and wagons then in use, Robert Woodruff entered into negotiations with Walter White for a fleet of trucks. White took such a financial beating in the concluded deal that he decided to hire the shrewd Robert Woodruff. Eager to be on his own, Robert accepted White's offer and became White's sales representative in south Georgia.

Twenty-three-year-old Woodruff was a very successful salesman and began to receive promotions successively to Georgia manager, then Southeastern manager, Southern regional manager, assistant to the president (in Cleveland, Ohio). Finally, in 1919, Robert Woodruff became vice-president and general manager of White Motors.

Also, in 1919 Robert's father, Ernest, headed the group that purchased The Coca-Cola Company for $25,000,000. At the time of the transaction there were many who thought that Candler's son had made a good deal by selling for $25,000,000 a company his father had paid only $2,300 for twenty-seven years earlier. That thesis was further enhanced by the fact that although Coca-Cola was a nationally distributed product, The Coca-Cola Company had no effective national sales organization. There was also the suspicion that Coca-Cola had reached its peak.

Ernest Woodruff and his partners selected Asa Candler's nephew, Samuel Dobbs, to head their newly acquired beverage business, and in 1920 The Coca-Cola Company rose in gross sales to $32,000,000. Dobbs, however, made several errors, including a large purchase of sugar just before the sugar market collapsed. He was replaced as president in October of 1920 by Charles H. Candler, who had previously been president from 1916 until 1919, when the company was sold to Ernest Woodruff. By 1922 gross sales had fallen to $21,000,000. The $11,000,000 decrease in sales convinced Ernest Woodruff and his fellow investors that The Coca-Cola Company needed new leadership. For this reason certain members of the board of directors proposed that Robert be offered the presidency. Ernest Woodruff, his father, objected.

It was early in 1923 when the board of directors formally met to consider Robert's election as president of the company. With Ernest wisely abstaining, the board voted unanimously to offer the position to Robert. Robert considered the offer, realizing that he had progressed with White Motors as far as he could, and made the decision to leave White for the bigger job with The Coca-Cola Company.

Thus, at the age of thirty-three, Robert Winship Woodruff became president of The Coca-Cola Company. He formally took over the thirty-seven-year-old business on April 28, 1923. Robert very quickly formulated some ideas and initiated some policies that put the giant firm back on its financial feet, and made it grow. His three basic ideas, which resulted in numerous policies, were these: (1) basic loyalty to the product Coca-Cola rather than the company; (2) no merging or taking over of related enterprises—Coca-Cola would be the only product; and (3) every man associated with Coca-Cola would make money.

Robert Woodruff's loyalty to the product as opposed to loyalty to a money-making corporation was consistently put into effect, and as a result the firm did make money. When Robert took over in 1923, the company's slumping sales record in 1922 of $21,000,000 had increased to $24,000,000 in 1923. From 1923 to 1930, however, sales rose from $24,000,000 to a high of $35,000,000. While the rise in sales was significant, it was in the area of profit that Robert Woodruff's leadership clearly showed; in the 1923-to-1930 period profits rose from $5,000,000 to $13,000,000. In his first annual report to the stockholders, Robert Woodruff said: "All of our equipment might be replaced more easily than . . . our good will." The wisdom of that loyalty-to-product statement can be readily ascertained by moving ahead in time forty-eight years to 1971 and noting that at that time The Coca-Cola Company valued its intangible assets at $1,107,000,000.

The policy that The Coca-Cola Company would not merge or take over any related enterprises, while unusual for a firm of such a size, was a successful one for many years. Woodruff made sure that all effort went into the production and distribution of syrup. He wanted to make Coca-Cola available to those who wanted it, anywhere in the world. It is, in fact, for his idea of making Coca-Cola an international beverage that Robert Woodruff will be best remembered. John S. Pemberton invented Coca-Cola, Asa G. Candler made it a national beverage, and Robert W. Woodruff made it an international drink. The company's "Foreign Department" was established in 1926 by Mr. Woodruff; however, in 1930 the Coca-Cola Export Corporation, a wholly owned subsidiary of The Coca-Cola Company, was formed to handle the promotion and sales of Coca-Cola throughout the world, with the exception of the United States, Canada, and Cuba.

Woodruff's idea that every man associated with Coca-Cola should make money was not original, but he made it a reality. Except for John S. Pemberton, the inventor of Coca-Cola, the vast majority of people involved in the business of producing or selling Coca-Cola directly or indirectly have made substantial amounts of money. Readers who desire specific information regarding the fortunes resulting from Coca-Cola are referred to a most interesting book addressing itself in part to the subject: *The Big Drink*, by E. J. Kahn, Jr.

It has been virtually impossible to discuss post-1923 Coca-Cola history elsewhere in this book without mentioning the numerous contributions made by Robert W. Woodruff. He recognized the potential of bottled Coca-Cola and promoted the concept successfully. He promoted innovative ideas in advertising: Billboards were first used during Woodruff's administration; he pioneered in the use of radio to advertise Coca-Cola; a stereotyped Santa Claus advertising Coca-Cola was due in part to Woodruff's leadership. His many innovations further include the development of coolers from ice boxes to electric refrigerators, to coin-operated bottle-vending machines, to premix machines. He supported and pushed the efforts of the Standardization Committee. He led the pioneering efforts to develop take-home cartons.

Robert W. Woodruff served as president of The Coca-Cola Company from 1923 to 1939, but he has controlled the company in one way or another since 1923. Below is a listing of Woodruff's titles, which illustrates how he retained actual control while not always serving as president:

April 28, 1923, to May 1, 1939	President
May 1, 1939, to May 4, 1942	Chairman of the Board and Chairman of the Executive Committee
May 4, 1942, to November 5, 1945	Chairman of the Executive Committee
November 5, 1945, to May 6, 1946	President and Chairman of the Executive Committee
May 6, 1946, to December 31, 1954	Chairman of the Executive Committee

December 31, 1954, to present	Chairman of the Finance Committee
Also:	
August 2, 1952, to February 5, 1955	Acting Chairman of the Board

Although the presidents have led the business activities of the firm, they have done so with Robert Woodruff in the background exerting his will in major corporate decisions. Regarding the presidents since Woodruff, let it suffice here to provide only a listing:

A. A. Acklin	May 1, 1939, to September 19, 1945
R. W. Woodruff	November 5, 1945, to May 6, 1946
William J. Hobbs	May 6, 1946, to August 2, 1952
H. B. Nicholson	August 2, 1952, to February 5, 1955
William E. Robinson	February 5, 1955, to May 6, 1958
Lee Tally	May 6, 1958, to May 8, 1962
J. Paul Austin	May 8, 1962, to November 15, 1971
Charles W. Duncan, Jr.	November 15, 1971, to present

Over the years Robert W. Woodruff has purposely stayed out of public life. Because of this, very little is known about Woodruff, and what is known has been repeated in articles and by word of mouth until each of the stories resembles a legend.

A favorite story illustrating the leadership techniques of Robert Woodruff took place in 1926. In that year Woodruff decided that his syrup salesmen had become merely order-takers. As the story goes, he recalled all of his salesmen from all parts of the country to Atlanta for a meeting. At that meeting he announced that it had been decided that The Coca-Cola Company no longer needed salesmen and that their jobs, therefore, had been terminated. He added, however, that a new department had been formed and that he would describe it to those interested at a meeting the next day. To those who came back the next day he outlined his plan for a new service department which would devote itself to helping owners of soda fountains make more profit from the sales of Coca-Cola. He then suggested that any of the ex-salesmen interested in a job in the new department could apply after the meeting. The ex-salesmen, of course, did apply and were rehired as service representatives. The psychological effect of the temporary dismissal was certainly much greater than a mere change in job title, and the new service-department concept was very successful.

Another story that is often told about Woodruff, one which illustrates his tremendous capacity for work, took place in 1929. Woodruff's long-time friend and former employer Walter White was killed in an automobile accident. The board of directors of White Motors immediately asked Woodruff to assume the presidency. Woodruff accepted, and for more than a year he was the head of both White Motors and The Coca-Cola Company. That in itself would have been a tremendous job for one person, but to make matters worse Woodruff was forced to spend three out of four days on trains commuting between Cleveland, Ohio, and Atlanta, Georgia. He accomplished the work involved in operating the two companies while on the train between the two cities.

Part of the Woodruff legend is his interest in philanthropy. Since the late 1930's Robert Woodruff has been as generous with extensive amounts of money as his father Ernest was not. Because of his desire for anonymity it is not possible to describe the extent to which he has given his money to worthy causes. He is known to have contributed heavily and frequently to education, research, and medicine. His first major philanthropic deed was in 1938. Woodruff and Walter White began acquiring plantation acreage in Baker County, Georgia, in 1928, which eventually totaled 36,000 acres. The plantation was called Ichauway. After White's tragic death in 1929 Woodruff purchased White's portion of the old plantation, and upon his discovery of malaria among the people of the area he spent a fortune on medicine and medical research to rectify the situation. Both of the giants of Coca-Cola —Candler and Woodruff—met what many people feel is the responsibility of wealth and poured a great deal of their fortunes into philanthropy. Asa Griggs Candler retained the idea that Coca-Cola was primarily a drink most successfully sold at soda fountains in glasses. Robert Woodruff proved Candler's idea wrong but went on to affirm that The Coca-Cola Company would be most successful as a one-product, one-price, and one-package firm. His ideas were correct for the 1920's, the 1930's, and the 1940's, but by 1950 the concept no longer fit a rapidly changing beverage industry.

By the early 1950's Pepsi-Cola began to capture a larger portion of the market that had previously belonged to Coca-Cola. By 1954 an ex-vice-president of The Coca-Cola Company, Alfred N. Steele, had led Pepsi-Cola to a very competitive position in the cola market. Coca-Cola previously controlled about 69 percent of the market but by 1954 was reduced 17 percentage points to around 52 percent. Steele did not believe in Woodruff's one-product, one-price, one-package concept and took 17 percent of the Coca-Cola market by offering Pepsi-Cola to consumers in various bottle sizes at varying prices.

In 1955 Woodruff was convinced by his top executives to step aside and let them operate the firm as they saw fit. Woodruff retained final control but did not exert his power very often. A variety of sizes and types of packages for Coca-Cola were introduced which successfully competed in the market; related enterprises were merged with The Coca-Cola Company; a new advertising agency was employed; and numerous new products were introduced. The end result was a regaining of most of what had been lost. Today, through constant awareness of the market changes, The Coca-Cola Company retains leadership in volume of sales.

Ernest Woodruff, who organized the purchase of The Coca-Cola Company in 1919 and whose son, Robert Winship Woodruff, became president in 1923. A banker and investor, Ernest Woodruff owned a big interest in The Coca-Cola Company, but he never held a company office. (*Archives, The Coca-Cola Company, Atlanta, Georgia*)

INCORPORATED UNDER THE LAWS OF THE STATE OF GEORGIA

No.

THE Coca-Cola Company.

SHARES
500

TRADE MARK REGISTERED JUNE 28th 1887 Delicious, Refreshing, Exhilarating, Invigorating.

This is to Certify that The Trust Co. of Georgia is entitled to Five hundred fully paid up Non-assessable Shares of One Hundred Dollars each of the Capital Stock of THE COCA-COLA COMPANY, transferable only on the books of said Company in person or by attorney on the surrender of this Certificate.

Witness our hand and the seal of the Company at Atlanta, Ga. this Sept 13 - 1919

President. Secy.

This is the legal transfer document representing the sale of The Coca-Cola Company (a Georgia corporation) on September 13, 1919, for $25,000,000 to The Coca-Cola Company (a Delaware corporation).

This one-of-a-kind collectible is the seal of The Coca-Cola Company. After the sale of the company in 1919 this seal was no longer official.

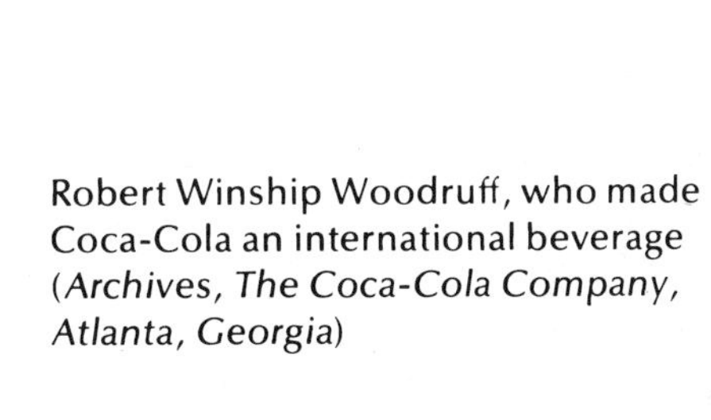

Robert Winship Woodruff, who made Coca-Cola an international beverage *(Archives, The Coca-Cola Company, Atlanta, Georgia)*

CHAPTER 7

TRADEMARKS OF THE COCA-COLA COMPANY

A trademark is a word, letter, device, or symbol used by one company to distinguish its product from that of another company. Trademarks are also symbols of good will and have value as such. A firm obtains exclusive rights to a trademark by using it to identify its product(s) before another company does. Trademarks can also be registered with the U.S. Patent Office, but only approximately 10 percent of the trademarks in the United States are. A registered trademark can be lost if not used for two years *or* if used by the public habitually as a general term for all similar products.

"Coca-Cola," "Coke," and the basic *shape* of the standard contoured Coca-Cola bottle are all registered trademarks of The Coca-Cola Company. No history of The Coca-Cola Company could be considered complete without a study of its three most famous trademarks. Coca-Cola became the company's first registered trademark on January 31, 1893; Coke, the second trademark of the firm, was registered on August 14, 1945; and the basic shape of the Coca-Cola bottle became the third registered trademark of The Coca-Cola Company in 1960.

The importance of The Coca-Cola Company's trademarks can hardly be overstated. The company spends hundreds of thousands of dollars each year protecting its trademarks, which in 1967 were listed as part of the firm's intangible assets valued at three billion dollars.

Throughout the business history of the United States there are examples of trademarks that have been lost to their originators because they became common words for similar products. The National Biscuit Company's "Shredded Wheat" is now just "shredded wheat," a term applied to similar products; the Bayer Company lost the exclusive rights to "aspirin" in 1921; the A. B. Dick Company's "Mimeograph" became the generic term "mimeograph" in 1948; the Kellogg Company lost "corn flakes" in 1915; the Charles H. Phillips Company lost "milk of magnesia" in 1932; and the duPont Company was forced to concede that both "cellophane" and "nylon" had become generic terms for all similar products. The list goes on to include many other one-time brand names which are now generic terms in the public domain: pocket book, cube steak, linoleum, escalator, mineral oil, lanolin, phonograph, and kerosene. Although a company wants to do, and generally does, all it can to make its trademark well known, it does not want its trademark to become so well known that people begin to use it, without a capital letter, to represent all similar products.

During the late 1930's and early 1940's The Coca-Cola Company led other large corporations in the fight to protect trademarks. The continuous battle by The Coca-Cola Company to keep "Coca-Cola" and "Coke" as registered trademarks is paralleled by other firms' trying to retain exclusive rights to such brand names as Adrenalin, Band-Aid, Benzedrine, Dacron, Deepfreeze, Dictograph, Dictaphone, Dry Ice, Fiberglas, Frigidaire, Jeep, Jell-O, Laundromat, Levi's, Mercurochrome, Photostat, Ping-Pong, Pyrex, Simonize, Spray Net, Tabasco, Technicolor, Teletype, Thermo-Fax, Vaseline, Victrola, and Windbreaker. One can see that it may already be a losing battle for some of the brand names listed.

Over the years The Coca-Cola Company has been besieged by imitations. It would take many pages just to list them. The Coca-Cola Company has ignored some and has actively fought others in court. In 1921 a judge, while defending Coca-Cola against an imitator called Taka-Kola, spoke at length about his decision:

> In the instant case the defendant's mark "Taka-Kola" consists, as does "Coca-Cola," of two words, each of four letters and of two syllables. In each phrase a consonant and a vowel alternate, there being in each four of the one and four of the other. Plaintiff's "a" and "o" each appear twice. Defendant's has three "a's" and one "o." The consonant "l" is common to both and in each is the seventh letter from the beginning. Plaintiff's contains three "c's," having in every instance the hard or "k" sound. Twice defendant replaces the "c" with a "k," and once by a "t," the use of which last must be relied upon to distinguish the two words, for in every other respect they are for all practical purposes identical. The two words of plaintiff's are united by a hyphen; so are those of the defendant. The plaintiff displays its [mark] in script. The defendant has followed suit. . . . It taxes credulity to believe that so close a resemblance was accidental.

In the 1880's a woman named Diva Brown, for a brief period, was a business associate of John S. Pemberton, the inventor of Coca-Cola. As a result of the association, Mrs. Brown claimed that Pemberton had sold her the original Coca-Cola formula. To the chagrin of The Coca-Cola Company she traveled the South manufacturing such imitations as Celery-Cola, Better-Cola, Lime-Cola, My-Cola, Vera-Cola, and the like. Mrs. Brown died in 1914.

A product called "Koke" gave The Coca-Cola Company fits for years. The Coca-Cola Company took the Koke Company to court in 1909, and the arguments went on until they had reached the United States Supreme Court. In 1920 The Coca-Cola Company finally won the case, with Supreme Court Justice Oliver Wendell Holmes stating that Coca-Cola is a "single thing coming from a single source and well known to the community."

The Koke case was not the last for The Coca-Cola Company; since 1920 the company has been involved in more than four hundred cases to protect its trademarks. Of all its cases, however, one more than any other taught the company a lesson the hard way.

In 1931 a chain of candy stores owned by a company called Loft, Inc., become upset because The Coca-Cola Company would not sell them syrup at a discount. To combat what they considered a problem, Loft, Inc., purchased the almost bankrupt Pepsi-Cola Company for twelve thousand dollars. The Coca-Cola Company had previously passed up the opportunity to buy Pepsi-Cola for the same amount. Because Loft, Inc., was selling its customers Pepsi-Cola when they ordered Coca-Cola, The Coca-Cola Company became upset. Within a year the two firms were engaged in more than thirty lawsuits in over a dozen countries. It took ten years for the courts to come to a final decision. On March 19, 1942, the Privy Council of England upheld a series of decisions made in 1939 by the Supreme Court of Canada.

The result was a real blow to a perhaps overconfident Coca-Cola Company. The decision was that "Pepsi-Cola" was not an infringement on the trademark "Coca-Cola." The loss by The Coca-Cola Company of the "Cola" part of its trademark resulted. So in 1942 the trademark "Cola" became the generic word "cola." Shortly thereafter, to prevent further assault on its trademark, The Coca-Cola Company removed "Trade Mark Registered" from the tail of the "C" in "Coca" and positioned it above the entire trademark "Coca-Cola." While other firms may use "cola" as part of their trademark (and many have), the trademark "Coca-Cola" remains the property of The Coca-Cola Company.

Even the ultimate court decision against Coca-Cola in 1942 might not have hurt The Coca-Cola Company if in 1939 the Pepsi-Cola Company had not hit upon the merchandising scheme that was to put it in a position to compete successfully with Coca-Cola. The Pepsi-Cola Company introduced its classic twelve-ounce bottle and the jingle "Twice as much for a nickel, too."

The battle between Coca-Cola and Pepsi-Cola has been a continuous one since the early skirmishes in 1931. Of special interest to collectors is a court battle between the two firms that began in November, 1957, in England and was not resolved until February, 1959. The problem centered on a bottle design that the Pepsi-Cola Company had planned to issue in England. The Coca-Cola Company felt that the new Pepsi-Cola bottle too closely resembled its classic Coca-Cola bottle and went to court to prove it. Whether the bottle was ever actually used remains a mystery; collectors feeling that the questionable bottle was indeed used are constantly searching for a specimen to add to their collections. The outcome of the court case was equally mysterious. The settlement was made out of court. It was so secret that a clause in the agreement read, "No party to this agreement shall publish or cause to be published for public distribution the terms of this agreement." All that is publicly known for sure is that the objectionable bottle was eliminated. The full story will have to await a future time. Meanwhile collectors still search for the mysterious bottle.

How The Coca-Cola Company continues to do battle to protect its trademarks can be seen in a number of ways. There are numerous stories of how The Coca-Cola Company reacts when somebody violates its trademark by not capitalizing its name. One story deals with the famous American novelist John Steinbeck. In 1947 Steinbeck wrote a book called *The Wayward Bus.* Throughout the book there are references to "Pepsi-Cola," all properly capitalized, but on page 128 Steinbeck wrote:

" 'Now, let's have a couple of cups of coffee,' he said. And to the blonde, 'You rather have a coke?'

" 'No. Coffee. Cokes make me fat.' "

Then again, on page 182, Steinbeck wrote:

" 'Got any coke?' he asked.

" 'No,' said Breed. 'Few bottles of Pepsi-Cola. Haven't had any coke for a month. It's the same stuff. You can't tell them apart.' "

To the letter from The Coca-Cola Company

protesting Steinbeck's use of its trademark without a capital letter, he replied, "In English when a word is spelled with a small 'c' and is still acceptable, it has become a great word. Only the small need to capitalize."

Since its loss to the Pepsi-Cola Company, The Coca-Cola Company has constantly issued pamphlets, booklets, and the like explaining to editors, announcers, and so forth the correct use of its trademark. In most cases the company overstates its requirements and greatly handicaps those involved in the use of its trademarks. Some typical examples can be found in a pamphlet produced in 1956 entitled *Conversational Guidelines about "Coca-Cola" & "Coke"* and subtitled, "For the confidential use of radio announcers, disc jockeys and other program personnel." The seven points made in this booklet are reproduced here.

1. Coca-Cola and its companion trade-mark, Coke, identify a particular brand of refreshment. These trade-marks may be used any time you wish to talk about a situation in which something good to drink is appropriate, such as, "Man, wouldn't an ice cold bottle of Coke go good right about now"!

(Never use Coca-Cola or Coke as a generic term or as a general name for refreshment. The two trade-marks, Coca-Cola and Coke, refer only to the product of The Coca-Cola Company.)

2. As trade-marks for the world's most popular soft drink, Coca-Cola and Coke should be used as any other brand name, such as, "It's time for a Coke" or "Serve plenty of Coca-Cola at your next party".

(Never use either trade-mark as a common adjective, such as, "Coke time", "Coke party" or the like. This encourages general use of the trade-marks in place of specific identification of the product.)

3. Like deer and elk and a host of other words, Coke and Coca-Cola are both singular and plural. Use each mark to represent one or many. The container (bottles, glasses or cups) Coke comes in may vary, but the trade-mark is always "Coke" or "Coca-Cola".

(Never say, "All the cats had Cokes". Instead, say, "All the cats had bottles—or glasses—of Coke"!)

4. In the same way, since trade-marks identify or refer only to the product, they should not be personalized or personified. The Company that makes the product is The Coca-Cola Company; the Company that distributes the product is The Coca-Cola Bottling Company. These Companies do things like sponsoring programs, the product Coca-Cola does not. Thus, a name for a show would be "Refreshment Time, brought to you by your friendly neighbor who bottles Coca-Cola"!

(Never say, "Coca-Cola's Saturday Recording Show" or "Coke's Announcer".)

5. The product, Coca-Cola, is available in containers of many different sizes, but the product is the same great drink in each and does not vary. When you talk about the various sizes of containers, be sure you identify the *container* and not the product. For example, Coca-Cola is sold in Regular Size, King Size, Half Quart and Family Size bottles, both returnable and one-way. Coke is also served in King Size and Jumbo Size drinks at the fountain. Be sure to check your area to see which size bottles are available and which you should talk about.

(Never say, "King Size Coke" or "Big Coke", say instead, "Coke in thrifty Half Quarts" or "Coke in big Half Quart Bottles".)

6. Advertising copy for any product changes from time to time. For example, we use the advertising slogan "The Pause That Refreshes" from time to time. Instead, the phrase "Things Go Better with Coke" is used prominently, and specific suggestions are often coupled with this slogan. Slogans, however, never take the place of the trade-mark.

(Never say, "Coca-Cola is the Pause That Refreshes", instead say, "Ice cold Coca-Cola for the Pause That Refreshes", if you are using this slogan!)

7. Coca-Cola and Coke are of equal status trade-mark-wise and may be used interchangeably, but the trade-mark Coca-Cola must be used at least *once* in every commercial message.

(Never use Coke only, instead say Coke and then refer to the product as Coca-Cola the next time you mention the brand name".)

Advertising & Sales Promotion Department

THE COCA-COLA COMPANY

P.O. Drawer 1734, Atlanta 1, Ga.

"COCA-COLA" AND "COKE" ARE REGISTERED TRADE-MARKS WHICH IDENTIFY ONLY THE PRODUCT OF THE COCA-COLA COMPANY.

CHAPTER 8

COCA-COLA AS A "PROPRIETARY ELIXIR"

When Charles Howard Candler—son of the first president of The Coca-Cola Company, Asa Griggs Candler—told of how his father "purchased a one-third interest in the formula of an almost completely unknown *proprietary elixir* [italics added] known as Coca-Cola" in a biography entitled *Asa Griggs Candler* (Emory University, Atlanta, 1950), he confirmed what historians, collectors, and others had suspected for years: The carbonated soft drink we know today as Coca-Cola was originally a "proprietary elixir" or a "patent medicine."

"Dr." (as he was often called) John S. Pemberton, the inventor of Coca-Cola, got his start in Atlanta by producing and marketing a line of compounds he described as "the panaceas for a multitude of human frailties." Some of his most famous mixtures were Extract of Styllinger, Gingerine, Globe of Flower Cough Syrup, Indian Queen Hair Dye, and Triplex Liver Pills. What was to become his most famous mixture, Coca-Cola, was (according to E. J. Kahn, Jr., in *The Big Drink*) a modification of a mixture Pemberton had patented in 1885 as French Wine Coca, an "ideal nerve and tonic stimulant." Pemberton, according to Kahn, had taken out the wine and substituted "a pinch of caffeine," some extract of cola, and other oils.

When Asa Griggs Candler purchased the "proprietary elixir" known as Coca-Cola in 1891, he was acquiring a product similar to other proprietary products he had owned in the past. His three most famous products were Botanic Blood Balm, Delectalave, and Everlasting Cologne.

Other pioneers came to The Coca-Cola Company with proprietary products in their backgrounds. Benjamin F. Thomas manufactured a proprietary product known as Sofas. Joseph B. Whitehead was president of a firm called the Bowden Lithia Springs Water Company which bottled a Lithia water that was supposed to have medicinal properties. John T. Lupton was vice-president of the Chattanooga Medicine Company, which had as two of its products the famous Black Draught and Wine of Cardui, a patent medicine with quite a history, according to an 1892 almanac:

> Many years ago an immigrant from North Carolina camped for a night near an Indian Village in Georgia. A girl, about fifteen, just passing into womanhood, was with him. During the night she was attacked with violent pains and could get no relief. An old Indian squaw witnessed it, and without saying a word, went to her wigwam, selected some herbs from her store, prepared a decoction and administered it to the suffering girl. In a short time the girl was entirely relieved. Before resuming their journey, the mother of the girl obtained from the squaw a quantity of the herbs, in which she found a bud containing seeds. These she planted and raised more herbs from year to year. This practice was continued by her descendants.
>
> Rev. R. L. McElree, a minister of the Cumberland Presbyterian Church, in Tennessee, in visiting his parishioners, became acquainted with the virtues of these herbs and their history. He procured some of the seeds and planted them in his garden. He furnished afflicted ladies with wine made from the herbs and witnessed many remarkable cures of those who used it.
>
> In 1879 the Rev. McElree solicited the Chattanooga Medicine Company to take charge of the manufacture of the wine and put it within reach of afflicted women everywhere.
>
> To test the wine, it was furnished free of charge in the treatment of about 7,000 selected cases of female diseases. Among these cases were every class of female disease—some of them chronic cases of 20 years standing. The results were beyond the most sanguine expectations. Less than 500 failures to cure were reported. Ladies who had despaired of ever regaining health, were completely restored. Young girls were carried over a critical period in their lives in perfect health and safety. Weak, nervous, debilitated women discovered that the wine restored their strength, quieted their nerves, and increased their energy. Since that day, McElree's Wine of Cardui has been used by many thousands of women with entire satisfaction, and is confidently recommended as a tonic that has no equal in medical science.

At the time Coca-Cola was invented, developed, and marketed, proprietary (or patent) medicines were enjoying their heyday. Soda water, while popular during the late 1800's, was not comparable in a business sense to proprietary medicines. In the 1870's advertising as we know it today began to blossom. By 1900 few publications could financially survive without paid advertising, and most of the advertising was for proprietary medicines. It is hard to say whether the phenomenal development of the advertising industry was caused by proprietary medicine advertising or just the reverse. While it is true that the majority of proprietary medicines on the market at that time did not do what their owners claimed they would, most people who purchased them firmly believed in their worth. From that standpoint it is easy to see why people would purchase a tonic they felt was good for them and why they might not purchase a soft drink just for pleasure. The "Puritan ethic" of hard work and thriftiness was also involved. To some people it was just not right to indulge in the simple pleasure of a soft drink; it was all right, however, to purchase a "medicine."

Pemberton, Candler, and others may have thought they could get the best business mileage out of Coca-Cola by selling it both as a soft drink to be consumed for pleasure *and* as a proprietary medicine to be consumed for medicinal reasons. An examination of some of the early advertising slogans and statements for Coca-Cola seems to back this thesis. Many of the slogans and statements were written to appeal to both a pleasure-seeking and a medicine-seeking market.

During the few years that Pemberton controlled Coca-Cola, the company made few medicinal claims. Asa Candler, however, advertised it right along with his other proprietary products, Botanic Blood Balm, Delectalave, and Everlasting Cologne. (In the following discussion of specific slogans and statements all italics have been added.) An 1886 slogan, "Delicious! Refreshing! *Exhilarating! Invigorating!*," has a slight medicinal flavor to it. By 1890 a more direct approach was used, with the slogans "The wonderful *nerve* and *brain tonic* and remarkable *therapeutic* agent" and "For *headache* or tired feeling summer or winter." The slogans "Relieves mental and physical exhaustion" and "For *headache* or tired feeling" of 1891 carry on the same theme. In 1893 "For *headache* and exhaustion, drink Coca-Cola" and "The ideal *brain tonic*" continue the promotion of the drink along medicinal lines. More evidence that Coca-Cola was promoted as a proprietary medicine can be found in a third 1893 slogan: "*Specific* for *Headache*." The use of "specific" is important because all ready-made medicines in those days could be placed in one of two general categories—single-purpose and all-purpose, or in medicine-men language, "specifics" and "cures." On that basis it seems fair to take the 1893 "Specific for Headache" literally.

In 1899 the slogan "Coca-Cola makes flow of thought more easy and reasoning power more vigorous" was used to promote Coca-Cola as a product that would do more than just give pleasure and quench thirst. Such words as "pure," "healthful," and "palatable" were used in 1904. By 1905 the medicinal approach was a bit more evident in such slogans as "The favorite drink for *ladies when* thirsty, weary and *despondent*," and "Refreshes the weary, *brightens the intellect, clears the brain*." Of a more oblique nature are these 1906 slogans: "It is a charming, *healthful* drink," "Relieves fatigue," "Restores energy," "Something more than thirst-slaking," "Strengthens the nerves," and "A toast to *health* and happiness."

In 1906 the Pure Food and Drug Act was passed. This historic legislation eventually had a great effect on the proprietary medicine industry, and further examination of the slogans and statements used to promote Coca-Cola will reveal that it had its effects on The Coca-Cola Company as well.

Before the effect of the Pure Food and Drug Act of 1906 was felt and the new law was greatly implemented, The Coca-Cola Company used the following slogans in 1907: "It sustains because it is a true food. It refreshes because it has a *slightly* [note the softening adjective] *tonic* effect on the system. It invigorates because it supplies the elements for physical and mental exertion," "A liquid food for *brain*, body and *nerves*," "Physically sustaining, good to the taste, and *an aid to the digestion*," and "Relieves fatigue and *calms overwrought nerves* without undue stimulation." In 1909 the slogan "Relieves *fatigue* of *brain*, body and *nerves*" was used.

While slogans somewhat open to interpretation have been used by The Coca-Cola Company right up to the present, perhaps one of the last statements that could be considered definitely to contain medicinal claims for Coca-Cola is the following one used in 1910:

> When you feel all hot and sticky and tired and "*headachy*," when the life and energy seems to be oozing out of your pores with each drop of perspiration and it just seems you can't go a step further or do a lick more of work, step into any place and Drink a Bottle of COCA-COLA. You'll wonder first thing who turned on the cool wave—*your headache will disappear*—that *nervous*, exhausted feeling will be replaced by a general all round "brace-up," the rough spots will be smoothed out of your temper and you'll feel refreshed and exhilarated. The great *temperance*, tonic beverage for men, women, and children—now try a bottle today.

For the next bit of evidence that Coca-Cola

could at one time have been truly labeled a proprietary medicine, we must go back to the Civil War. In 1862 the United States government put into effect a series of excise taxes. Schedule "C" of the Revenue Act of 1862 required that revenue stamps be affixed to such items as printed legal and business documents, playing cards, matches, perfume, cosmetics, *and* proprietary medicines to indicate prepayment of taxes. The 1862 act was repealed in 1883 but revived again on June 13, 1898, and was in force for a second time from July 1, 1898, until April 2, 1901. Proudly displayed in the archives of The Coca-Cola Company and in numerous revenue stamp collections are Proprietary Revenue Stamps with a Coca-Cola cancellation. The specific example framed and displayed in the archives of The Coca-Cola Company bears a December 28, 1899, cancellation. The existence of these stamps by itself seems to offer indisputable evidence that even if The Coca-Cola Company did not consider Coca-Cola a proprietary medicine, the United States government did and taxed the product as such.

Coca-Cola was not the only combination soft drink and proprietary medicine in the field during the late 1800's and early 1900's. The very famous beverage Moxie could probably be placed in the category since it was advertised as "Moxie Nerve Food," as could Pepsi-Cola. In the words of E. J. Kahn, Jr., in *The Big Drink*, "Like John Pemberton, the Coca-Cola pioneer, Bradham [the inventor of Pepsi-Cola] was often called 'Doc'; and like Doc Pemberton, Doc Bradham had thought of his drink at the start not primarily as a refreshment but rather as an aid to stimulating appetite and easing indigestion. (There is no pepsin in Pepsi-Cola, incidentally.)"

During the Spanish-American War the government taxed Coca-Cola as a proprietary medicine. The Coca-Cola Company disagreed on the classification, and in 1902, according to E. J. Kahn, Jr.,

> the company sued the government then for a refund of nearly eleven thousand dollars in federal taxes that had been imposed on it because the drink was classified as a medicinal proprietary. . . . In the years just preceding the trial, Coke had been advertised as a "remarkable therapeutic agent," a "sovereign remedy," and a cure for, among other indispositions, headaches, neuralgia, hysteria, melancholy, insomnia, biliousness, and spring fever. But despite this panacean past, the jury gave the nod to Coca-Cola, which not only got back its tax money but received a couple of thousand dollars in interest.

A number of firms, including The Coca-Cola Company, misused the new drug law by claiming that it guaranteed their products. One specific example is an advertisement for Coca-Cola in 1907 that proclaimed the beverage to be "Guaranteed under the Pure Food and Drug Act, June 30th, 1906, Serial #3324." As soon as the government found out about it, such advertising was stopped on the basis that it was misleading and illegal. Because the government had not prosecuted the makers of various products, this was not to be taken as an endorsement.

The vast majority of patent medicines of turn-of-the-century America contained substantial amounts of alcohol. Despite the fact that The Coca-Cola Company loudly advertised as early as 1906 that Coca-Cola was "The great temperance beverage—a liquid food for brain, body, and nerves"; despite the 1907 slogan "Coca-Cola—the great temperance beverage—it has none of the ill effects or 'let down' qualities of alcoholic stimulants" (alcohol is a depressant); and despite the claim in 1908 that Coca-Cola is "The drink that cheers but does not inebriate"—nevertheless many people felt that Coca-Cola contained alcohol. A possible explanation is that many people thought that all patent medicines contained alcohol. Another possible explanation is that during the early 1900's Coca-Cola was frequently advertised by local bottlers and others as being a fine alcoholic drink mixer; as a result, the Coca-Cola highball and gin ricky became popular drinks. The mistaken association of Coca-Cola and alcohol was so prevalent that in 1907 the War Department banished Coca-Cola from Army posts. The injunction remained in effect for two years.

In 1906, when the Pure Food and Drug Act was signed into law, Dr. Harvey W. Wiley was the head of the Bureau of Chemistry of the Department of Agriculture. It was his duty to enforce the new law that he had helped formulate. Wiley had a profound dislike for Coca-Cola and is quoted as having called its makers "dope peddlers." When questioned about this statement, he asserted that he would be glad to replace "dope peddlers" with "poisoners." In 1909 Wiley, representing the government, formally accused The Coca-Cola Company of violating the Pure Food and Drug Act of 1906. The famous case is known as the *United States v. Forty Barrels and Twenty Kegs of Coca-Cola*. The barrels and kegs of Coca-Cola syrup were impounded by federal agents while they were being transported from Atlanta to Chattanooga. Wiley's charges were adulteration and misbranding. More specifically, the charge of adulteration was based on the portion of the new law which forbade the addition of caffeine to a product; the charge of misbranding was based on the government's opinion that Coca-Cola contained no coca and very little cola.

The historic case between the government and Coca-Cola dragged through the courts for nine years. The Coca-Cola Company won in two lower courts with the arguments (1) that caffeine was not an additive but an essential part of Coca-Cola and (2) that if such things as butternuts, pineapples, and Grape-Nuts, which contained no butter, pines, apples, grapes, or nuts, were not misbranded, then neither was Coca-Cola. But when the government pushed the case on to the U.S. Supreme Court, that body did not agree with the lower courts' decisions. Justice Charles Evans Hughes explained the Supreme Court's logic by pointing out that it would be illegal to produce and sell a product called "chocolate" that contained no chocolate or one called "vanilla" that contained no vanilla. His logic was further expanded when he concluded that if The Coca-Cola Company was right in its arguments, then it would be all right to label a product "chocolate-vanilla" when it contained neither substance.

The Supreme Court, upon making the final decision, remanded the case back to a federal district court in Chattanooga, where the original trial had been held, for disposition. Luckily for The Coca-Cola Company, however, Dr. Wiley had by then left government service, and his successor was just as anxious as The Coca-Cola Company to settle the nine-year-old fight. To settle the case, as ordered by the Supreme Court, The Coca-Cola Company agreed to make slight modifications in its syrup-manufacturing processes and paid all costs of the protracted trial. Since the settlement in 1918, Coca-Cola has had little trouble with the government.

Perhaps the final part of the *United States v. Forty Barrels and Twenty Kegs of Coca-Cola* story came in 1946 when Dr. Orville E. May was appointed vice-president in charge of quality control of The Coca-Cola Company. Dr. May had previously spent twenty-three years in the Bureau of Chemistry of the U.S. Department of Agriculture and for his last two years was the bureau's head—the position first held by Dr. Harvey W. Wiley.

The Coca-Cola Company has always managed to maintain leadership in the beverage industry by initiating necessary change. While it may have been good business to promote its product in the late 1800's and early 1900's as both a soft drink and a proprietary medicine, the company changed with the times and today finds it good business to promote its products in close connection with the philosophies of the "now" generation. Racial, ecological, and other current issues are very much a part of the company's advertising.

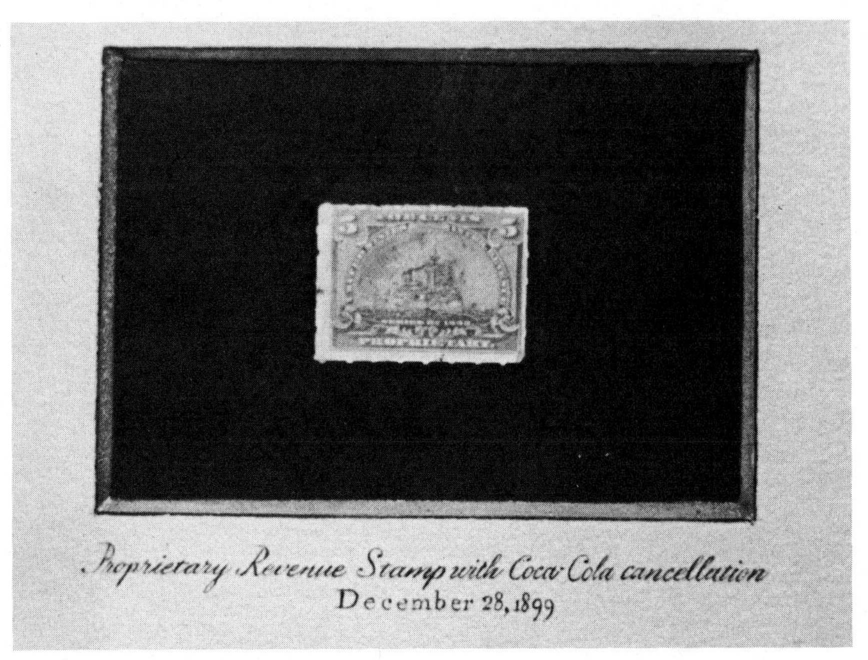

This is a U.S. Proprietary Revenue Stamp, the type commonly used during the Spanish-American War, with a Coca-Cola cancellation. During the period from 1898 to 1901, Coca-Cola was taxed by the government as a proprietary medicine.

These two magazine advertisements of June, 1969, illustrate how The Coca-Cola Company retains its leadership in the soft-drink field by changing with the times. The advertisement featuring black models was run in a magazine with a black readership, while the advertisement featuring white models was run in a magazine with a predominantly white readership.

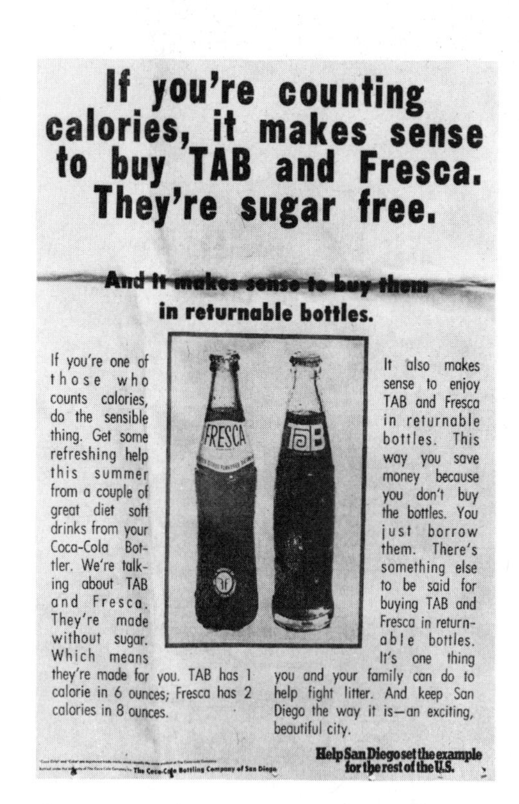

The Coca-Cola Company retains its leadership in the soft-drink industry in many ways. It is always aware of current trends and philosophies. These 1971 full-page newspaper advertisements emphasize the interest in ecology. Both advertisements stress ecology by promoting the company's returnable bottles (Coke is sold in nonreturnable bottles, too).

How to order Fashion Squares.

Original Fashion Squares—commissioned by The Coca-Cola Company from today's leading designers.

Order as many accessories as you wish. Simply fill out the form below and send check or money order (no cash or stamps, please) to:

Fashion Squares
P.O. Box 1178
Brooklyn, N.Y. 11202

Gentlemen: Please rush to me immediately the Fashion Square accessories I have checked below. Enclosed is my ☐ check ☐ money order in the amount of $_______.

Item	Price	Quantity
Endura® Dynasty Bracelet Watch (Retail value $25)	$11.00 each	☐
6-foot Silk Maxi Scarf by Ray Strauss (Retail value $14)	$ 5.00 each	☐
Lucite Placque on heavy anodized chain designed by Eye Plus (Retail value $12.50)	$ 4.25 each	☐
Mirror-Finish Clasp Bracelet with lucite square from Eye Plus (Retail value $12)	$ 3.75 each	☐
Pair of Fashion Square silvery and lucite Rings by Eye Plus (Retail value $7.50)	$ 2.00 for both	☐

Allow 4 to 6 weeks for delivery.

Name

Address

City State Zip

"Coca-Cola" and "Coke" are registered trade-marks of The Coca-Cola Company. This offer expires October 31, 1970.

In 1970, when The Coca-Cola Company refurbished its image, one of the new promotional items was jewelry. Five of the pieces featuring the new "dynamic contour" that was added to the trademark are featured in this order form passed out by the millions. These items are choice collectors' pieces.

Part III

PRODUCTION AND MERCHANDISING ITEMS

CHAPTER 9

CIGARS, RAZOR BLADES, AND CHEWING GUM

At least three products other than Coca-Cola were produced and marketed with the Coca-Cola trademark in the early 1900's. Records for the early years of The Coca-Cola Company are incomplete and, as a result, early history is sketchy and heavily dependent on what can be learned from such related primary sources as city directories, catalogs, periodical advertising, and relics of the period.

In the area of tobacco there are references to a cigar featuring the trademark "Coca-Cola" which is supposed to have been produced and marketed during the early years of this century. It is unlikely that very many specimens of such a perishable product have survived for today's collectors, but if such a cigar was ever marketed, it is likely that cigar bands, boxes, inside-cover labels, and loose labels with the Coca-Cola trademark prominently displayed on them can be located. Collectors of cigar bands and other tobacco relics have been around for many years. An extensive search of their varied collections has not revealed any trace of the early 1900's cigar featuring the Coca-Cola trademark. However, two different types of cigar bands used for advertising by The Coca-Cola Company have been located. The two types of cigar bands—one featuring a hobbleskirt bottle of Coke and one featuring a glass of Coke—were produced intermittently by special request of The Coca-Cola Company, in lots of ten thousand, from 1927 to 1944. These specialized bands were manufactured by Consolidated Lithographing Company, of Brooklyn, New York (now located on Long Island), for promotion or convention purposes.

Safety razor blades are another early 1900's

product which prominently bore the Coca-Cola trademark. The small red packages with white lettering contained five steel double-edged safety razor blades "for OLD and NEW Type Razors." In 1895 King C. Gillette invented the safety razor. Gillette, a salesman for the Crown Cork & Seal Company, of Baltimore, Maryland, in the 1890's, was a personal friend of William Painter's, the inventor of the crown cap. Painter inspired Gillette to invent the double-edged safety razor blade, although it did not reach the market until 1903. Only 51 razors and 168 blades were sold during the first year. In 1904, however, the product caught on, and 90,844 razors and 123,648 blades were sold. Gillette's razor initially sold for five dollars, but soon two-dollar and one-dollar razors were introduced; then razors at fifty cents and at twenty-five cents; and finally came the ten-cent razor, complete with blades. The razor blade for Coca-Cola was produced and marketed in about 1910. It is hard to determine the quality of these razor blades because so few exist today. The occasional advertisements indicate that the razor blades were a relatively small and short venture.

Chewing gum was invented by Thomas Adams in the mid-1800's from chicle (dried sap of sapodilla trees), given to him as a possible rubber substitute by the famous Mexican general Antonio López de Santa Anna. By the 1870's there were several chewing-gum manufacturers. In 1875 John Colgan, a Louisville, Kentucky, druggist, made one of the first flavored chewing gums by adding aromatic balsam to chicle. In 1880 another druggist, Edward E. Beeman, introduced a pepsin compound which he manufactured into gum. In 1908 a "Coca-Cola Pepsin Gum" was produced by the Franklin Manufacturing Company, of Richmond, Virginia. In the 1908 drug catalog (page 556) of Peter Van Schaack & Sons, of Chicago, there is an advertisement for Coca-Cola Pepsin Gum, in which a Buster Brown–type boy stands with his hands in his pockets (a habit frowned on in the early 1900's by most parents). Beneath him is the slogan "Suits Me by Gum." The catalog explains among other things that Coca-Cola Pepsin Gum "aids digestion and gives comfort after a hearty meal" and that twenty five-cent packages (a box) cost sixty cents wholesale.

In addition to a few well-preserved packages of Coca-Cola gum, collectors have recently discovered a number of clear-glass display jars embossed "Coca-Cola Pepsin Gum" (on the obverse) and "MANUFACTURED BY FRANKLIN MFG. CO., RICHMOND, VA." (on the reverse). Another type of jar known to exist is of identical shape, glass, and measurements but with the embossment (on the obverse) "Coca-Cola Chewing Gum."

Chewing gum was apparently the most successful of the products known to have carried the Coca-Cola trademark in the early 1900's. The advertisements, display jars, and the relatively large number of packages of gum still in existence suggest that the selling of this gum was most likely not just a small venture; it was marketed for at least eight years, from 1908 to 1916.

This is a proof of the first cigar band made as a promotion or convention item by Consolidated Lithographing Company, of Brooklyn, New York, in 1927. The proof was rejected by The Coca-Cola Company because the entire trademark was not shown on the bottle.

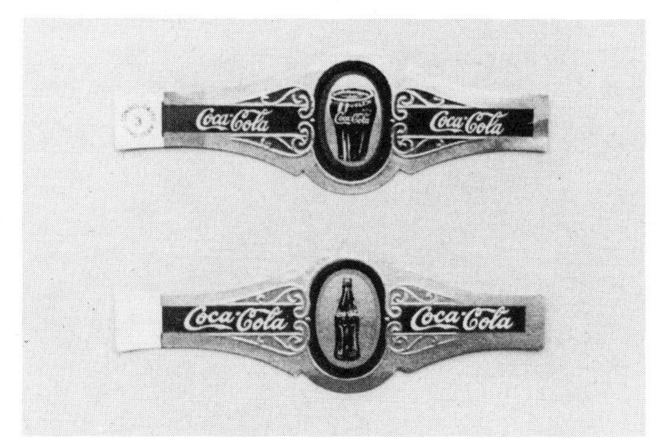

These are the two different cigar bands manufactured intermittently from 1927 to 1944 for The Coca-Cola Company by the Consolidated Lithographing Company. These bands were produced in lots of ten thousand each and were used to promote the sales of Coke in glasses (top) and Coke in bottles (bottom).

A box of safety razor blades produced and marketed around 1910. The box is red, with white lettering. Razor blades were one of three products, in addition to Coke, that were marketed under the trademark of "Coca-Cola."

COCA-COLA PEPSIN GUM

suits the boy. It will suit you and your boy. No adulteration in Coca-Cola Gum. It is all gum and stays big. Don't melt. Made of the best grade of Mexican chicle gum and finest flavorings and Pepsin used in its preparation. It aids digestion and gives comfort after a hearty meal.

COCA-COLA PEPSIN GUM HAS A LASTING FLAVOR

20 5-cent packages, box - - - - 60c

An advertisement for Coca-Cola Pepsin Gum on page 556 of the 1908 drug catalog of Peter Van Schaack & Sons, of Chicago (*Jack K. Rimalover, Stonybrook Associates, Princeton Junction, New Jersey*)

A clear glass display jar made in 1908. The obverse (*left*) is embossed "Coca-Cola Pepsin Gum," and the reverse (*right*) is embossed "MANUFACTURED BY FRANKLIN MFG. CO., RICHMOND, VA." The jar measures 4½ by 11 inches and features a ground glass stopper embossed on the obverse with "Coca-Cola."

A clear glass display jar, 4½ by 11 inches, with embossing "Coca-Cola Chewing Gum" (*Thurman Maness, Maness House, Inc., Valatie, New York*)

A stick of Coca-Cola Gum, spearmint flavor, measuring 2¾ inches in length. The package is red, with white lettering.

CHAPTER 10

WAGONS AND TRUCKS

The Coca-Cola Company has always used heavy-duty vehicles to transport either syrup in kegs and barrels *or* the bottled beverage in cases. Some collectors of the memorabilia of Coca-Cola are very much interested in the early vehicles used by The Coca-Cola Company, especially vehicles used prior to World War II.

Wagons were the first vehicles used to transport Coca-Cola; as such they are of prime collecting interest. There is no such thing as a Coca-Cola wagon; only wagons used by The Coca-Cola Company. The company did not have wagons built to its specifications, but hundreds of horse-drawn vehicles were modified to fit the requirements of delivering Coca-Cola in kegs, barrels, or bottles. The key to distinguishing a collectible wagon from the average old collectible wagon lies in the painting. Since approximately 1885 to 1915, wagons used by The Coca-Cola Company and its bottlers were almost always painted with the trademark "Coca-Cola" and other advertising for the product. Sometimes special signs were separately painted and attached to the wagon. Other keys are the modifications made to make the vehicle a more workable transporter of Coca-Cola.

A highly desirable accessory that was often found attached to these old wagons is the large umbrella employed to shield the driver from the sun. Such umbrellas (about the size of beach umbrellas) were often brightly painted with advertisements for Coca-Cola. They are not usually found with the old wagons but may be discovered elsewhere.

Motor-driven trucks have long been the prime movers of the products of Coca-Cola. Early in the 1900's the more successful bottlers began to use various types of trucks. These trucks may also be identified by painted advertisements and alterations in structure. As might be expected, many trucks of pre-World War II vintage have already been collected.

The Coca-Cola Company runs the world's second-largest fleet of trucks. First place goes to the United States Postal Service.

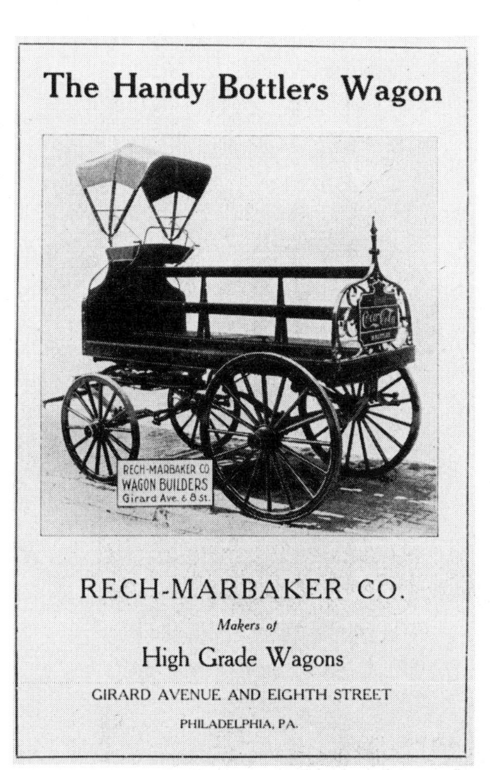

Left: This full-page advertisement from the April, 1909, issue of *The Coca-Cola Bottler* magazine shows one of the many wagons that were used as carriers of Coca-Cola.

Right: This 1913 photograph shows a wagon used for delivering bottled Coca-Cola. The umbrella over the driver's seat was used to shade the driver and advertise Coca-Cola. (*Archives, The Coca-Cola Company, Atlanta, Georgia*)

Right: This photograph, taken in 1914, shows a wagon that has been modified to accommodate cases of bottled Coca-Cola. (*Archives, The Coca-Cola Company, Atlanta, Georgia*)

The truck shown in this 1909 photograph is one of the first used to transport bottled Coca-Cola from bottling plants to retail outlets. Such vehicles are very valuable and have long been the interest of collectors of old vehicles. (*Archives, The Coca-Cola Company, Atlanta, Georgia*)

The truck pictured here was typical of those used to deliver bottled Coca-Cola in 1920. This particular photograph was taken in New Orleans, Louisiana. (*Archives, The Coca-Cola Company, Atlanta, Georgia*)

This 1934 photograph, taken in Cincinnati, Ohio, shows a truck used in the 1930's to deliver Coca-Cola. The truck is painted according to the specifications adopted by the Standardization Committee of The Coca-Cola Company. (*Archives, The Coca-Cola Company, Atlanta, Georgia*)

CHAPTER 11

GLASSES AND GLASS HOLDERS

Glasses manufactured specifically to hold Coca-Cola are almost as old as the beverage itself. When the drink was first marketed in 1886, plain unmarked glasses were used at soda fountains. In the early 1890's, after Asa G. Candler founded The Coca-Cola Company, the brand name was displayed on glasses and holders.

All of what is known about glasses and holders for Coca-Cola before the turn of the century has been gleaned from advertisements of the period. For some pre- and post-1900 glasses or holders, no actual specimens are known to exist. One theory is that the advertising illustrations, which lend evidence to the hope that there were glasses and holders before 1900, may very well be the figment of an overenthusiastic company and its ambitious advertising department, which in this case may have been Asa G. Candler himself.

At any rate, advertisements of the early 1890's picture wasp-waisted glasses etched with the trademark "Coca-Cola" and encircled with a holder that was a silver band and handle. In some illustrations the silver band only partially encircles the glass and appears easy to remove so that the glass could be washed.

Several 1901 and 1902 advertisements picture a straight-sided glass in a very ornate silver holder. The holder is highlighted with the trademark "Coca-Cola." The same holder is pictured in an advertising brochure as well, along with the information "Supplied either direct or by the trade at the following Net Cash price list: . . . ."

The earliest glasses of which there are currently actual specimens appeared around 1900. These glasses have a relatively straight and cylindrical base and taper out to a flared lip. While all of these glasses featured the "Coca-Cola" trademark, some read "Drink Coca-Cola," some "Drink Coca-Cola 5¢," and many had a syrup line about a half-inch from the base.

In the early 1920's a new design was introduced. The new glasses were practically the same as the older ones except that there was a slight inward tapering of the lip. Glass engineers had shown officials of The Coca-Cola Company that the slightly revised design was stronger and would greatly reduce breakage.

The glass shape of the 1920's proved so successful that in the early 1930's a more modified version of the 1920's design was introduced. Without careful inspection the newest model is hard to distinguish from its earlier counterpart by its shape alone. Syrup dispensers in the 1930's would measure the proper amount of syrup, so that a syrup line on the glass was no longer necessary. The lack of this distinguishing mark is the best way to identify a post-1930 fountain glass. Except for several size modifications, fountain glasses have remained unchanged since the 1930's.

Thus far the discussion has been limited to glasses specifically used at soda fountains and similar outlets where Coca-Cola was sold in glasses. In the early 1930's, when bottled Coca-Cola began to outstrip fountain sales, advertisements for the beverage began to stress a variety of glasses for home use. None of these glasses were marked or produced by The Coca-Cola Company; they were just a variety obtainable at most department stores. The company has not made great attempts to develop and market glasses for home use. Although a number of glasses have been produced and distributed for advertising purposes, they were limited issues and do not resemble the traditional fountain glasses. Several times The Coca-Cola Company has allowed other firms to produce glasses with its trademark on them. Such glasses were either given away as promotional items by the firms that ordered them or sold retail on the open market. There are also glasses produced by individual bottlers for general and localized advertising reasons or those made by local bottlers to commemorate special occasions.

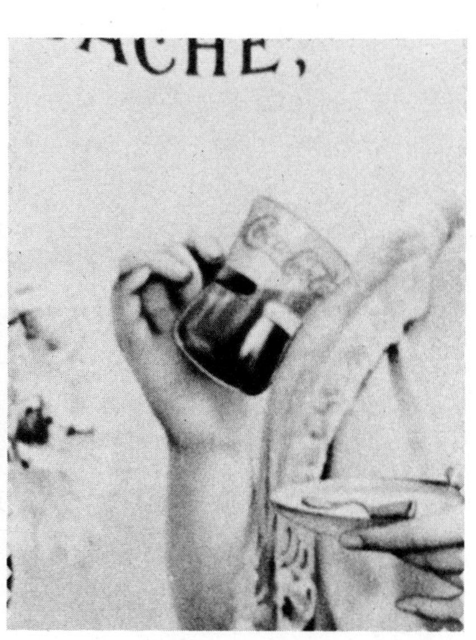

During the mid-1890's The Coca-Cola Company displayed these glasses and holders in their advertisements. Since no examples of either are currently known to exist, there is speculation that they were planned but never produced.

This glass holder first appeared in company advertising in 1901. Although many such holders may have been manufactured, only two specimens are currently known to exist. (*Archives, The Coca-Cola Company, Atlanta, Georgia*)

Calendars for 1901 (*left*) and 1902 (*right*) pictured a plain, cylindrically shaped glass and a sterling-silver glass-holder featuring the trademark "Coca-Cola."

The Coca-Cola tray for 1912 pictures a glass marked with the trademark "Coca-Cola" encircled by a large "5." Few of these glasses were made, and as a result, few have survived. Those still in existence are considered quite valuable by collectors.

This glass is pictured in advertisements for 1922, but no actual specimens are currently known to exist. The glass may have been only an advertising illustration and may never have been actually produced.

Two identical miniature glasses, 1½ inches high, made in 1925 as an advertising item. Unlike real Coca-Cola glasses, these feature an embossment of the trademark "Coca-Cola."

A fountain glass typical of 1900–1920. Such glasses were always marked with the trademark "Coca-Cola." There were sometimes other markings, such as "Drink" and/or a syrup line near the bottom, as in this example. (*Archives, The Coca-Cola Company, Atlanta, Georgia*)

A glass of the 1900–1920 period. This particular specimen, with the arrow-shaped "5," was first produced in 1905 and probably last made in 1915. (*Archives, The Coca-Cola Company, Atlanta, Georgia*)

An example of a modified version of the early 1900's fountain glass. This type, with a modified flared lip, was first produced in 1923. (*Archives, The Coca-Cola Company, Atlanta, Georgia*)

A modified version of the 1920's fountain glass, first produced in 1935. The lack of a syrup mark near the bottom of the glass (typical of earlier glasses) is an easy way to identify this model. These glasses have been used into the 1970's, and reproductions have been distributed on the open market for home use. (*Archives, The Coca-Cola Company, Atlanta, Georgia*)

Glasses of this shape have been used for Coca-Cola since the mid-1930's. These examples were made in the late 1960's and early 1970's. The obverses (*top*) are marked "Drink Coca-Cola," and the reverses (*bottom*) are identified by "Enjoy Coke." From left to right the glasses measure 4, 4¾, 5, and 6 inches in height.

A glass for home use, designed and distributed as a promotional item. Similar glasses have been produced with company permission and sold on the retail market by independent firms.

Two glasses produced in the early 1960's by The Coca-Cola Company for advertising purposes. Such glasses were designed for home use, whereas the traditional glasses were used exclusively for fountain drinks.

CHAPTER 12

BOTTLES AND BOTTLE CAPS

Because John S. Pemberton and Asa Griggs Candler did not envision the tremendous potential for Coca-Cola in bottles and Robert W. Woodruff's administration did not start until 1923, a study of the history of Coca-Cola bottles must begin with Joseph A. Biedenharn, of Vicksburg, Mississippi, who in 1894 was the first man to bottle Coca-Cola.

The first bottles to contain ready-to-drink Coca-Cola were not identified by the product's trademark. The first Coca-Cola bottles were short six-ounce bottles utilizing the popular Hutchinson stopper. The stopper consisted of a rubber gasket (which came in five sizes to accommodate various neck diameters) held between two metal plates and attached to a spring wire stem (which came in three sizes to accommodate various neck lengths). A portion of the looped wire stem protruded above the mouth of the bottle, and the lower end with the gasket and plates extended far enough into the bottle to allow the gasket to fall below the neck. To seal the bottle after it had been filled, the rubber disk was pulled up by the wire stem. The bottle was then inverted and righted. This motion formed the seal; the pressure of the carbonation forced the rubber gasket to remain against the shoulder of the bottle. The first bottles used by Biedenharn for Coca-Cola were also used for the other beverages he manufactured. Consequently they were identified with only the embossments "REGISTERED" across the shoulder of the bottles, and "BIEDENHARN CANDY CO. VICKSBURG MISS." in a circle on the bottles.

Although Joseph Biedenharn's bottling of

Coca-Cola was limited, his total line of bottled soda water was fairly extensive. As a result, bottles used by the Biedenharn Candy Company are not impossible for today's collectors to obtain.

The second bottles to contain Coca-Cola are from Valdosta, Georgia. As briefly mentioned in a previous chapter, R. H. Holmes and E. R. Barber, of the Valdosta Bottling Works, were owners of the second soda-water bottling company to put Coca-Cola in bottles; the year they added Coca-Cola to their line was 1897.

In a letter written in 1954, one of the pioneering partners of the Valdosta firm described the venture as follows:

> We started bottling Coca-Cola in the old Hutchinson soda water bottle with an iron stopper with a rubber washer attached. The majority of our business was out of town and merchandise was shipped in crates that held seventy-two bottles. At first we would include *only six bottles of Coca-Cola in each crate* [italics added]. The drink was well accepted on the trade and our customers requested larger shipments of Coca-Cola. . . .

Similarly, the Holmes and Barber bottles from Valdosta were not embossed with the Coca-Cola trademark, because the firm bottled a number of beverages and as a result only used one type of bottle. Because neither the Vicksburg nor the Valdosta Hutchinson-stoppered soda-water bottles were specifically identified with the Coca-Cola trademark, the inclusion of these bottles in a collection of Coca-Cola bottles is questioned by a few collectors. Such collectors do have a point, especially since Biedenharn began bottling soda water in 1891 (Coca-Cola in 1894) and Holmes and Barber began in 1894 (Coca-Cola in 1897). Any objections to including the earliest bottles of these two firms in a collection of Coca-Cola bottles is probably not significant when it is realized that the sturdy Hutchinson-type bottles were returnable and reused for a number of years. Furthermore, the odds are very strong that if a bottle was reused, it would eventually have been used to hold Coca-Cola.

Before continuing this chronological study of Coca-Cola bottles, it seems important to make a parenthetical examination of the bottling industry of the late 1800's and the early 1900's.

One of the main problems of the period was finding a suitable bottle closure. Although hundreds of closing devices were invented during the last decades of the nineteenth century, relatively few were used to any extent. Almost without exception every stopper had some objectionable feature, and more often than not the major objections were related to initial expense, poor sanitation, and/or impracticality. One of the most popular bottle closures of turn-of-the-century America was the Hutchinson stopper, which was invented by Charles G. Hutchinson, of Chicago, in 1879. As mentioned, Hutchinson bottles were used for the first bottlings of Coca-Cola. Regarding these first attempts, E. R. Barber, of the Valdosta Bottling Works, explained, "We soon discovered that we were running into a great deal of trouble [with Hutchinson bottles] due to the fact that the rubber washer on the stopper caused a not-too-wholesome odor in the drink [Coca-Cola] after it had been bottled for a period of ten days or two weeks."

In 1891 William Painter, of Baltimore, Maryland, invented his third and what was to become the most popular and practical beverage bottle closure of the first half of the twentieth century —the crown cork. Even though the crown cork was patented in 1891, it was not until a decade later that it began to enjoy widespread use. E. R. Barber, of Valdosta, Georgia, describes his experiences with the crown cork in relationship to Coca-Cola:

> A new bottling machine was invented by the old Crown, [sic] Cork, and Seal Company that used the present day [1954] type of crown and we placed an order for two or [sic] three machines around 1900. However, we were unable

> to obtain but one of these machines due to the large amount of orders which they had on hand and the salesman advised us that this machine was the first one sold in the state of Georgia. As soon as this foot power machine arrived, it was put into immediate operation and was used to bottle Coca-Cola exclusively. This new process enabled us to ship Coca-Cola by the case without any fear of spoilage of merchandise and for the first time we were able to supply the demand for Coca-Cola.

The original bottling plant in Chattanooga, Tennessee, and the others that followed generally used the Hutchinson-stoppered bottles because the more practical, more sanitary, and less expensive crown-cork bottles and machines did not become accepted in the bottling industry until around 1905 or 1910.

It is interesting to note that the Chattanooga, Tennessee, firm used two different types of Hutchinson-stoppered bottles before they switched to the crown-cork bottle. Both types were embossed around the bottle base with "CHATTANOOGA, TENN.," and one was embossed with the Spencerian-script Coca-Cola trademark on the shoulder and the other type on the bottle base opposing the geographical marking. History reveals that the Chattanooga firm used plain unembossed Hutchinson-stoppered bottles; these, of course, may be found but cannot be positively identified as being from Chattanooga or as having contained Coca-Cola.

Bottle caps took the bottling industry by surprise shortly after the turn of the century. With the aid of state laws which gradually outlawed most other closures as being unsanitary, they became the most popular closure of the beverage industry. The Coca-Cola Company encouraged crown-type caps until 1915, when its standardized bottle was invented, and then crown-type caps became mandatory.

Until recent years collectors have not shown much interest in gathering Coca-Cola bottle caps because they were all essentially the same regardless of the firm that manufactured them. There are differences in the crown-type caps of the various manufacturers, but variations are so slight that they have for the most part escaped collectors' notice.

In the 1950's Coca-Cola bottle caps began to capture collectors' attention. The Coca-Cola Company periodically lithographed various pictures on the interior of its caps. After removal of the cork disk a collector (usually a youngster) could note which in the series he had. A gathering of an entire series certainly makes an interesting collection. Because children have saved such bottle caps, there are a number available today for adult collectors. In addition, caps used on bottles of Coca-Cola sold in foreign countries feature numerous languages. Collectors have casually collected examples from the countries represented (well over one hundred), and these are frequently available today. Coca-Cola crown-type caps of a pre-World War II vintage are scarce and considered quite valuable today by collectors.

Until 1916 Coca-Cola bottles were very much a matter of each individual bottler's choice. Consequently, from 1899 until 1916 a large variety of shapes were produced and used by the various bottlers. Along with the variety in shapes there are differences in glass color. It will be recalled that Thomas and Whitehead (and Lupton) each preferred a different-color bottle for Coca-Cola. Thomas insisted that Coca-Cola should be packaged in amber glass and Whitehead and Lupton maintained that clear flint glass should be the color of Coca-Cola bottles. Generally the bottlers honored the wishes of Thomas and Whitehead (and Lupton), and many bottles of the period were made either of amber or of clear glass. Still, it is not unusual to locate Coca-Cola bottles of the 1899–1916 period, from either of the two territories, made in the more common and less expensive light green or aqua glass. Because of their variety, the bottles of this early period make up the bulk of almost any collection of Coca-Cola bottles.

During the first decade of the nineteenth century Coca-Cola bottles differed only slightly from the hundreds of other beverage bottles of the time, and it was relatively simple for a bottler to produce and market an imitation of the Coca-Cola bottle. The growing number of imitators annoyed the producers of Coca-Cola, and they began to ponder ways of putting a stop to the parasitic mimics.

Benjamin Franklin Thomas made the suggestion that ultimately solved the problem. He is quoted as saying, "We need a distinctive package that will help us fight substitution. We need a bottle which a person can recognize as a Coca-Cola bottle when he feels it in the dark. The Coca-Cola bottle should be so shaped that, even if broken, it would be recognized at a glance for what it is." Furthermore, in July, 1913, Harold Hirsch, whose law firm served as general counsel for The Coca-Cola Company and some of the parent bottlers, wrote a letter to all of the parent bottlers and advised them that from a legal standpoint it would be advantageous to develop and adopt a uniform bottle for Coca-Cola.

Beginning in 1913, the various bottle manufacturers who were supplying the Coca-Cola industry were asked to design the unique Coca-Cola bottle. Almost a dozen designs were submitted and studied by a committee of seven bottlers, who met at the 1916 bottlers' convention in Atlanta, Georgia. The committee's final selection was a design submitted by the Root Glass Company, of Terre Haute, Indiana.

During the summer of 1913 the Root Glass Company was idle because of excessive heat, and the president of the company, Chapman J. Root, assembled his supervisory staff and read them the challenge issued by The Coca-Cola Company. The entire supervisory staff spent the two-month period developing the needed bottle. The staff consisted of Alexander Samuelson, plant superintendent; T. Clyde Edwards, auditor; Roy Hurt, secretary; Earl R. Dean, mold shop supervisor; and William Root, son of the president. T. Clyde Edwards did the necessary research, and Earl Dean developed a bottle design from the research which featured a bulging middle with parallel vertical grooves and tapered ends. The first model was made of wood, and from the wooden model Dean made the necessary iron mold. A small number of bottles were blown in the experimental design shape. However, they were found to be too large around the shoulder to fit existing bottling machinery, and most of the experimental bottles were destroyed. Both Dean and Samuelson each kept one of the experimental bottles. Dean's bottle is still kept by his descendants, and Samuelson's has been given to the archives of The Coca-Cola Company by his son.

In 1971 the Owens-Illinois Glass Company in Toledo, Ohio, made a mold from the original Coca-Cola bottle in the archives of The Coca-Cola Company and produced five thousand bottles. These reproductions are identical to the original except that the dates "1915–1965" are embossed on the bottom. The reproduced bottles were distributed at a belated fiftieth anniversary celebration of the bottle's creation. A number have recently appeared on the collectors' market priced at several hundred dollars. In some instances the dates embossed on the bottoms of the bottles have been carefully ground away, and the bottles are sold as originals. It is highly unlikely that any of the original bottles, other than the two already mentioned, are still in existence and even more unlikely that collectors would ever have the opportunity to obtain an original bottle.

Bottles were blown in the shape of the final design, which was patented in Alex Samuelson's name on November 16, 1915 (U.S. Patent #48160), and tested at the Coca-Cola bottling plants in Birmingham and Anniston, Alabama, Augusta, Georgia, and Nashville, Tennessee, on a confidential basis at night, with only the bottlers and superintendents present.

Shortly after the modified bottle was selected

by the assigned committee, the new bottle was put into production. For the first year, as contracted, the Root Glass Company was the only firm allowed to manufacture the new bottle. After that period other firms were allowed to produce Coca-Cola bottles under the supervision of the Root Glass Company. Subsequently supervision was taken over by The Coca-Cola Company.

It was almost 1920 before the new contoured bottle, which had quickly picked up the nicknames Mae West and hobble skirt, was being used almost universally throughout the Coca-Cola bottling industry. The reason for the delay was that there were literally millions of straight-sided Coca-Cola bottles in circulation at the time of the adoption, and each bottler wanted to continue to use these as long as they were serviceable. Bottlers ordered the new bottles as they needed them, and within a two- to three-year period, bottlers ended up with a complete set of the new "hobble-skirt" or "Mae West" bottles.

Until 1923 the Coca-Cola bottle went unchanged, and then Chapman J. Root patented the bottle in his name (U.S. Patent #63657), and for the next fourteen years The Coca-Cola Company paid Root a five-cent royalty on every gross of bottles manufactured. The only noticeable change was the replacement of the embossed November 16, 1915, patent date with one that read "December 25, 1923." Because of the December 25 dating, the 1923 specimen is often called the Christmas Coke bottle.

Such a romantic patent dating could not help stirring the imaginations of many people. For many years the tale was told of a shrewd man who noticed the Christmas dating and quietly patented the bottle himself on a nonholiday. He then went to Atlanta and asked the officials of The Coca-Cola Company if they liked their bottle and if they wanted to continue using it. The company assured the man that they liked the bottle and did want to continue using it. The man then ambled out of Coca-Cola headquarters about $500,000 richer after selling the company his patent rights on their bottle. The story is not true. The U.S. Patent Office always issues patents on Tuesdays, even if they are not actually working on that day. In 1923 Christmas happened to fall on Tuesday—thus the reason for the romantic patent date.

In 1937 The Coca-Cola Company acquired the patent for the contour bottle from Chapman J. Root. A slight change was the replacement of the December 25, 1923, bottle embossment with "BOTTLE PAT. D105529," which is the March 24, 1937, identifying patent number.

The 1937 patent ran out in 1951, and for nine years, or until 1960, the Coca-Cola bottle was protected under common law rights. In 1960 the U.S. Patent Office registered the classic contoured Coca-Cola bottle shape as the third trademark identified with the product Coca-Cola. Until 1960 only one other bottle had ever been registered by the U.S. Patent Office as a trademark—the Haig & Haig pinch bottle, which was registered in 1958.

The first change in the bottle as patented in 1937 came in 1948 when the State of New York passed a law that stipulated that all packages sold in that state containing liquid contents must be identified with the actual liquid contents. Until that time Coca-Cola bottles were embossed "MINIMUM CONTENTS 6 FL. OZS." Rather than producing only some bottles that would specifically comply with the new New York law, the company just changed all Coca-Cola bottles. The replacement embossment, therefore, became "6½ FL. OZS."

The next change of the 1937 bottle came in 1951 when the fourteen-year patent ran out. At that time the "BOTTLE PAT. D105529" embossment was dropped, and "IN U.S. PATENT OFFICE" was put in its place.

From the first use of the Samuelson hobble-skirt bottle in 1916 until 1955, the name of the city and state in which the Coca-Cola was initially bottled was embossed on the bottom. In 1955 the practice was halted because it seemed to serve no function; once a bottle was initially filled there was no guarantee that it would not be carried to another town and rebottled there. Coca-Cola bottlers do not even attempt to exchange bottles.

The Coca-Cola Company had not taken into consideration the consumer's fascination and fondness for the bottler's address on the Coca-Cola bottle. It is a favorite American pastime to drink a bottle of Coca-Cola and then compare the city and state embossment with someone else who has just finished one also. The game is to see who has the bottle embossed with the name of a place the greatest distance away. The public's insistence that the bottler's town be a part of a Coke bottle was finally heeded, and in 1963, eight years after its removal, the favored embossment was put back on the bottle. At first it was an optional feature left up to individual bottlers who were willing to pay for it. Shortly thereafter, bottle manufacturers dropped the extra charge. Furthermore, most bottlers not only approved and requested city and state embossments, but they asked for a mix of all cities and states.

In 1957 The Coca-Cola Company decided to eliminate the traditional embossing of its trademark, "Coca-Cola," on the bottle and replace it with "Coca-Cola" in white Applied Color Labeling (ACL). The remainder of the information remained an embossed feature on the bottle. The ACL process was first developed in the United States around 1920. It was not until the 1930's, however, that it began to replace the popular mold-created embossments as a means of decoration and identification. By 1957, when The Coca-Cola Company adopted the process for its bottles, the process had been refined to the point that a bottle could be imprinted during a single trip through the automatic printing machine instead of the previous two trips. The actual process consists of powdering a borosilicate, which has a low melting point, mixing it with an oxide for color, and adding a thermoplastic wax or plastic resin. The resulting paste is applied to the bottle through a stainless-steel screen similar to the screen used in silk-screening.

In 1958 the traditional bottle was produced with an ACL "Coke" on the throat, but that was not a universal action. Some of the bottles continued to be produced without the trademark "Coke" on the throat. After 1961 the ACL "Coke" became standard. The only change in the bottle that came with registration of the Coca-Cola bottle in 1960 was the addition of the "registration dimple," on the bottom of the bottle, which is a circle around a capital "R." After 1960 all Coca-Cola bottles have been marked with "TRADE MARK" and the registration dimple.

Beginning in 1963, along with the reappearance of the town embossment already discussed, "Coke" in ACL was placed on the shoulder panel of the bottle, opposite a panel containing "Coca-Cola" in ACL; "6½ oz." was then placed on one side panel. In 1965 another marking of "6½ oz." was added to the other side panel of the classic contoured bottle. Although the basic bottle shape patented in 1915 in Alex Samuelson's name has not been altered throughout the years, a number of other changes have occurred and can be used by collectors to date bottles.

Another excellent method of dating bottles from 1916 to the present is by examining the series of manufacturer's numbers near the base or on the bottom of the bottles. On the older bottles a series of four numbers can usually be found, such as "14–29." The first two indicate the mold number ("14" in the example) and the second two the year of manufacture ("29"—or 1929—in the example). Recent Coca-Cola bottles have a refined system. Four digits are still used, the first digit indicating the year; the second, the mold; the third, the manufacturer's symbol; and the fourth digit, the glass plant of origin.

Appendix A in this book lists Coca-Cola bottling firms alphabetically by state and city, along with the date they started in business. By noting the starting date of a firm, collectors can determine when bottles were first used. This information, coupled with the material presented in this chapter, should provide accurate dating, especially for the older bottles.

From its inception in 1916 a light-green glass has been consistently used as the color for the classic contoured bottle. This color has been called Georgia-green by The Coca-Cola Company. As will happen, however, manufacturing "mistakes" have been made over the years, and it is not impossible to obtain Coca-Cola bottles produced in an ice-blue or emerald-green color. Additionally, there are some bottles that were produced on an experimental basis in dark amber in the United States. There were some bottles, made in Indochina by the Japanese during World War II, with confiscated Coca-Cola bottle molds. They were used to contain soy sauce. These bottles are easily identified because they feature the glass plant number (19) on the left side of the manufacturer's design symbol and the year number (44) on the right side of the symbol.

In parts of the world outside the United States, clear glass Coca-Cola bottles are often used. In fact, between 1915 and the end of World War II, whenever Coca-Cola was introduced into a foreign country, clear glass bottles were used; after World War II the Georgia-green glass bottle was usually used in foreign countries.

A few of the pre-1916 bottlers sold Coca-Cola in quart bottles they had specially made for the purpose. In 1955 The Coca-Cola Company introduced the king-size line. Bottles were produced to hold ten, twelve, sixteen, and twenty-six ounces of Coca-Cola. Although larger, the four king-size bottles each retained the classical Coca-Cola bottle shape. Market research had showed that the competition was making inroads and taking business with their variety of products and package sizes. After much research, testing, and evaluation The Coca-Cola Company made what was probably one of the biggest decisions in its history—it decided to offer Coca-Cola in a variety of larger packages.

The second decision was to revive a beverage called Fanta which had been sold in Germany during World War II when Coca-Cola syrup was unavailable there. The Fanta Division was actually formed in 1960 as a line of fruit flavors, including the lemon-lime Sprite. To compete with the diet-cola competition, The Coca-Cola Company next introduced Tab. More diversification came in 1960 when The Coca-Cola Company acquired the Minute Maid Corporation. In addition to being one of the nation's leading producers of fruit juices, the Minute Maid Corporation owned an instant coffee company. This acquisition instantly put The Coca-Cola Company in the coffee business. In 1964 The Coca-Cola Company purchased Duncan Foods Company, which made and distributed coffee products. Another drink was introduced in 1966—Fresca. More recently, Simba was added to the beverage line, and in May, 1970, The Coca-Cola Company purchased Aqua-Chem, Inc., of Milwaukee, Wisconsin. Aqua-Chem is a leading maker of water purification equipment.

From 1955 to 1970 the bottle changes and diversifications of The Coca-Cola Company have provided collectors with a number of unusual bottles to collect. Many of the more than 250 new products resulting from this fifteen-year period are bottled products. Gold Coca-Cola bottles are another unusual type that can be collected. Since 1949, when the Coca-Cola bottling industry celebrated its fiftieth anniversary, it has been the policy of the bottle manufacturers to supply bottlers with a limited quantity of bottles dipped in gold with gold-washed crown caps. The souvenir bottles are rarely discarded after the usual celebration, and they are often found in bottle collections. Gold bottles are most often found in the $6^1/_2$-ounce size, but other sizes are known.

For advertising purposes, The Coca-Cola Company has often produced its famous contoured bottle in a variety of miniature sizes. Oversized bottles for advertising have also been produced from time to time. Generally the miniature and oversize bottles are identical to the regular bottles.

Another unusual series of bottles that are considered interesting by collectors of Coca-Cola bottles are "flavor" bottles. Many bottlers of Coca-Cola also handle other beverages such as orange, grape, cherry; the bottles used to contain the subsidiary beverage are called flavor bottles. Because the bottles are marked with the name of the Coca-Cola bottler, they are often thought to be unusual bottles used for Coca-Cola. Such an assumption is generally wrong; only in emergencies were such bottles ever to be filled with Coca-Cola. Since the 1930's it would be next to impossible to find a flavor bottle that was ever used for Coca-Cola. A good rule of thumb regarding flavor bottles is that if the words "Coca-Cola" are marked on the bottle in block lettering, the bottle was used for some flavor other than Coca-Cola. There are exceptions to that rule, and bottles used for flavors other than Coca-Cola with the Spencerian script trademark "Coca-Cola" marked on them can be considered very unusual and excellent collectors' items.

Conversely, it is unusual to discover pre-1916 Coca-Cola bottles without the Spencerian script trademark embossed on them. Nevertheless such bottles were produced for bottlers unaware of their obligation to The Coca-Cola Company and its first registered trademark. Such unusual and unauthorized bottles are extremely interesting collectors' items.

In the early 1960's The Coca-Cola Company began to produce its first one-way or nonreturnable glass bottles for domestic use. The first bottles were straight-sided, a deviation from the traditional contoured bottle. Shortly thereafter nonreturnable bottles were produced in the classic contoured hobble-skirt shape and featured Applied Color Labeling (ACL), whereas the first one-way bottles were identified with embossing. In 1970 The Coca-Cola Company marketed its first one-way plastic bottle. These bottles were produced by the Monsanto (chemical) Company and were made of a plastic called Lopac.

Because of their unusual shape and weight, Coca-Cola bottles, like the beverage itself, have been used in rather esoteric ways by clever people. Perhaps the best example of an imaginative use of Coca-Cola bottles on the basis of shape took place during World War II, when the Seabees converted empty bottles into electrical insulators (p. 77). Weight seems to have been an important factor. Standard hobble-skirt Coca-Cola bottles have changed over the years in their empty weight but have always been relatively heavy:

1916–1936	empty weight—14.24 ounces
1937–1956	empty weight—14.01
1957–1958	empty weight—13.80
1958–1962	empty weight—13.65
1963–Present	empty weight—13.26

While there are easier methods of dating Coca-Cola bottles, a consideration of weight can be an effective tool for collectors. The relatively heavy Coca-Cola bottle has been used successfully as a hammer, a drumstick, and in various ways as a weapon.

Coca-Cola and its classical bottle have long been recognized by many people as a symbol of America and the American way of life. In 1940 Oglethorpe University in Atlanta, Georgia, put together a "Crypt of Civilization" to be opened in the year 8113. Among the symbols of American culture was a bottle of Coca-Cola. The bottle was especially prepared for its long rest in the time capsule. The cap was securely affixed with molten asphaltum and several layers of silicate. It was then hermetically sealed in a glass container, wrapped in asbestos, and finally the whole thing was embedded in a stainless-steel cylinder.

It is interesting to examine material produced for "the world's most famous bottle" at the golden anniversary dinner of The Coca-Cola Bottling Company (Thomas), Inc., in New York City in 1949. It read:

> Many billions of drinks of Coca-Cola have flowed from bottling plant to consumer in the standard package. The bottle designed on the banks of the Wabash has made its way into every corner of America and into most of the countries of the world. In the minds of millions beyond the seas, the famous bottle—like the bathtub, the automobile, and the refrigerator—is now a symbol of America and the rich abundant life of its people.

During the same year, the Parker Pen Company conducted what it called a Product Recognition Study. Four hundred people, randomly selected, were shown pictures of a Parker Pen, a Ronson cigarette lighter, a Ford automobile, and a Coca-Cola bottle. The results were revealing: 64.5 percent identified the pen, 75 percent the car, 81.75 percent the lighter, and 99 percent identified the Coca-Cola bottle.

Highlights in the History of Bottles Used to Contain Coca-Cola

Date	*Type*	*Remarks*
1894	Hutchinson-stoppered bottle from Beidenharn Candy Co. (Vicksburg, Mississippi).	First bottle to contain Coca-Cola.
1897	Hutchinson-stoppered bottle from Valdosta Bottling Works (Valdosta, Georgia).	Second bottle to contain Coca-Cola.
1899	Hutchinson-stoppered bottle from Chattanooga, Tennessee: 1. Unembossed 2. Embossed "Coca-Cola" in script on shoulder. 3. Embossed "Coca-Cola" in script around base.	First bottle to be marked with trademark "Coca-Cola" in script.
ca. 1899–1910	Hutchinson-stoppered bottle.	This bottle type was used but was being phased out.
ca. 1905–1916	Crown-cork bottle.	Generally straight-sided with paper labels in amber, clear, aqua, and light-green colors.
1916	Classical contoured ("Mae West" or "hobble-skirt") bottle: embossed "BOTTLE PAT'D NOV 16, 1915."	First of contoured bottles (shape was registered as a trademark in 1960).
1916–present tified by "Coca-Cola" in block letters.	Flavor bottle used by bottlers on an individual basis (variety of shapes, colors, and sizes), almost always identified by "Coca-Cola" in block letters.	Generalization.
ca. 1920	Contoured bottle.	Universally used throughout Coca-Cola bottling industry.
1924	Coutoured bottle: embossed "BOTTLE PAT'D DEC. 1923" (Xmas Coke).	Second contoured bottle.

Date	*Type*	*Remarks*
1937	Contoured bottle: embossed "BOTTLE PAT. D105529."	Third contoured bottle.
1948	Contoured bottle: embossment of "MINIMUM CONTENTS 6 FL. OZS." changed to "6½ FL. OZ."	Fourth contoured bottle.
1949	Contoured bottle: gold-dipped bottles to commemorate bottlers' fiftieth year in business.	Produced in limited quantities.
ca. 1950	Contoured bottle: elimination of clear glass bottles for foreign countries.	This is a generalization that applies only to countries that have obtained bottling plants after World War II.
1951	Contoured bottle: "BOTTLE PAT. D105529" embossment changed to "IN U.S. PATENT OFFICE."	Fifth contoured bottle.
1955	Contoured bottle: city and state embossment, used since 1916, was removed.	Sixth contoured bottle.
1955	King-size bottle: contoured bottles in 10-, 12-, 16-, and 26-ounce sizes.	First bottles since 1916 designed for more than 6½ ounces.
1958	Contoured bottle: "Coke" in ACL on neck.	Seventh contoured bottle.
1960	Contoured bottle: "IN U.S. PATENT OFFICE" embossment replaced with "TRADE MARK ®."	Eighth contoured bottle.
1960	Fanta, Sprite, and other fruit flavors plus Tab.	First time The Coca-Cola Company produced subsidiary beverages (something individual bottlers had been doing since 1900).
1963	Contoured bottle: 1. Reappearance of city and state embossment on bottom. 2. "Coke" in ACL moved from neck to shoulder opposing panel containing "Coca-Cola" in ACL. 3. "6½ oz." in ACL added to one panel.	Ninth contoured bottle.
ca. 1964	Straight-sided one-way or nonreturnable bottle with "Coca-Cola" embossment.	First no-deposit bottle for domestic use.
1965	Contoured bottle: Another "6½ oz." in ACL added to another shoulder panel.	Tenth contoured bottle.
1966	Fresca.	
ca. 1966	Contoured: one-way or nonreturnable bottle with ACL markings.	First in nonreturnable glass bottle of contoured design.
1970	Simba.	
1970	Contoured: one-way plastic bottle.	First one-way bottle of plastic.

The first bottle to contain Coca-Cola. The Biedenharn Candy Company, of Vicksburg, Mississippi, began bottling Coca-Cola in these six-ounce Hutchinson-stoppered bottles in 1894. Although these bottles are the oldest, they are not the rarest. The Biedenharn Candy Company bottled a number of beverages in these bottles, and as a result, there are many specimens still in existence.

An array of bottles illustrating general shapes and colors used throughout the years (*Archives, The Coca-Cola Company, Atlanta, Georgia*)

A 1902 Hutchinson-stoppered bottle from Birmingham, Alabama

A 1904 Hutchinson-stoppered bottle from Talladega, Alabama. The Coca-Cola Bottling Company of Talladega was one of the few plants that was not financially successful. In 1922 it was absorbed by the Alabama Coca-Cola Bottling Company, of Anniston, Alabama. (*A. N. Shpil, Castro Valley, California*)

Hard To Beat

COCA COLA
CROWN CORK

A UNIVERSAL CORK

The quality of a beverage is
judged by the seal

The Crown Cork Always
Seals the Best

SOLE MAKERS
The Crown Cork and Seal Co.
BALTIMORE MD.

A page from *The Coca-Cola Bottler* of April, 1909, advertising the closure that became the universal one on beverage bottles. The crown cork was so named because it looked like a crown with a layer of cork inside. This bottle closure was invented in 1891 by William Painter, a Baltimore machine-shop foreman. Before the invention of the crown cork there were over 1,500 patented bottle closures.

Executives of the Crown Cork & Seal Company. Photograph taken in the main office in Baltimore in 1900. Standing, left to right: C. S. Greensfelder; G. E. Sturgis; M. Morris; M. G. Gillette; King Camp Gillette (encircled), who became famous for his 1895 invention of the safety razor; Henry Scarborough; J. T. Hawkins; and B. S. Greensfelder. Seated, left to right: O. C. Painter; Harvey Coale; Joseph Friedenwald; William Painter (encircled), inventor of the Baltimore loop seal and the crown cork; and L. S. Greensfelder. (Soft Drinks *magazine*)

William Painter, inventor of several beverage-bottle closures, including the Baltimore loop seal in 1887 and the crown cork in 1891 (Soft Drinks *magazine—formerly the* National Bottlers' Gazette)

A page from *The Coca-Cola Bottler* of April, 1959, advertising crown corks for Coca-Cola bottles. Crown corks were first manufactured by the Crown Cork & Seal Company, Inc., of Philadelphia, Pennsylvania. This company is still the leading producer today.

Another firm involved in the manufacturing of crown-type caps is Armstrong Packaging, a division of the Armstrong Cork Company, of Lancaster, Pennsylvania. Armstrong crowns are popular with bottlers. This advertisement is from the April, 1959, issue of *The Coca-Cola Bottler.*

Above: Advertisement from the April, 1959, issue of *The Coca-Cola Bottler* promotes the Hutchinson crown cap. W.H. Hutchinson & Son, Inc., was a pioneer in bottle closures, and the firm dates from the mid-1800's. Just before the turn of the century Hutchinson soda-water bottles and closures were the most popular of those used by beverage bottlers at the time. The invention of the crown cork in 1891 and its successful marketing in the early 1900's forced W. H. Hutchinson & Son, Inc., to abandon its bottle and closure. The company began manufacturing its own crown cork. Hutchinson crowns are very popular today.

Advertisement from the April, 1959, issue of *The Coca-Cola Bottler* for Custom crowns, manufactured by Bond Crown & Cork, a division of Continental Can Company. This firm claims to have produced caps for Coca-Cola bottles since 1909.

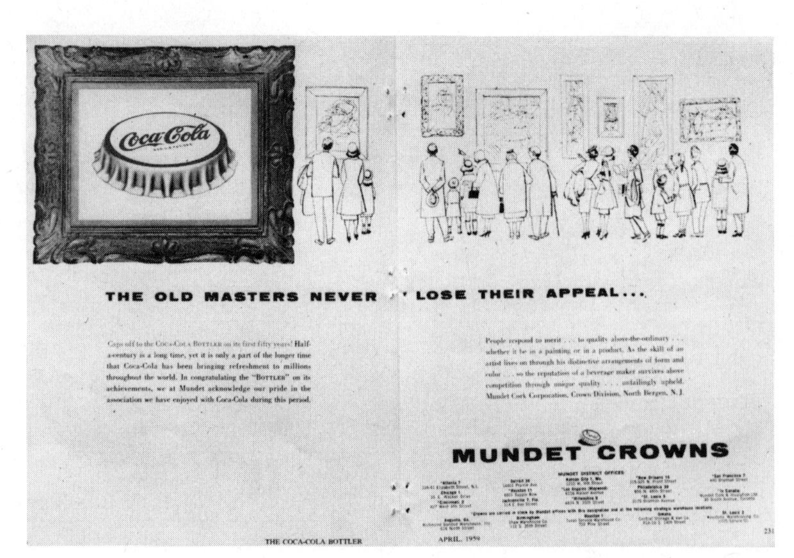

Advertisement for Mundet crowns in the April, 1959, issue of *The Coca-Cola Bottler.* Mundet crowns are made by the Mundet Cork Corporation, of North Bergen, New Jersey.

A "Koke" bottle. This is one of the many imitations that have been put on the market over the years. The Coca-Cola Company has often prosecuted such products to protect its trademark.

A circa 1905 bottle (left) embossed "Coca-Cola" in a circling arrow and "REGISTERED COCA-COLA BOTTLING WKS, 2ND" on the obverse and "COCA-COLA, LOUISVILLE, KY." on the reverse. A circa 1905 bottle (right) embossed "Coca-Cola TRADE MARK REGISTERED SAVANNAH, GA." Both bottles, typical of the period, are 7⅝ inches tall and made of amber (left) and light-green (right) glass.

Examples of clear and light-green glass bottles typical of those used from about 1900 to 1910. Such bottles were also typical of the Whitehead/Lupton territory until the standardized package was adopted in 1916. (*Chris' Studio of Photography, Roseburg, Oregon*)

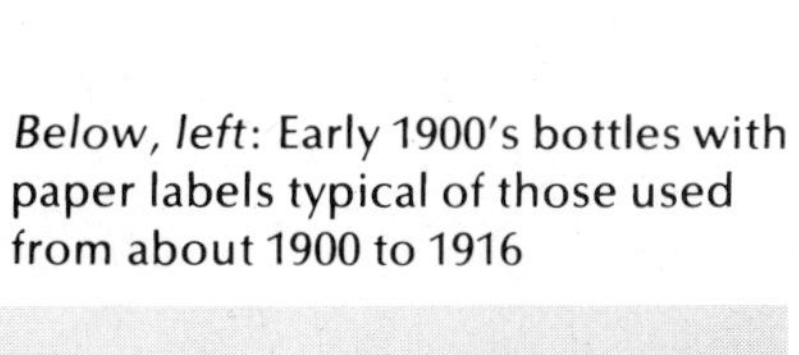

Below, left: Early 1900's bottles with paper labels typical of those used from about 1900 to 1916

An amber glass bottle made circa 1908 in Bristol, Virginia

Typical bottles and paper labels used during the first fifteen years of the twentieth century. Both are made in light-green glass. Left: Atlanta, Georgia, 7½ inches tall. Right: Tampa, Florida, 7⅞ inches tall.

Early 1900's bottles. These illustrate how unorganized the Coca-Cola bottling industry was at the time. Each bottle is marked with a different capacity (left to right): 6 ounces, 6½ ounces, 7 ounces. (*Chris' Studio of Photography, Roseburg, Oregon*)

Early 1900's amber glass bottles typical of those used throughout the Thomas territory until a standardized package was adopted in 1916. (*Dr. Julian H. Toulouse, Hemet, California*)

Unusually tall (nine inches) bottles used in Greenville, South Carolina, during the early 1900's. These and other bottles graphically point out the need, during the early years of this century, for some sort of bottle size, shape, and color standardization. (*Dr. Julian H. Toulouse, Hemet, California*)

Two unusual bottles. The bottle on the left was made in 1936 to commemorate the completion of Boulder Dam, now known as Hoover Dam. The slogan "The Best by a Dam Site" was frowned upon by The Coca-Cola Company in Atlanta, but since the bottle was designed by Boulder Products, of Las Vegas, Nevada, to contain fruit flavors (although it was used during peak periods for Coca-Cola) there was nothing the parent company could do. On the right is an early green glass bottle illustrating a block-lettered Coca-Cola trademark. Such presentations of the company's trademark were discouraged by the parent company. They realized that such displays of the trademark increased the possibility of its becoming a common term. (*Lou Alvarado, San Diego, California*)

Two syrup bottles circa 1900–1920 used at soda fountains. The bottle on the left features a label sealed under a curved piece of glass, and the bottle on the right features a durable applied metal-covered paper label. Both bottles are twelve inches tall and have measuring caps.

This twelve-inch-high fountain syrup bottle (circa 1900–1920) features an interesting variation of the Coca-Cola trademark. The bottle may not have been produced under parent-company supervision.

A twelve-inch-tall syrup bottle (circa 1900–1920) featuring the trademark encircled by a wreath in Applied Color Labeling (ACL) and an aluminum measuring cap

Before the adoption of a standardized bottle in 1916, some bottling works sold Coca-Cola in quart bottles. The parent company did not encourage the merchandising of Coca-Cola in such sizes, but they had little control over such matters until 1916. This early 1900's ice-blue quart bottle, 11⅜ inches in height, was produced by The Coca-Cola Bottling Company of Chicago.

Among the unusual bottles used for Coca-Cola are the very colorful seltzer bottles. Almost all bottlers sold seltzer water to bars, fountains, and restaurants in brightly colored bottles that were returned and refilled. This bottle is emerald-green, twelve inches tall, and acid-etched "Coca-Cola BOTTLING CO., INC., WINONA, MINN., CONT. 26 FL. OZ. SELTZER CARBONATED WATER."

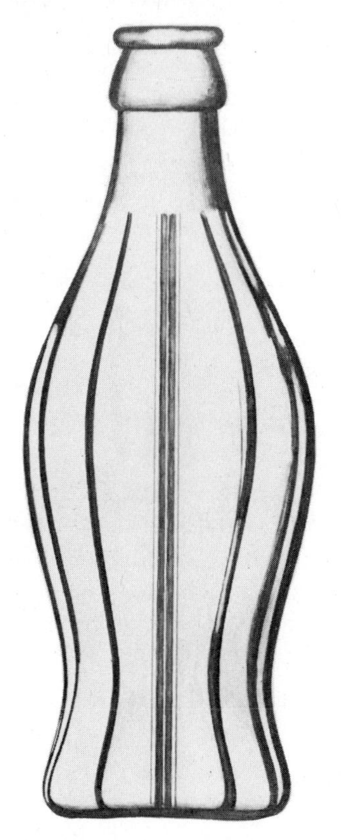

The original design for the standardized Coca-Cola bottle. This design was submitted by Earl R. Dean, of the Root Glass Company in Terre Haute, Indiana. The design was made in the summer of 1913, but it was not accepted by The Coca-Cola Company (in modified form) until 1916. (*Archives, The Coca-Cola Company, Atlanta, Georgia*)

The standardized bottle (left) and one of the many (right) used before its adoption (*Archives, The Coca-Cola Company, Atlanta, Georgia*)

From the original Earl Dean design a wooden model and an iron bottle mold were created. A small number of bottles were blown in the mold and submitted to The Coca-Cola Company. Because the bottles were too large around the shoulder to fit existing bottling machinery, the samples were rejected. Only two of these original bottles are known to exist today. In 1971, however, five thousand reproductions were made for a celebration; these bottles can be identified by the embossment "1915-1965" on the bottom. Collectors should be aware that if the embossed dates are carefully ground away, the reproductions are identical to the originals. (*Archives, The Coca-Cola Company, Atlanta, Georgia*)

The standardized bottle, because of its shape, was nicknamed the hobble-skirt or Mae West bottle. (*Whistl'n Dixie, Atlanta, Georgia*)

A sketch of the modified version of Earl Dean's design. This bottle was adopted in 1916 by The Coca-Cola Company, and although some modifications have since been made, the basic shape has remained the same. In 1960 the shape became the third registered trademark of The Coca-Cola Company. (*Archives, The Coca-Cola Company, Atlanta, Georgia*)

105,529
DESIGN FOR A BOTTLE
Eugene Kelly, Toronto, Ontario, Canada, assignor to The Coca-Cola Company, Wilmington, Del., a corporation of Delaware
Application March 24, 1937, Serial No. 68,391
Term of patent 14 years

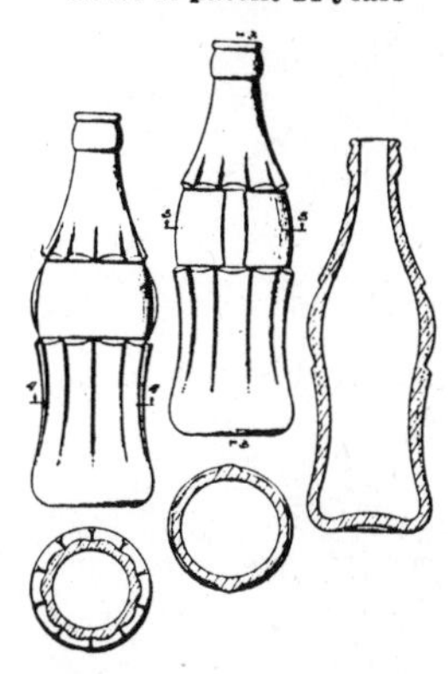

An iconic description of the bottle as it was patented in 1937 for the third time

The first one-way bottles were made after 1927. This bottle comes from Hartford, Connecticut, and was designed for use on luxury liners sailing to Europe.

These two experimental cans tried in the 1930's are almost always displayed with their glass counterparts. Extensive costs and lack of public acceptance postponed use of cans until after World War II.

Bottles of the hobble-skirt type are supposed to be made of Georgia-green glass. Occasionally, however, bottles of unusual colors are produced (left to right): ice-blue, amber (this bottle was made as part of an experiment to determine if amber glass would preserve the beverage better than the Georgia-green glass normally used), and grass-green.

Although the various glass companies that produce Coca-Cola bottles try to make sure that only perfect specimens get on the market, some mistakes are made. This poorly formed 1951 bottle is one that was overlooked by the maker and the bottler. The bottles are unusual collectors' items.

Although the classic contoured hobble-skirt bottle is the same shape in all parts of the world, the markings are different. These two foreign bottles represent the wide range of foreign bottles that collectors find desirable.

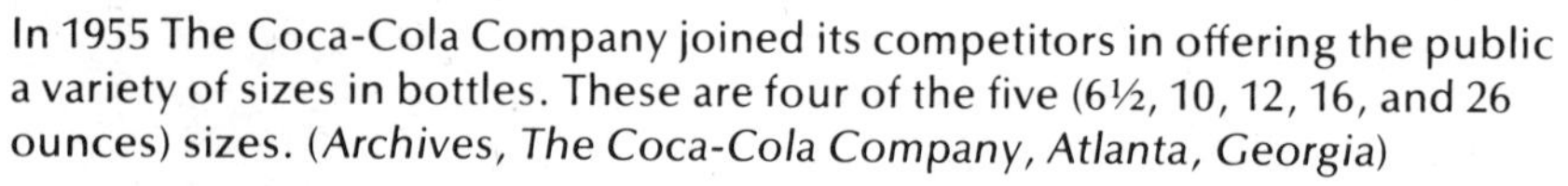

In 1955 The Coca-Cola Company joined its competitors in offering the public a variety of sizes in bottles. These are four of the five (6½, 10, 12, 16, and 26 ounces) sizes. (*Archives, The Coca-Cola Company, Atlanta, Georgia*)

In the mid-1960's The Coca-Cola Company began to produce its first domestic no-deposit bottles. These are seven of the many subsequently used. Because these bottles are designed to be discarded after use, many collectors predict that specimens saved now will be extremely rare and valuable in only a few years. (*Archives, The Coca-Cola Company, Atlanta, Georgia*)

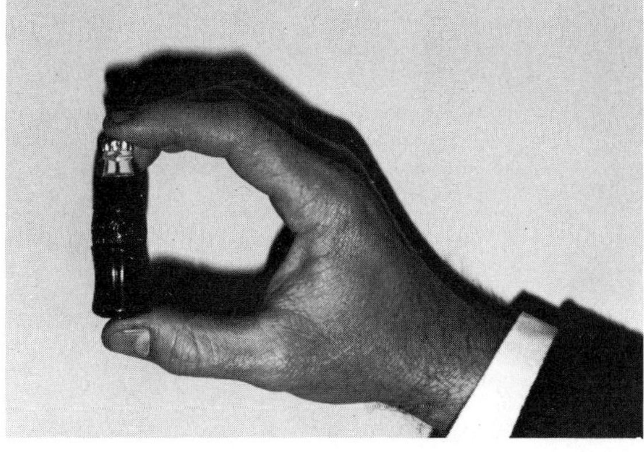

Bottles of various sizes have been produced by The Coca-Cola Company over the years for advertising purposes. This is a miniature Coke bottle. (*Herman "Bill" Berner, San Diego, California*)

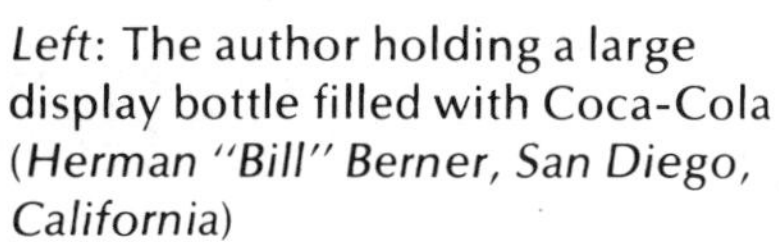
Left: An experimental plastic bottle made by the Monsanto Company of a material called Lopac. Collectors should always be watchful for such experimental bottles.

A miniature six-pack of bottles. These particular bottles are clear glass and partially painted to give the appearance of being full. They were made by Bill's Novelties Premiums, of Milwaukee, Wisconsin.

Left: The author holding a large display bottle filled with Coca-Cola (*Herman "Bill" Berner, San Diego, California*)

This miniature bottle (3½ inches high) was made in 1951 of solid plastic and used for advertising.

A miniature glass perfume bottle (3½ inches high) with stopper

Miniature bottles and case. The case measures 4⅜ by 3⅜ inches, and the bottles are 2½ inches high. The case is made of ceramic, and the bottles are glass.

Miniature bottles and case. The plastic case has yellow and red lettering and measures 3½ by 2½ inches. The twenty-four bottles are made of solid plastic.

Beginning in 1949, glass manufacturers have honored individual bottlers who have been in business for fifty years by making limited numbers of gold-dipped bottles. Since these are modified glass bottles, dating rules are the same as for undipped bottles. Gold bottles are most often found in the 6½-ounce size.

Two different fiftieth-anniversary gold-dipped 26-ounce bottles, complete with contents and gold-washed crown caps

Although most fiftieth-anniversary bottles are regular bottles dipped in gold, occasionally there are more elaborate examples. This bottle (circa 1949) is inscribed "PACIFIC COAST COCA-COLA BOTTLING CO., Ray E. Stauffer, Fiftieth Anniversary."

Marking any bottle with the trademark "Coca-Cola" in Spencerian script is not allowed by the parent company. Occasionally an unthinking bottler will go against company policy and incorrectly mark a bottle designed for beverages other than Coca-Cola. This specimen not only is an example of trademark misuse but also has a cobalt-blue glass neck and lip. (*Russ Leadabrand, Pasadena, California*)

A commemorative Hutchinson-stoppered bottle typical of the type used in the late 1800's. This bottle was produced in 1961 for the 75th anniversary celebration held in Miami Beach, Florida.

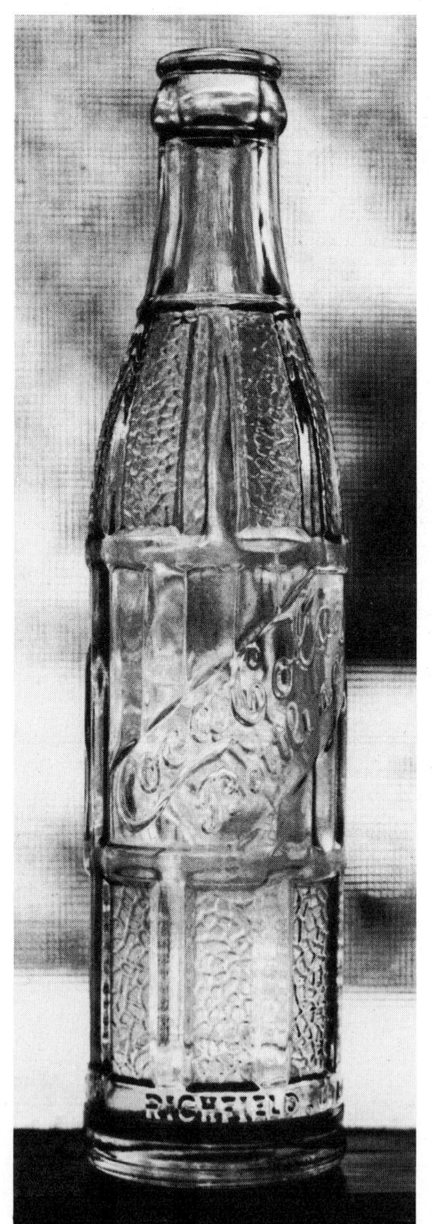

This bottle was designed to contain fruit-flavored beverages produced by the Richfield, Utah, Coca-Cola Bottling Company, and it should not have been marked with the Spencerian script trademark. Such unusual bottles are very much in demand by collectors.

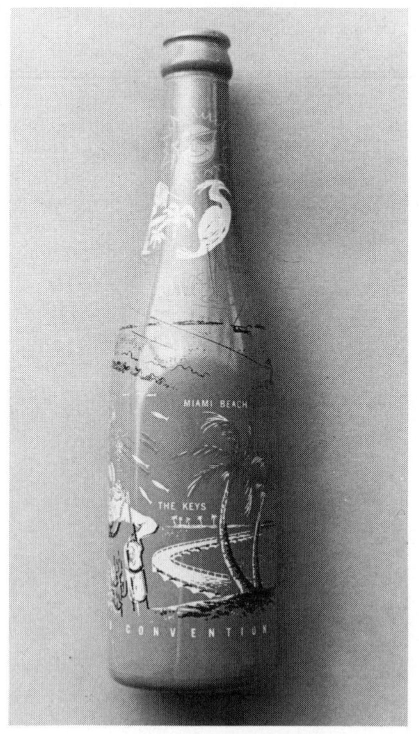

Commemorative bottle given away at the 1965 Miami, Florida, convention of the American Bottlers of Carbonated Beverages. The bottle is 9¾ inches tall and painted pink, with yellow, white, green, and brown decorations.

Commemorative bottle given away at the 1966 convention of the American Bottlers of Carbonated Beverages, held in Atlantic City, New Jersey. The bottle is mostly green.

Commemorative bottle given away at the 1967 National Soft Drink Association convention. This 9¾-inch-high bottle is multicolored with applied color labeling (ACL) decoration.

Commemorative bottle given away at the 1968 convention of the National Soft Drink Association in Detroit, Michigan. The bottle is red, and the design and lettering are multicolored.

Below: Commemorative bottle given away at the 1969 convention of the National Soft Drink Association. This gold bottle is 9½ inches high, with white and salmon-colored lettering and design.

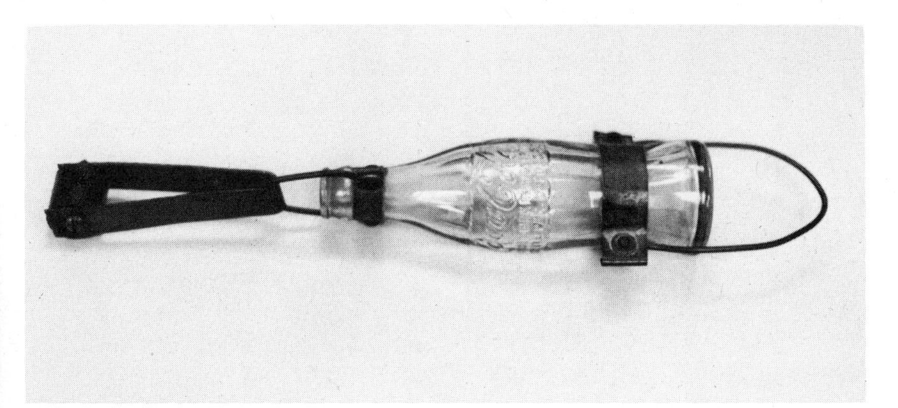

The hobble-skirt bottle has been used for many things other than to contain Coca-Cola. The bottle shown here was converted into an electrical insulator by the Seabees during World War II.

CHAPTER 13

STATIONERY

In 1924 a standardization committee was formed by The Coca-Cola Company and its individual bottlers. One of the items considered most important was the development of a uniform letterhead for use throughout the Coca-Cola industry.

In 1924 the Standardization Committee adopted a uniform letterhead. For years each bottler of Coca-Cola was allowed to create his own letterhead. The result was a conglomeration of types. Some were simple while others were complicated; some were clear, others were confused; some were rather homely, some quite beautiful; and some were in good taste, whereas others were more questionable.

The highly individualized stationery of Coca-Cola bottlers, before the standardized type featuring a bottle in hand (pictured in Chapter 16) was adopted in 1924, presents an interesting challenge for the collector. For that reason the collecting of letterheads has for the most part been limited to those produced before 1924.

Unlike advertising items and other objects that are widely scattered, stationery generally becomes part of company records. Only when such records are disposed of do letters become available. For that reason stationery generally comes on the collector market in spurts. It is not uncommon to note limited supplies of such paper goods being offered for sale in any of the collector periodicals.

A study of examples of the pre-1924 individualized stationery of the Coca-Cola industry gives a great deal of insight into conditions of the times. Steel engravings often show buildings, bottles, caps, and labels. Letterhead slogans and statements provide highly pertinent information about promotion. Addresses printed on early stationery can sometimes provide further important historical data. Names and titles can also provide the history-oriented collector with valuable information.

Collectors who feel that letterheads are a significant part of a collection should not overlook envelopes, bills, receipts, and other paper goods which in some way are representative of The Coca-Cola Company. Such items may appear to be of little consequence individually, but when gathered into collections they make an impressive showing.

A plain letterhead used in 1909 by The Coca-Cola Bottling Company of Chicago

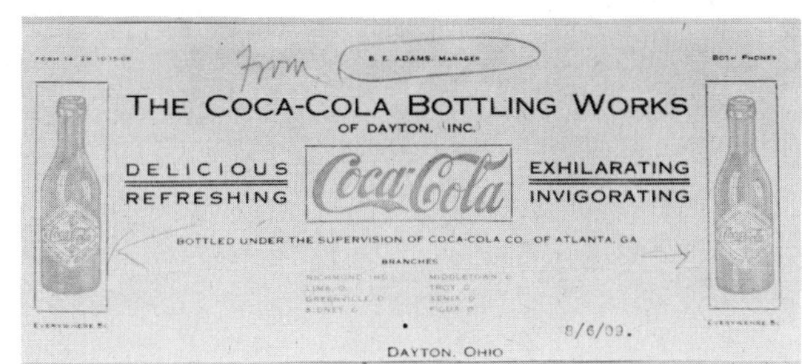

In addition to two interesting advertising slogans, this Dayton, Ohio, letterhead of 1909 pictures bottles typical of the period and geographical location.

A 1909 letterhead of The Coca-Cola Company in Atlanta. This fine example is illustrated with steel engravings of the company's major offices.

A St. Louis, Missouri, letterhead of 1911

A 1909 letterhead from Rockford, Illinois, indicates that this firm was also in the wholesale crushed fruit and syrup business.

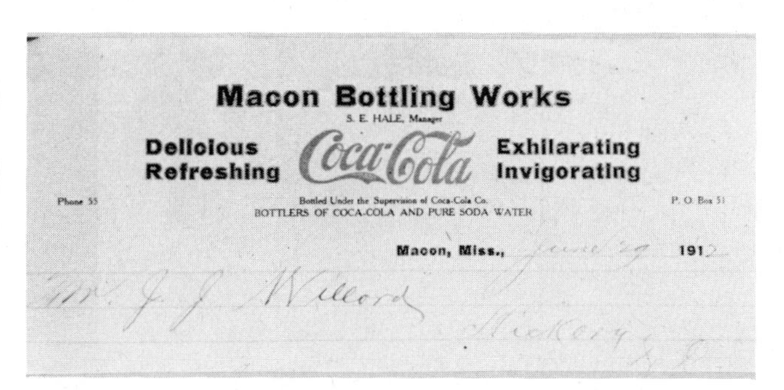

1912 Macon, Mississippi, letterhead

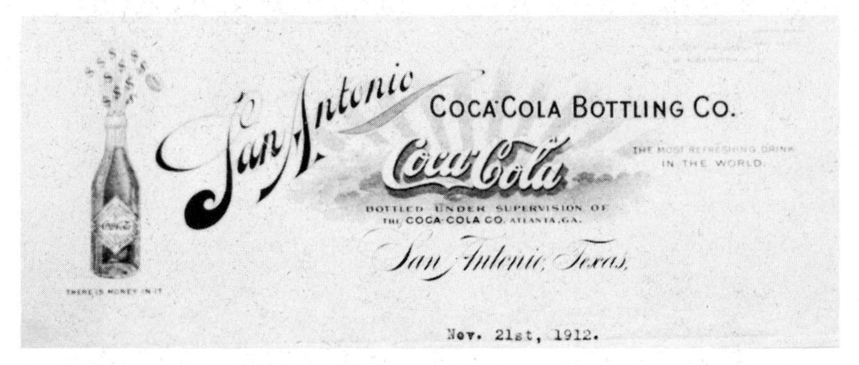

1912 letterhead of the San Antonio Coca-Cola Bottling Co.

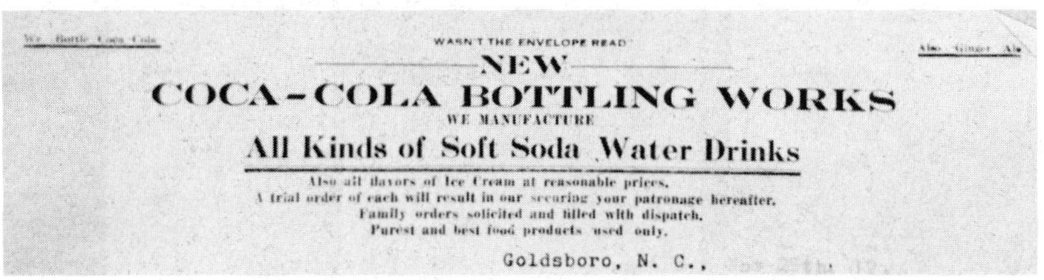

1912 Goldsboro, North Carolina, letterhead

1914 Henderson, North Carolina, letterhead

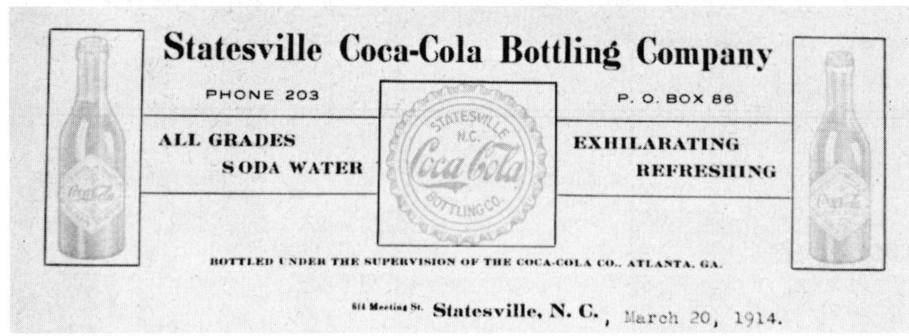

In 1914 the Statesville Coca-Cola Bottling Company in North Carolina sold all grades of soda water. The bottle cap is a rare specimen of the period.

The 1914 Coca-Cola bottler in Washington, D.C., sold, in addition to Coca-Cola, high-grade ginger ale, lemon soda, and sarsaparilla. Unusually shaped bottles are represented here.

1916 letterhead from Logan, West Virginia

The Coca-Cola Bottling Works of Jackson, Tennessee, appeared to have been exclusively a dealer in Coca-Cola in 1916. This letterhead is one of the few that displayed the arrow advertising slogan.

1916 letterhead of the Shelby Coca-Cola Bottling Co., Inc., in North Carolina

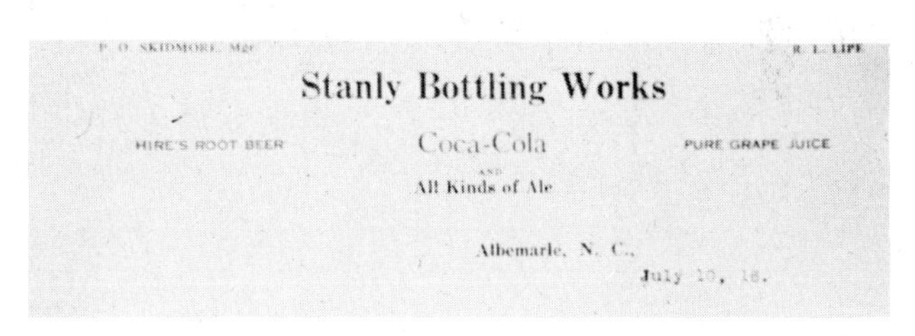

1916 letterhead from Albemarle, North Carolina

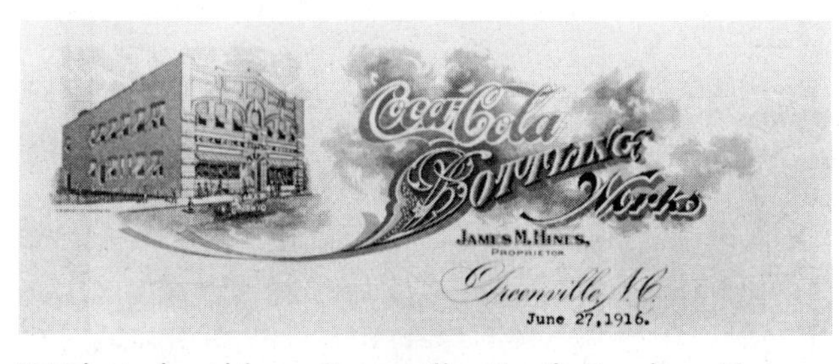

1916 letterhead from Greenville, North Carolina. Note the beautiful steel engraving of the company building and a truck.

1916 letterhead from Mobile, Alabama

1916 letterhead from Carrollton, Georgia

CHAPTER 14

KEGS, CARTONS, CASES, AND DISPLAY RACKS

The romantic stories about the first years of Coca-Cola include one which maintains that the first Coca-Cola syrup manufactured by John S. Pemberton in 1886 was carried to market in empty beer bottles. This method of transporting syrup, if it truly was the method, must have been short-lived, because as the demand for Coca-Cola grew the use of wooden kegs and barrels to market syrup became standard. Since the first kegs and barrels were used whiskey containers, which by law could only be used for whiskey once, they were painted red to cover any markings reminiscent of their original use. The red barrel thus became a symbol in the Coca-Cola industry. In later years a monthly publication of The Coca-Cola Company was even named *The Red Barrel.* Kegs and barrels were a part of the company's production equipment until after World War II and are collectible items.

In the late 1920's more Coca-Cola was sold in bottles than at soda fountains. The increase in the bottled product can be credited to Robert W. Woodruff. Shortly after his take-over in 1923, Woodruff predicted that the real potential for Coca-Cola was in bottles and encouraged innovative marketing ideas for the bottled beverage.

As early as 1922 the idea of capturing the home market for Coca-Cola with a handy take-home carton was conceived. It wasn't, however, until Robert Woodruff took over that the idea became a reality. Under the guidance of Harrison Jones, then vice-president in charge of sales, the six-bottle carton was created. The first cardboard carton was patented on September 23,

1924, and manufactured by the Empire Box Company, of Atlanta.

Shortly after the first cardboard carton was developed in 1924, it was test marketed in Tampa, Miami, Mobile, New Orleans, Shreveport, Oklahoma City, and Asheville. In spite of special promotional crews that were sent to each of the test cities to pass out free coupons, build displays, and set up booths staffed with attractive young girls, the results were not startling. In most cases it was not until 1928 that the take-home carton began to catch on. In New Orleans, however, by 1927 carton sales were more than 180,000 annually.

Collectors who consider production and merchandising items a part of their collection will certainly have, or be looking for, examples of early cardboard six-bottle take-home cartons. Areas in and around the eight test cities provide the best sources for such items, especially New Orleans.

In 1928 take-home cartons caught the public fancy. With the aid of a merchandising brochure (for bottlers), a consumer folder (for customers), cardboard display cutouts, and window displays, take-home cartons became an integral part of the merchandising of Coca-Cola. But perhaps the one advertising gimmick that gave the take-home carton a permanent place in the industry was a book, *When You Entertain,* by Ida Bailey Allen, which was sponsored by The Coca-Cola Company in 1932. That small book truly helped create the demand for bottled Coca-Cola for home use and for the convenient cardboard six-bottle take-home carton.

Because of initial cost the first take-home cardboard cartons were marked with such instructions as "Save the Carton," and consumers were encouraged to reuse the cardboard package. That proved a somewhat impractical idea and was soon abandoned. A one-time-use concept replaced the returnable carton idea and made it possible for The Coca-Cola Company to employ the carton as a medium for seasonal and other timely advertising. Hence a larger variety of cardboard cartons are available for collectors. At first a variety of advertising messages were lithographed on sleeves in which the basic carton was slipped. That soon gave way to cartons made specifically for special campaigns.

In 1934 the basic design of 1924 was modified. The modification was caused by the high cost (several cents) of producing the 1924 type. The 1934 model, by superior design, was able to serve the same function as the earlier model but had the distinct advantage of costing bottlers only one cent. The 1934 take-home carton is easily identified by its open ends and white border.

In 1937 The Coca-Cola Company produced an attractive carton sales manual, which is a collectible itself. The manual was the result of a two-year project. Also in 1937 "Singin' Sam" was employed to promote home sales of cartons on the radio; this campaign was so successful that Sam continued on radio for five years. At one point his commercials were sponsored by 450 bottlers of Coca-Cola.

In 1939, with the introduction of an improved open type of returnable carrier called the end-strap carton, home sales on a carton basis reached seventy million a year. While the end-strap carton was practical in many ways, it was not especially successful, mostly because the consumer did not seem to want to bother with the chore of returning it for refill. Consumers returned the bottles for the deposit, but frequently would not return the carton or case.

Each year for three years—1940, 1941, and 1942—The Coca-Cola Company produced and distributed a different flower book. The four million books increased carton sales of bottled Coca-Cola and provided today's collector population with another collectible.

Early in 1941 an aluminum-foil-covered take-home carton was developed and showed great promise. Unfortunately World War II forced The Coca-Cola Company to take this carton off the market because the materials involved were needed for the war effort. A comparatively small number of these cartons were used and have been saved.

During World War II wooden take-home cartons were introduced because of paper shortages and used for several years. Because of initial expense and maintenance costs these were abandoned after the war, and The Coca-Cola Company returned to the use of cardboard cartons that, in some cases, required the consumer to advance a deposit.

Since World War II, cardboard six-bottle take-home cartons have been used extensively and almost universally in home sales and were produced in a number of types. Collector interest in these postwar cartons has not been great, and they are not easy to locate. Future collectors will no doubt lament their earlier colleagues' lack of interest.

While it is proper to consider twenty-four-bottle carrying cases as collectible items, there has not been enough of a variety used in recent years to excite much collecting interest. When The Coca-Cola Company and its bottlers formed the Standardization Committee in 1924, one of the first things this group did was adopt a standardized case for bottled Coca-Cola. The initial adoption determined how cases were to be constructed and painted. As a result only a few minor changes were made in the ensuing years. One notable exception is the series of plastic cases developed in the late 1950's. Plastic did not replace wood, however, and wooden cases still prevail.

Cases made prior to 1924 offer the collector variety, but very few specimens seem to have survived the ravages of time and use. As a result only the very determined collector will be able to amass a respectable gathering of such cases.

Display racks, generally made of heavy-duty wire, were not used much before the 1920's and are even more discouraging to collect because so few have been saved. In addition, many collectors overlook these items, because of their comparative plainness. They were generally designed to be as compact as possible and are not especially attractive. They do not, for the most part, display more than one small sign.

A forty-gallon red barrel used during the 1920's and early 1930's to ship syrup to market. Specimens with full labels such as this one are very difficult to find. (*Archives, The Coca-Cola Company, Atlanta, Georgia*)

PRICE LIST COCA-COLA.

Coca-Cola

1-gallon jugs, per gallon........................$1 85
5-gallon kegs, per gallon........................1 75
10-gallon kegs, per gallon........................1 65
35-gallon barrels, per gallon........................1 50

Freight allowed on barrel shipments.

Increase trade at your fountain by dispensing the delicious, refreshing beverage. No fountain beverage ever increased in popularity so rapidly. None will draw so many customers to your fountain.

IRRESISTIBLY DELICIOUS

A page from the Peter Van Schaack & Sons catalog of 1908. This Chicago-based wholesale drug firm sold Coca-Cola in jugs, two keg sizes, and barrels. (*Jack K. Rimalover, Stonybrook Associates, Princeton Junction, New Jersey*)

Patented on September 23, 1924, this paper carton was the first in a long line of take-home packages that helped The Coca-Cola Company capture the lucrative home market. Examples of this first carton are quite rare and command a good price on the collectibles market. (*Archives, The Coca-Cola Company, Atlanta, Georgia*)

A 1931 take-home six-bottle carton designed for the Christmas trade. The Christmas message was printed on a sleeve into which the carton was slipped. (*Archives, The Coca-Cola Company, Atlanta, Georgia*)

Below: In 1931 artist Haddon Sundblom created the first of the famous Santa Clauses for The Coca-Cola Company. (*Archives, The Coca-Cola Company, Atlanta, Georgia*)

THE PACKAGE

OPEN TYPE CARTON

HERE is the new open type carton in red and white, a brilliant design that will attract attention anywhere. It is simple in construction, low in cost, and yet quite strong and durable.

ADVANTAGES

1. *A One Trip Package*—As the open type carton is used only once it is always a fresh, clean, unused package when displayed in the dealer's store and when carried into the home by the housewife. Coca-Cola as a food product demands that any package in which it is sold to the home market reflect the high sanitary standards of our industry.

2. *Eliminates Possibility of Spreading Diseases*—In certain localities where very strict health regulations are imposed possible complaint might be registered against repeated use of cartons on the theory that they might be instrumental in transmitting contagious diseases from one home to another. While we do not believe or subscribe to this, nevertheless the open type one trip carton completely eliminates this possibility of complaint.

3. *A Remarkable Display Value*—The red and white color combination of the new package is

The New Open Type Carton

The New Open Type Carton Gives Remarkable Display Value.

In 1934 The Coca-Cola Company offered bottlers this new take-home six-bottle carton for a penny apiece. This durable and inexpensive carton further stimulated bottlers to promote Coca-Cola in take-home cartons. (*Archives, The Coca-Cola Company, Atlanta, Georgia*)

In 1937 The Coca-Cola Company discarded the sleeve method of advertising on take-home cartons in favor of producing entire cartons for special campaigns. (*Archives, The Coca-Cola Company, Atlanta, Georgia*)

A foil-covered carton produced in 1941. Because of the advent of World War II, when the use of aluminum was restricted, this carton was discontinued. (*Archives, The Coca-Cola Company, Atlanta, Georgia*)

This open-type carton was introduced in the 1940's and was used for several years. (*Archives, The Coca-Cola Company, Atlanta, Georgia*)

Two of the wooden take-home cartons used during the early 1940's. Although very durable, they were expensive and difficult to store and maintain.

Two paper take-home cartons typical of the type used during the early 1950's

Left: An advertisement from the April, 1959, issue of *The Coca-Cola Bottler* illustrating a series of paper take-home cartons typical of those used in the late 1950's and early 1960's

Advertisements from the April, 1959, issue of *The Coca-Cola Bottler* showing typical take-home cartons

A wooden twenty-four bottle case used for transporting Coca-Cola. Standardized in 1924, such cases show little variation throughout the years and have consequently been neglected by collectors. This advertisement is from *The Coca-Cola Bottler* of April, 1959.

Advertisement from the April,, 1959, issue of *The Coca-Cola Bottler* showing some plastic cases that were popular in the late 1950's and early 1960's

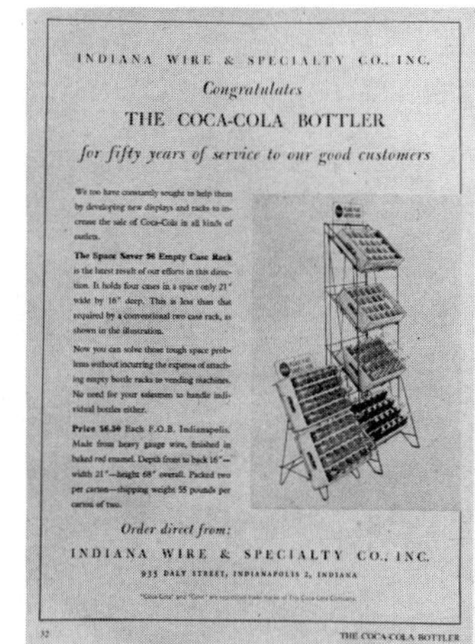

Advertisements from the April, 1959, issue of *The Coca-Cola Bottler* illustrating some typical display racks

CHAPTER 15

COOLERS

The collecting of memorabilia of The Coca-Cola Company involves objects of a wide variety; perhaps none of the other collecting specialties offers its participants as wide a range of object types and sizes as does this one. Coolers, while not the most cumbersome of the collectible Coca-Cola items, are far from the most convenient to collect and display. This fact, however, does not seem to bother the numerous collectors who add coolers to their assemblages of memorabilia of The Coca-Cola Company.

The importance of coolers historically in the successful merchandising of Coca-Cola (in bottles) is overshadowed only by bottles and cartons. Only the bottle precedes the cooler chronologically; cartons were a relatively late merchandising development. From the first bottling of Coca-Cola the need for coolers was evident. The first coolers were simple and rather crude devices developed, for the most part, by the vendors themselves. Bottled Coca-Cola was most successfully sold chilled, and vendors either just stocked the beverage in their ice boxes along with meat, fish, milk, butter, cheese, and similar perishables or dispensed the bottled drink from boxes or barrels loaded with ice.

Until the development of an electrically operated cooler in 1930, The Coca-Cola Company used numerous models that were refrigerated with ice. Such coolers ranged in complexity from simple barrels cut in half to coolers that dispensed bottles mechanically.

The first coin-operated vending machine for Coca-Cola was developed in 1910 by George S.

Cobb, a bottler from West Point, Georgia. He called his invention the Vend-all. The machine had a capacity of only twelve bottles and was activated by a five-cent piece. Although one of the few made was actually placed in operation in front of the bottling plant, the experiment was a failure because it was highly impractical to ice a cooler with such a small capacity. It is assumed that Cobb's Vend-all machines were eventually discarded. If one or more examples of these pioneering instruments were to be discovered by collectors, they would certainly be the most valuable of all the coolers.

During the 1920's a cooler industry blossomed, and trade magazines carried numerous advertisements for such unusually named machines as Freez a Bottle, Icebergdip, Goodwillie Ice Cooler, Walrus Cooler, and Icy-O. Although Coca-Cola bottlers bought and used a variety of the available coolers (costing at least $50 apiece), the Icy-O was the most popular at $90; it is a matter of record that during 1928 alone bottlers purchased 4,790 Icy-O coolers. The Icy-O is a mechanically operated machine. By turning the crank on the top a chilled bottle was moved into a position that enabled the purchaser to remove it from the machine. Empty bottles, as a sign on the front indicated, were placed in a case in the bottom of the machine.

In early 1928 The Coca-Cola Company decided to develop a standardized, inexpensive, simple cooler. The company purchased examples of all existing coolers and tested them for structural strength, ease of operation, durability, and the melting rate of ice. Each machine was disassembled and each part studied. Late in 1928 a model based on the test results was built and approved. The Glascock Bros. Mfg. Co., of Muncie, Indiana (a large sheet-metal firm), received the contract to build the standardized coolers; the low bid was for $25 apiece. Further negotiations brought the cost down to $17.50, and eventually it was lowered to $14.50, exclusive of signs. Final negotiations reduced the price to $12.50, f.o.b. Muncie. Although the firm was finally reduced to an 8-percent profit margin, they were not unhappy because they were aware of a tremendously large potential market.

The new inexpensive Glascock cooler was introduced to bottlers at their annual convention in Indianapolis, Indiana, in January, 1929. By the end of the year 32,000 Glascock coolers had been sold, or more than six times as many as any other cooler up to that time.

In 1930 Glascock developed the first electric cooler for Coca-Cola. This revolutionary new machine sold for $150 and was not an immediate success because of its initial cost. Along with the development of an electric cooler, Glascock developed an extensive line of coolers for The Coca-Cola Company. For five years Glascock made coolers exclusively for Coca-Cola and during that period sold more than 150,000 of its various models, many of which are to be found in collections today.

The Century of Progress Exposition was held in Chicago in 1933. The Coca-Cola Company presented an exhibit which included a fountain dispenser that had been created by the famous industrial designer Everett Worthington. The fountain dispenser was rather progressive looking for the times and attracted a great deal of attention. As a result Worthington was asked to design a cooler with similar lines. Everett Worthington quickly completed the design; the engineering departments of The Coca-Cola Company and the Westinghouse Electric & Manufacturing Company then collaborated to build the specified cooler. The prototype was accepted by The Coca-Cola Company, and Westinghouse quickly moved into full production. The manufacturing firm offered the Coca-Cola bottling industry a Junior Ice model at $7.65, a Standard Ice at $10.39, a Master Ice at $12.32, a Standard Electric at $76.50, and a Master Electric at $81.75. Thus in 1934 the classic red coolers were put on the market. Although the refrigerating-with-ice models have long been recalled from use and are available to collectors, a few electric models are still in use.

While the first coin-operated cooler for Coca-Cola was invented in 1910, it was not until 1931 that the first practical coin-operated machines were used. The first of these machines was produced by the Glascock Brothers Co. Between 1931 and 1936 over six thousand coin-operated coolers were purchased and used by bottlers. That number represents only a small percentage of the cooler population. This indicates that it would be difficult to locate examples of the early coin-operated machines. Coin-operated machines were not immediately popular for several reasons: (1) They were crude devices prone to mechanical malfunction. (2) They would accept almost any kind of a slug.

In 1936 Westinghouse produced an improved coin-operated cooler named Vendo Top. The Vendo Top was, as the name implies, a top. The coin-operated top could be purchased separately and locked on the open-type red cooler. Instead of operating a mechanism which moved all the bottles in the machines, the Vendo Top itself moved around, exposing the next bottle to be sold. The Vendo Top was activated with a five-cent piece and the pulling of an activating lever.

Coin-operated machines made before 1940 are difficult to locate because so few were made. While bottlers found it easy to sell icebox coolers and electrically operated coolers to distributors, they could not sell many coin-operated coolers. Because coin-operated coolers were prone to malfunctions and needed frequent repairs and/or adjustment, distributors resisted involvement. It was well into the 1950's before bottlers began to buy these machines in any great quantity and lend them to retailers. Bottlers were also forced to maintain their machines. What initially appeared to bottlers as a big problem for a small market has turned out to be just the opposite; machine sales of Coca-Cola today account for a great percentage of most bottlers' business.

World War II curtailed cooler production, but not as much as might be expected. Because vending machines placed in war plants increased production, the government allowed them to be produced for that purpose. During the war the Mills and Vendo companies joined the ranks of companies producing machines for Coca-Cola and produced a number of coin-operated machines. After the war, dry refrigeration was perfected; this method allowed taller machines to be built. The new, more vertical machines were popular because they took up less floor space. The upright models produced by the Mills Company were the most popular.

The latest development in vending has been the premix vendors. Beginning in the 1950's, The Coca-Cola Company began to promote premix machines. These machines offer the customer a cup of Coca-Cola mixed in the machine instead of bottled. As yet there is little collecting interest in such machines. One reason is that most premix machines are so well maintained that even the earliest ones are still in use. Another reason is that collectors are aware that such machines could have been used for other beverages. It is not uncommon for bottlers of different beverages to use the same brand of machine. Frequently bottlers will take old machines of a competitor as trade-ins from distributors who own machines, and will replace them with new machines selling their product. The traded-in machines are generally overhauled, repainted with the bottlers' product trademark, and resold as used machines. Thus a Coca-Cola machine may very well have been used by several leading competitors, and purists hesitate to include such machines in their collections.

Other coolers of interest are the small, portable picnic coolers. The Coca-Cola Company has had such coolers produced and distributed since the 1930's. While most picnic coolers are insulated metal boxes, plastic bags have also been issued since the 1960's.

Among the first and rather crude coolers for Coca-Cola was a barrel that had been cut in half and fitted with a hinged top. From such ice-filled coolers, vendors dispensed bottled Coca-Cola for a number of years before and after the turn of the century. (*Archives, The Coca-Cola Company, Atlanta, Georgia*)

The first coin-operated vending machine was invented in 1910 by George S. Cobb, a West Point, Georgia, bottler. The machine held twelve bottles of Coca-Cola, was chilled with ice, and was activated by a nickle. Because it was uneconomical to ice the small machine, only a few were produced, and only one (in front of Cobb's bottling plant) was ever used. No examples are known to have survived. (*Archives, The Coca-Cola Company, Atlanta, Georgia*)

This late 1920's ice-cooled vending machine, called the Icy-O, was the one purchased by bottlers at that time. Thousands of these machines were sold, and many are available to collectors today. (*Herman "Bill" Berner, San Diego, California*)

Another example of the Icy-O cooler. These mechanically operated vending machines held chilled bottles in the top half and empty bottles in the bottom half. (*Archives, The Coca-Cola Company, Atlanta, Georgia*)

A 1929 cooler built to specifications for The Coca-Cola Company by the Glascock Bros. Mfg. Co., of Muncie, Indiana. The cooler was only $12.50, and over 32,000 were sold in 1929. This was the first official cooler for Coca-Cola. (*Archives, The Coca-Cola Company, Atlanta, Georgia*)

In 1930 Glascock introduced an electric cooler for $150. The refrigeration unit was designed to fit into the base of their existing model. Few were sold because of the cost. (*Archives, The Coca-Cola Company, Atlanta, Georgia*)

GLASCOCK BROS. MFG. CO.

STANDARD COCA-COLA COOLER

Cooler holds 72 bottles. 4 cases in reserve. Ice capacity 50 pounds. Size 31½"x 23½"x40" high 10½" deep inside. Packed knocked down in crate. Shipping weight 130 pounds. . . Price $11.50

An ordinary 40 foot car will hold 192 Standard Coolers, and loads nearer to the required minimum than a 36 foot car.

Page Seven

The "Standard Coca-Cola Cooler" as illustrated in a Glascock Bros. Mfg. Co. catalog entitled *Coca-Cola Coolers for 1932*

GLASCOCK BROS. MFG. CO.

STANDARD PORTABLE COCA-COLA COOLER

Cooler holds 72 bottles, with 3 cases in reserve. Ice capacity 50 pounds. Height 40", length over all 53", width over all 28", 10½" deep inside. Large wheels 20" diameter. Small swivel wheel 8", all ball bearing, 1⅛" rubber tires. Packed in two crates. Shipping weight 235 pounds. . . . . . Price $30.00

This cooler is designed primarily for use in Industrial Plants, Filling Stations and other places where the surface over which it is moved is comparatively smooth. Owing to its weight when fully loaded—approximately 600 lbs., it is not recommended for use over rough streets, cobble stones, curbs, etc., as the construction is not sufficiently rugged to stand up at all times under such adverse conditions.

To save freight, the cooling box proper is packed in one crate weighing 97 pounds, and the wagon portion in another crate weighing 138 lbs. The assembly is a very simple matter, and no detailed instructions necessary. Care should be taken to have axle securely attached to frame, and see that large wheels revolve on their roller bearings on axle. No overflow pipe is furnished with this cooler.

Page Twelve

The "Standard Portable Coca-Cola Cooler" as illustrated in the same Glascock catalog

GLASCOCK BROS. MFG. CO.

STANDARD All Weather COCA-COLA COOLER

Hot galvanized finish inside and out. Built for continuous outside service. Holds 72 bottles, 4 cases in reserve. Ice capacity 50 pounds. Size 31½"x23½"x40" high, 10½" deep inside. Packed knocked down in crate. Shipping weight 135 pounds. . . . . Price $14.50

This cooler is exactly the same as regular Standard Cooler as to design, construction and capacity. The only difference is in the outside finish. All exposed parts are hot galvanized after fabrication, and as all bolts and nuts and other hardware are of brass, it will stand constant outdoor use without corrosion, and will not become unsightly.

Page Fourteen

The "Standard All Weather Coca-Cola Cooler" as illustrated in the Glascock Bros. Mfg. Co. catalog entitled *Coca-Cola Coolers for 1932*

GLASCOCK BROS. MFG. CO.

ENCLOSED BASE
STANDARD COCA-COLA COOLER

Capacity 72 bottles in ice water and storage in base for three cases. Ice capacity 50 pounds. Size 23½" wide, 31½" long, 40" high, 10½" deep. Shipped set up in crate. Shipping weight 190 lbs. . . . . . . Price $16.50

This model has same cooling capacity as the regular Standard Cooler. The enclosed base holds a removable can to catch empty bottles (see illustration opposite page) and has storage room for three cases full or empty.

It meets the demand of the better class of locations where the exposed cases and empty bottls are objectionable.

Page Sixteen

The "Enclosed Base Standard Coca-Cola Cooler" as illustrated in the same Glascock catalog

For advertising purposes the Glascock Bros. Mfg. Co. produced and distributed hundreds of these miniature coolers, 12½ by 7½ by 10½ inches. These models are eagerly sought by collectors, who will pay $100 for them. The miniatures are exact replicas of the real coolers and come with miniature cases and bottles.

A salesman's miniature sample of the 1934 Westinghouse cooler, 10 by 12 inches. These models, like their miniature Glascock counterparts, are generally valued at almost $100.

In 1936 Westinghouse produced the first large-selling coin-operated cooler. The Vendo Top sold either as a total unit (cooler and top) or as just a top that could be locked on the regular open-type Westinghouse cooler. In the Vendo Top, only parts of the top moved to expose a bottle, whereas in previous cooler models all the bottles moved until one was exposed. (*Archives, The Coca-Cola Company, Atlanta, Georgia*)

Above: The big red cooler designed by Everett Worthington and first manufactured in 1934 by Westinghouse. The design was marketed in five models: three ice-cooled and two electrically refrigerated. (*Archives, The Coca-Cola Company, Atlanta, Georgia*)

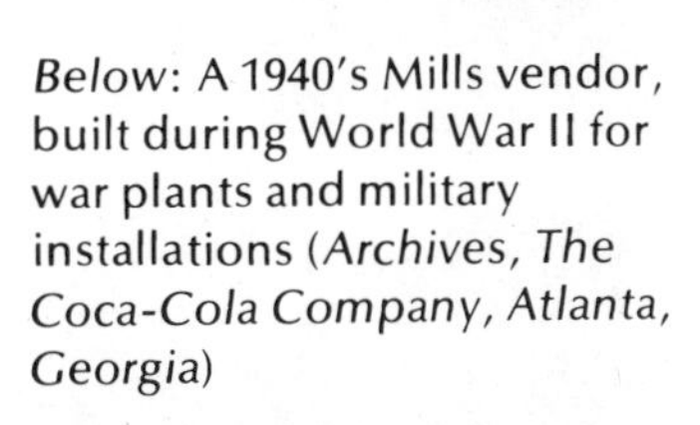

Below: A 1940's Mills vendor, built during World War II for war plants and military installations (*Archives, The Coca-Cola Company, Atlanta, Georgia*)

Typical bottle vending machine of the 1950's. This model was manufactured by the Vendo Company. (*Archives, The Coca-Cola Company, Atlanta, Georgia*)

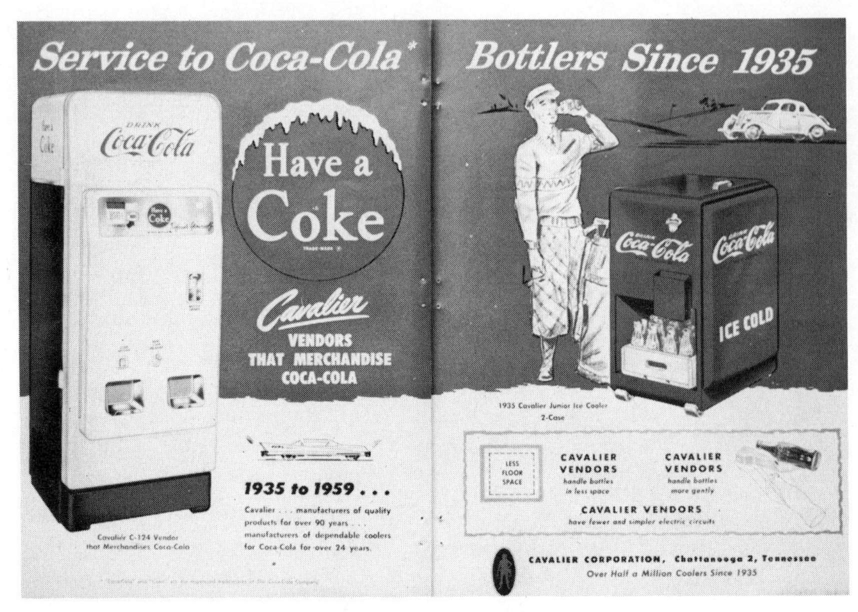

An advertisement from the April, 1959, issue of *The Coca-Cola Bottler* comparing a 1959 Cavalier vending machine with a 1935 Cavalier icebox cooler

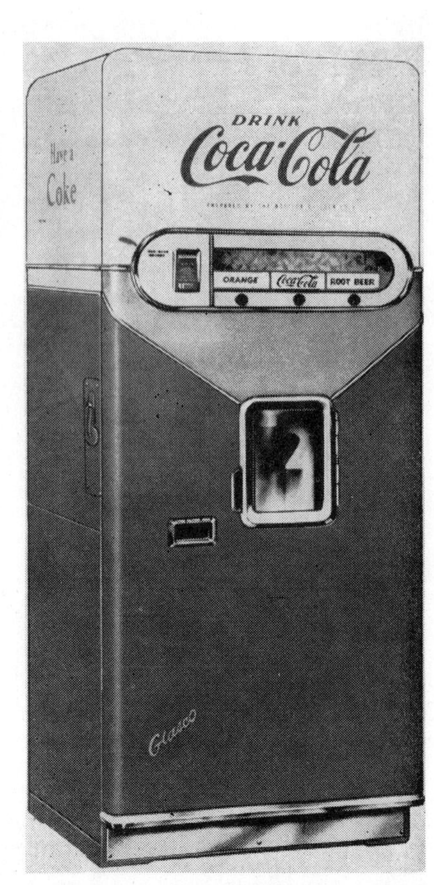

A 1959 Glassco pre-mix machine. Such machines generally stock about eight hundred drinks of Coca-Cola. (*Archives, The Coca-Cola Company, Atlanta, Georgia*)

Typical 1940 picnic cooler. These portable insulated boxes have been popular over the years and are easily collected.

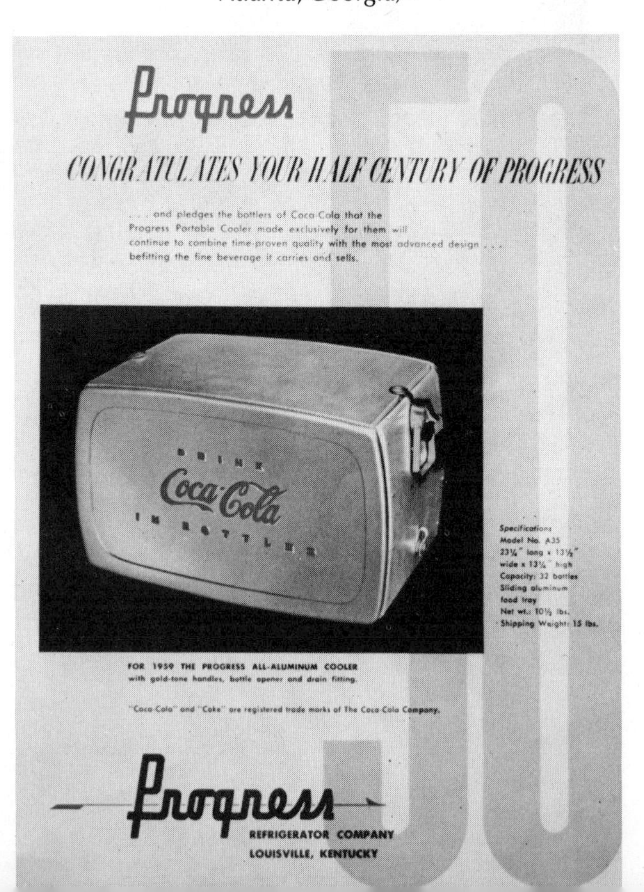

An advertisement from *The Coca-Cola Bottler* for April, 1959, illustrating the "Progress All-Aluminum Cooler"

CHAPTER 16

THE STANDARDIZATION COMMITTEE AND ITS EFFECTS ON COLLECTING

During its formative years The Coca-Cola Company concentrated its efforts on increasing production. Little attention was given to the idea of standardization. As a result the items related to the manufacturing of Coca-Cola varied greatly and reflected the nature of the individual dealer. Although the parent company offered a few guidelines, it didn't begin to enforce them until 1920.

This initial laissez-faire attitude of the parent company, along with the imagination of individual bottlers, helped to produce an abundance of collectibles, especially in the area of bottles and advertising.

By 1910 the company had grown to considerable size and had become aware of the need to standardize. However, it took a long time to convince individual bottlers that standardization was good for business. The first big breakthrough came in 1916 when the parent company adopted a standardized glass package (bottle). The second big push for standardization came in 1924, one year after Robert Woodruff became president of The Coca-Cola Company. It led to the formation of the Standardization Committee. The chairman of a bottlers' meeting held in March, 1924, Charles V. Rainwater, is quoted as saying:

> Gentlemen, there is, as you know, a wonderful effect in the uniformity of things. The Coca-Cola Company years ago established a certain color for its advertising. Other concerns throughout the world have established various standards, so that their business is immediately identified when that particular color or design is seen by the public. There are many great advantages in having all Coca-Cola Bottlers uniform in all things. We have placed the discussion of this question under the head of "Standardizing." It is a thing you are all interested in.

During the first meeting of the Standardization Committee, which was held nine months later, a standard design for stationery and checks and a standard color and design for the painting of cases and trucks were considered. The committee met for a second time in June, 1925. At that meeting it was decided that trucks would be painted yellow and red with black hoods, fenders, and radiators. A standardized uniform for truck drivers and factory employees was also discussed.

In March, 1926, the Standardization Committee held its annual meeting in Dallas, Texas. At this meeting a standardized white-and-green-striped cotton uniform for drivers and plant employees was approved. The highlight of the meeting, however, was the clarification of the previously adopted standardized letterhead which was being misused by a number of bottlers. The decision was ". . . to forbid the printing of anything on the standard letterhead advertising any other drink, bottled or otherwise, bottlers' supplies of any kind, real estate, etc., with the one exception that the insignia of the American Bottlers of Carbonated Beverages may be used." The Standardization Committee proved its power to make such decisions.

In November, 1927, an unofficial meeting of three members of the committee resulted in the contribution of six thousand dollars to pay for the development of several standardized plans for bottling plants. The Atlanta architectural firm of Pringle and Smith was employed to develop three plans, one for plants producing up to 1,500 cases per week, one for plants producing up to 3,000 cases per week, and one for plants producing up to 10,000 cases per week. Pringle and Smith presented four sets of plans instead. Their plans were for plants with *daily* capacities of 200 cases, 400 cases, 600 cases, and 1,350 cases. The submitted plans also provided a variation in northern and southern construction. The estimated costs of the four plants was from $10,000 to $35,000. It was decided by the Standardization Committee that the first plant would be constructed in Elberton, Georgia. It was completed in the fall of 1928.

The next meeting of the committee was held in September, 1928, in Elberton, Georgia, and the green-and-white-striped uniform was formally adopted. In May, 1929, McCampbell and Company, of New York, was selected to manufacture the material, while the Riverside Manufacturing Company, of Moultrie, Georgia, the H. D. Lee Mercantile Company, of Kansas City, and the Globe Superior Company, of Abingdon, Illinois, were selected to manufacture the standardized uniform. At the 1930 annual committee meeting the Richard Manufacturing Company, of Dallas, was added to the list of firms authorized to manufacture official uniforms.

In 1937 new plant specifications were adopted for northern bottling plants. In 1938 dark-green woolen material was adopted for winter uniforms. The Cleveland Worsted Mills was selected to manufacture the fabric. In 1939 Robert and Company, of Atlanta, was employed to develop architectural plans for six new types of bottling plants. From 1940 to 1944, standard truck body plans were developed. In 1945 specifications for the new truck were adopted, but because of postwar shortages the first trucks were not produced until 1947. The truck body was built by the Hobbs Manufacturing Company of San Antonio, Texas. The Hobbs truck was a failure, and only a few hundred were sold between 1947 and 1955; consequently these trucks are choice collectors' items for collectors of Coca-Cola memorabilia as well as collectors of old vehicles. By 1949 it was decided that no set of fixed plant plans could meet the individual needs of bottlers, so that the idea of standardized plant plans was abandoned in favor of plans drawn specifically to suit each bottler's needs. At the 1950 meeting a new stationery was adopted, featuring the red disk. In 1958 truck colors were changed to yellow, white, and red. This same light yellow was adopted for bottle cases as well.

From approximately 1920 until the present The Coca-Cola Company has continued its standardizing practices in many areas. The result for collectors has been a standardized collection; most collectors of Coca-Cola memorabilia gather the same objects from all parts of the country. The big variations in memorabilia collections thus come from the items produced generally before 1920, individual bottler advertising items, and collectibles from foreign countries.

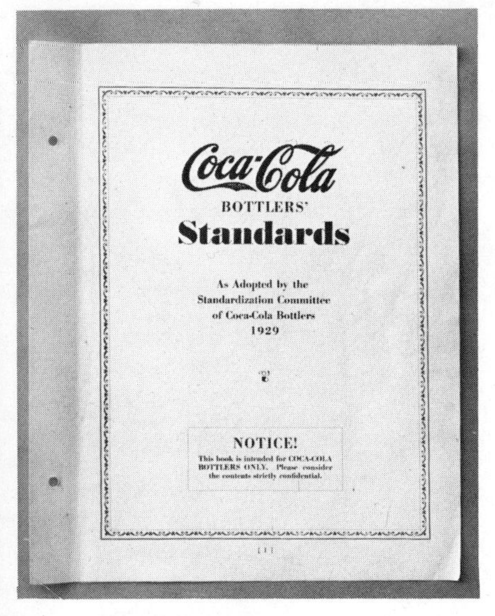

Coca-Cola

BOTTLERS'

Standards

As Adopted by the
Standardization Committee
of Coca-Cola Bottlers
1929

NOTICE!

This book is intended for COCA-COLA BOTTLERS ONLY. Please consider the contents strictly confidential.

[1]

By 1929 the Standardization Committee had instituted a number of rules. The new rules were presented in a booklet, 11½ by 9½ inches, entitled *Coca-Cola Bottlers' Standards* (*far left*). The title page (*near left*) of the booklet read "This book is intended for COCA-COLA BOTTLERS ONLY" and "strictly confidential." Because the booklets were considered confidential, most were destroyed as they became obsolete. Books that do exist are considered valuable by collectors.

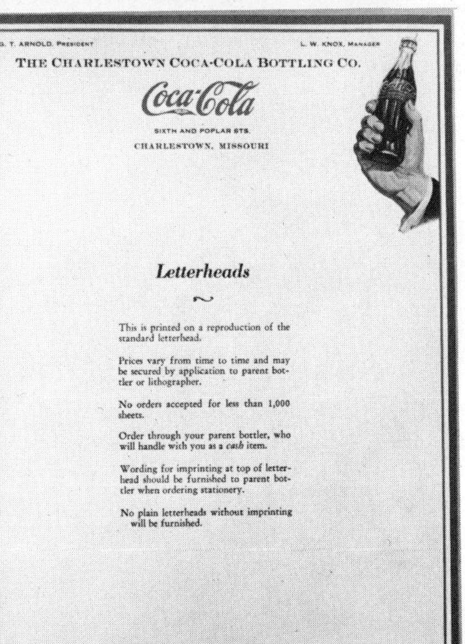

G. T. ARNOLD, PRESIDENT — L. W. KNOX, MANAGER

THE CHARLESTOWN COCA-COLA BOTTLING CO.

Coca-Cola

SIXTH AND POPLAR STS.
CHARLESTOWN, MISSOURI

Letterheads

This is printed on a reproduction of the standard letterhead.

Prices vary from time to time and may be secured by application to parent bottler or lithographer.

No orders accepted for less than 1,000 sheets.

Order through your parent bottler, who will handle with you as a *cash* item.

Wording for imprinting at top of letterhead should be furnished to parent bottler when ordering stationery.

No plain letterheads without imprinting will be furnished.

THE CHARLESTOWN COCA-COLA BOTTLING CO.
CHARLESTOWN, MISSOURI

One of the first adoptions of the Standardization Committee was uniform stationery. The standard letterhead (*left*) and envelope (*above*) both featured a bottle in hand. These remained from 1924 to 1950.

Right: Bottle delivery-case specifications were another adoption of the Standardization Committee. Illustrations and detailed instructions for manufacturers and bottlers were offered in 1929 on page 67 of *Coca-Cola Bottlers' Standards*.

Printing Specifications

The following words "Drink Coca-Cola In Bottles" to be printed on each side of case both on the inside and outside with Coca-Cola red stencil ink, in such a manner as to make a definite sunken impression in the wood. This printing to be done after the coat of yellow paint has been applied to the parts of the case named.

The arrangement of the words to be as per illustrations above.

Nothing other than the name of the town to be printed on the ends of the case, and this at the bottler's option.

Case manufacturers trade mark, identification seal or serial numbers, to be on the inside of the end.

Painting Specifications

FOR CASE MANUFACTURERS

Use the following method or a method that will give equally satisfactory results:

Spray one coat of Coca-Cola Case Yellow No. 33 (reduced with pure turpentine or universal thinner) on parts of case after they are cut but before they are assembled.

Drying time for this first coat, approximately eight hours.

Print with Coca-Cola red stencil ink (see printing) and after cases are assembled completely, spray one coat Coca-Cola Case Varnish No. 703 (reduce with universal thinner).

Varnish sets in four to five hours, drying over night sufficient to ship.

(NUMBERS REFERRED TO ABOVE ARE SHERWIN-WILLIAMS NUMBERS. YOU CAN USE THEIR PAINTS OR MATCH WHATEVER PAINT YOU USE WITH THEM FOR COLOR AND QUALITY.)

FOR BOTTLERS

Wood Primer—

The wood surface must be thoroughly dry on new cases not previously coated. Apply one coat Coca-Cola Standard Paste Yellow Primer No. 70, Sherwin-Williams Yellow Paste No. 70. Thin 75 per cent to 100 per cent with naphtha to make paint brushing consistency. Allow to dry 8 to 12 hours.

Note:—Primer optional in re-painting cases.

Second Coat—

Brush over entire surface one coat Coca-Cola Standard Case Yellow No. 33, Sherwin-Williams Yellow No. 33. Allow to dry 12 to 16 hours.

Stencil Color—

Use Coca-Cola Standard Red Stencil Color, No. 613, Sherwin-Williams No. 613. This material comes ready to use for stenciling. Dries to touch in one hour and to handle in 2½ to 3 hours.

NOTE:—Stencil is to be applied to sides of case.

[67]

Above: Uniform colors for trucks were adopted by the Standardization Committee in 1925. As specified and illustrated in *Coca-Cola Bottlers' Standards* in 1929, trucks were yellow and red, with black hoods, fenders, and radiators.

ARTIST'S DRAWING, PLANT NUMBER 1

The first bottling plant adopted by the Standardization Committee. This plant was designed for a daily capacity of two hundred cases and cost approximately $10,000 to build in 1929. Collectors actively seek the molded cement panels featuring the trademark which appeared on all plants built according to these plans.

ARTIST'S DRAWING, PLANT NUMBER 2.

The second bottling plant adopted by the Standardization Committee. This plant was designed for a daily capacity of four hundred cases and cost approximately $15,000 to build in 1929.

ARTIST'S DRAWING, PLANT NUMBER 3

The third bottling plant adopted by the Standardization Committee. This plant was designed for a daily capacity of six hundred cases and cost approximately $20,000 to build in 1929.

ARTIST'S DRAWING, PLANT NUMBER 4

The fourth bottling plant adopted by the Standardization Committee. This plant was designed for a daily capacity of 1,350 cases and cost approximately $30,000 to build in 1929.

White and green striped cotton uniforms were adopted by the Standardization Committee in 1928. The cloth was manufactured by McCampbell and Company, of New York City, and the uniforms were made by a number of firms, one of which was the H.D. Lee Mercantile Company, of Kansas City. This "Buddy Lee" doll was issued by the Kansas City firm to promote the sales of its uniforms to Coca-Cola bottlers. The doll is 12½ inches tall and is considered an excellent collectible by both collectors of dolls and collectors of Coca-Cola memorabilia.

Part IV

ADVERTISING ITEMS

CHAPTER 17

ADVERTISING HISTORY—AN OVERVIEW

Beginning with the originator of Coca-Cola, John S. Pemberton, all the men selling the beverage have invested heavily in advertising. Pemberton grossed approximately $50 from the sale of Coca-Cola during the first year and spent $73.96 on advertising. Pemberton's 1887 bill of sale for advertising included such items as 1,600 posters, 14 oilcloth signs, 45 tin signs, 500 streetcar cards, and one stencil plate for the Coca-Cola trademark.

From such humble beginnings The Coca-Cola Company has steadily increased its advertising expenditures over the years, and today the annual advertising budget is estimated to be somewhere between $70,000,000 and $100,000,000. Much of the money is, of course, spent on items that will become collectibles.

An alphabetized list of advertising slogans and statements with date of first use is offered in this book as Appendix B. Many of the advertising items collectors gather will display one of the numerous advertising slogans and statements used over the years by The Coca-Cola Company.

During the years between 1886 and 1892 (the year The Coca-Cola Company was formally created) not much is known about Coca-Cola advertising except that the product was advertised and that items of that period are occasionally located and considered quite rare and valuable. In 1892 records reveal that Asa Griggs Candler's newly formed company spent $11,401.48 on advertising items which included calendars and outdoor signs.

By 1896 Coca-Cola advertising items included metal serving trays, which are today among the most popular of all of the advertising items. Other items issued in 1896 were soda fountain urns for dispensing syrup (offered to dealers who bought and dispensed a minimum of one hundred gallons of Coca-Cola annually), clocks conspicuously promoting Coca-Cola, complimentary tickets for free samples of Coca-Cola, and a number of newspaper advertisements.

In 1901 records reveal that $100,000 was spent promoting Coca-Cola. Among the items issued by the firm were those which were rapidly becoming standard, such as metal serving trays, calendars, and outdoor signs.

By 1904 The Coca-Cola Company had begun advertising in nationally circulated magazines. Many of those advertisements (a number in full color) are available today to collectors who are willing to hunt through stacks of old magazines.

The now famous "Man on the Grass" cutout window display was produced in 1909, and in 1910 the "Lady on the Grass" was added to the ever-growing list of Coca-Cola advertising items. These two items, because of their lack of durability, did not survive the years well, and are cherished collectors' items today. Along with the "Man on the Grass" cutout, pencils, blotters, and rulers marked with advertising were given away to school children. The 1909 advertising budget reached the all-time high of $760,000. In addition to the above, eight-day clocks, watch fobs, knives, napkins, calendars, trays, matches, and palm-leaf fans were given away; $2,189.30 was spent on fans alone during 1909–1910.

The year 1912 saw the debut of the first bathing beauty; she appeared in Coca-Cola advertising wearing a bathing costume typical of the period, complete with long black stockings and beach shoes.

By 1910 oilcloth signs that hung from the awnings of drugstores were on their way out, being replaced with more durable and expensive metal signs. As early as 1910, the company recorded a ten-thousand-dollar expenditure for new metal signs (which are studied in detail in Chapter 26).

Individual distributors and bottlers have always had the option to produce their own advertising, and in many cases they did. Most advertising of Coca-Cola, however, was and is accomplished with items issued by the parent company. The historic contract awarded to B. F. Thomas and J. T. Lupton included provision for advertising money. The agreement was that ten cents of advertising was included in the price of each gallon of syrup sold by The Coca-Cola Company to The Coca-Cola Bottling Company. The amount was later changed to five cents. The money involved is usually called the "advertising allowance." Currently the parent company favors sharing advertising costs with bottlers on a fifty-fifty basis, with the bottler determining the extent of his advertising.

Shortly after the turn of the century The Coca-Cola Company produced for its bottlers two stained-glass leaded "chandeliers" of a Tiffany type. These chandeliers, or shades, are possibly the most sought-after advertising items the company has ever issued. Today the chandeliers sell for between one and two thousand dollars apiece. At such a price many collectors actively seek one for their collections but are secretly relieved to learn that these choice items are almost impossible to find. Because of the debossment on the circular lamps indicating that they were the property of The Coca-Cola Company, it is safe to assume that the few distributors and bottlers who purchased these expensive advertising items only lent them to customers. On the rectangular-shaped chandeliers there is no such debossment, which could mean that this is the earlier of the two and that the company learned a lesson about retailers' reluctance to return such handsome fixtures after they once had them in their stores. Of the two types known, the circular ones are the most popular and have been reproduced. Other light fixtures have been issued throughout the years by The Coca-Cola Company, but they are less interesting than the elaborate stained-glass models.

Around 1920 The Coca-Cola Company issued three-foot-tall stained-glass bottles. These items feature panels of ruby-red glass in a granite pattern, "Coca-Cola" in white opaque glass around the shoulder of the bottle, and two rows of green opaque glass near the top. Like their stained-glass chandelier cousins, these large replicas of the classic contoured bottle are true works of art and extremely rare and valuable. Few of these exist today, because they were very expensive and few bottlers took advantage of the opportunity to buy them.

Advertising records become more plentiful for the decades after World War I. In 1922, for instance, a portfolio entitled "Coca-Cola Opens the Door" featured two pages of illustrated advertising items that were offered to bottlers and distributors during that year. Among the items can be found four different metal signs, an aluminum and celluloid sign, a fiber sign, a transparent window sign, a sign to hang over the icebox, a leather wallet, a vendor's cap, an ice pick, several bottle openers, match books, blotters, pencils, a tray, and a calendar. Elsewhere in the 12½-by-17-inch portfolio of 1922 there are discussions and illustrated examples of period magazine and newspaper advertising. The forty-page publication also features illustrations of window signs, cutouts, direct-mail pieces, and painted walls. (A number of collectors gather bricks from such walls, and one collector has obtained, torn down, and reconstructed such a wall in his home. With the current popularity of used brick, esoteric collectors seeking such signs are finding the task a difficult one.)

An interesting sidelight of the 1922 brochure is the prediction that "the time will come when Coca-Cola bottling plants will be up to an equal standard of excellence—when the buildings of all will be painted alike in the red, white, and green—when a truck in Duluth will look like a truck in Miami—when a sales idea developed in the New York plant or anywhere else will be applied universally—when the volume of business done in bottled Coca-Cola will depend on the population of a territory rather than the bottler in it—when there will be big sales everywhere." This rather optimistic prediction was to become a reality sooner than expected, and the repercussions for collectors have been significant.

In July, 1925, a sixteen-page illustrated price list was published by The Coca-Cola Company. The booklet (a collectors' item itself) was one of the first separate price lists for advertising items for Coca-Cola. (An earlier price list was produced in 1920.) The 1925 booklet was 6 by 8 inches and sported a cover like the ones typically used on *The Red Barrel,* which was the company publication at that time. In the catalog were thirty-five different advertising items, illustrated mostly in full color. Such a catalog was expensive to produce, but the company justified the expense by eliminating the practice of sending each bottler samples of new advertising items as they were created. In addition to eliminating the costly practice of sending samples, the new booklet showed bottlers for the first time all the available advertising material in one place at one time. The words in the booklet explain the new format in this way: "This is the first edition of our price list in book form. We have gone to considerable expense to get up this issue with the intention of showing the bottler exactly how the different pieces look that we have to offer him. We hope you will read it through carefully and make your selections from it."

The first part of the illustrated price list discussed the billboard-poster campaign, which was the company's first attempt to use this medium. Following that, there were illustrations of such bottler advertising as a 12-by-36-inch flat metal sign ($0.14), a 12-by-18-inch metal flange sign ($0.19), the "Carrier Boy" lithographed cutout ($0.37 1/2), and two composition signs called "barkers," 21 by 60 inches ($0.60) and 36 by 60 inches ($1.13). Large 4-by-10-foot metal signs were next shown, and then a large 4-by-10-foot privilege panel ($7.35). As encouragement the book explained that in the previous year (1924), 2,045 large (4 by 10 feet) signs had been purchased with the privilege panel and 2,471 without.

Some of the other novelties offered in the 1925 booklet were flower cards, book matches, rulers, bottle openers, ice picks, trays, calendars, jazz caps, visor caps, card cases, needle cases and thimbles, the *Little Gem* pocket dictionary, and a booklet titled *The Charm of Purity*.

The 6-by-8-inch booklet in *The Red Barrel* format issued in 1925 was revised and reissued for the next eight years with occasional supplemental bulletins. These booklets and bulletins are not only highly desirable collectors' items but are also wonderful tools for dating Coca-Cola advertising memorabilia. Collectors using such materials for dating objects should *be aware that items were often issued year after year for as long as they were popular*. To most accurately place a collector-type date on an item, the first catalog to contain the item would have to be located.

Along with the usual advertising materials, the 1927 catalog, entitled *Coca-Cola Bottler Advertising 1927*, shows illustrations of a variety of metal signs. Offered were signs measuring 8 by 11 inches, 6 by 18 inches, 20 by 28 inches, 12 by 36 inches, 18 by 54 inches, 3 by 5 feet, and the large 4 by 10 feet.

In 1934 the format of the catalogs of bottler advertising items was changed. The new format, which is still being used, was mostly in full color. (In 1935 the catalog page size was standardized at 11 by 15 inches.) Again, any of the catalogs are excellent reference sources for collectors of Coca-Cola advertising material.

The new 1934 production featured a startling eighty-one items. To summarize the list somewhat it can be noted that bottlers had a choice of thirty-two metal signs (four of which were cooler signs). Also in 1934 a menu board, a plywood hanger, a new arrow sign, and a 4-by-10-foot "Silver Bar Sign" were introduced. Eleven lithographed pieces were offered, the most popular of which were display pieces featuring such movie stars as Jackie Cooper, Wallace Beery, and Jean Harlow. There was also a festoon for hanging on the wall behind soda fountains which pictured movie stars Benita Hume, Joan Crawford, Maureen O'Sullivan, and Jean Harlow. Still another piece of lithography was a hanging piece for home use illustrated with pictures of Johnny Weissmuller (the current movieland Tarzan) and Joan Crawford. Miss Crawford later married Alfred Steele, a one-time vice-president of The Coca-Cola Company who became president and chief executive officer of the Pepsi-Cola Company. During the 1950's Miss Crawford was an inexhaustible missionary for Pepsi-Cola and was elected a director of the company on May 6, 1959, one month after her husband died unexpectedly. Some executives of The Coca-Cola Company delight in reminding people that their company used Joan Crawford before Pepsi-Cola. (Along the same lines, The Coca-Cola Company can brag that in 1907–1908, for one year only, it used the advertising slogan "Good to the last drop" before Maxwell House Coffee and that it used skywriting before Pepsi-Cola did.) Some other movie stars employed during the 1930's to advertise Coca-Cola include Wynne Gibson, Randolph Scott, Claudette Colbert, Sari Maritza, Cary Grant, Clark Gable, and Florine McKinney. Advertisements featuring movie stars are greatly appreciated collectors' items; movie buffs have been saving such items from the time they were first issued.

Other 1934 advertising material listed in the enlarged eighty-one-item catalog included twelve wood, fiber, and transparent signs. Also listed were twenty-three specialty items. The 1934 price list even offered wall paint for Coca-Cola signs in units enough for signs measuring five, ten, and twenty-five square feet.

Each year since 1934 the lists of advertising materials for bottlers have grown and grown. In recent years there have been well over a thousand items available. In 1947 the company stopped issuing its annual catalog and switched to an ongoing catalog in two loose-leaf binders. As items are cancelled and/or added, bottlers are notified, and each bottler is responsible for maintaining his own catalog.

Robert Winship Woodruff introduced many advertising innovations that were highly successful in promoting Coca-Cola. Woodruff was responsible, in 1925, for the first billboard advertising ever done by The Coca-Cola Company, a thirty-thousand-dollar cash-prize contest in 1927, as well as radio advertising. Coca-Cola began to sponsor numerous radio programs in 1927.

Any study of advertising for Coca-Cola would be incomplete without an examination of the advertising agencies that were lucky enough to have had the Coca-Cola account. It was the D'Arcy Company that handled the majority of advertising from August 23, 1906, until March 31, 1956.

During the three-year period from 1904 through 1906 The Coca-Cola Company spent $107,000 on streetcar card advertising. During those years W. C. D'Arcy was a salesman for such advertising. D'Arcy was very much impressed with The Coca-Cola Company and the amount of money they put into streetcar cards, so he went after their business for the streetcar companies he represented. After securing some of The Coca-Cola Company account, D'Arcy formed an advertising agency in 1906 which has become world famous. The newly formed agency started with an order from The Coca-Cola Company of $2,500 for newspaper advertisements in Texas.

Although much of the advertising for Coca-Cola during the first decades of the twentieth century originated with the D'Arcy Company, there was another advertising agency working for The Coca-Cola Company. The other was the Massengale Advertising Agency in Atlanta. It is important for collectors to know that a great deal of this latter agency's advertising art carries the credit "MASSENGALE, ATLANTA," which is valuable information in dating Coca-Cola periodical advertisements of the period.

D'Arcy and his company did not have the entire advertising account for Coca-Cola, but the D'Arcy Company was involved in most phases of the advertising. Most of the advertising slogans (see Appendix B) used over the years to promote Coca-Cola were at least partially the ideas of W. C. D'Arcy and/or Archie Lee, a member of the D'Arcy staff.

When Robert W. Woodruff became president of The Coca-Cola Company in 1923, he began to work closely with the D'Arcy Company in stressing bottled Coca-Cola. Until 1923 the company did not really accept the fact that bottled Coca-Cola would eventually outsell Coca-Cola in glasses and become the backbone of the company's business. Woodruff's many innovative advertising ideas were made a reality under the guidance of the D'Arcy Company. Woodruff's prediction about the future of bottled Coca-Cola became a fact in 1928. From 1923 to 1928 fountain sales grew 20 percent, but bottle sales grew 65 percent. In 1928 bottle sales exceeded fountain sales and have done so every year since.

Archie Laney Lee, who began work for the D'Arcy agency in 1919, became the leader in putting Woodruff's advertising dreams into reality. Lee headed the Coca-Cola account for the

D'Arcy Company until his death in 1950. It was Archie Lee who was responsible for the Santa Claus series launched in 1930 and continued over the years.

"It had to be good to get where it is" was another of Lee's outstanding contributions. A collector of magazine advertisements will surely have a number of examples of "It had to be good to get where it is" advertisements which pictured bottles of Coca-Cola in numerous famous places all over the world. The complete series would certainly be a valuable collectors' item.

Other important Archie Lee contributions include the popular 1932 booklet *When You Entertain* by Ida Bailey Allen; the famous flower books of 1940, 1941, and 1942; the traditional summer advertisements (first painted by the famous artist N. C. Wyeth) picturing a bottle of Coca-Cola sitting in snow; and the development of the slogan "The pause that refreshes." (This last phrase, even though mimicked in many ways, has served to keep the image of Coca-Cola before the public as did "flivver" jokes with the Ford automobile.)

With the death of Archie Lee in 1950 and the tremendous problems of continuing to successfully meet and beat the competition, The Coca-Cola Company began to examine itself carefully.

In 1953 the company decided to make a survey of *each* of its 1,600,000 retail outlets for Coca-Cola in the country, or in other words to make the largest single private census ever made. Another survey conducted shortly afterward consisted of studying 20,861 motorists who stopped at 287 service stations in fourteen states. The results of this survey showed that clean restrooms and soft drinks are a motorist's main concerns. Still another survey of approximately 53,000 grocery-shopping housewives revealed that generally a housewife is worth about $0.40 a minute while she is in the store, $0.02 more if the store gives her a free Coke, and $0.02 more a minute if she buys a Coke herself.

These and other surveys taken in the early 1950's gave The Coca-Cola Company the information necessary to make profitable changes. Thus, with Robert Woodruff's retirement as the active leader of the firm in 1954, it was decided that some cataclysmic changes were imperative. One involved changing the advertising account from the D'Arcy Company to McCann-Erickson, Inc., in 1956. Many new ideas were successfully tried, and The Coca-Cola Company rather quickly regained its position of leadership in the beverage industry. For collectors the flow of advertising items continued at an exhilarating pace. Devoted collectors of memorabilia made hearty attempts to keep up, but new hobbyists were discouraged until 1970, when The Coca-Cola Company announced that it was initiating a multimillion-dollar project intended to refurbish its image. Almost everything changed except the shape of the traditional hobble-skirt bottle. A new twisting white ribbon (called the dynamic contour) was added under both trademarks, "Coca-Cola" and "Coke."

For collectors the new image was an ideal stopping point (at least for a few years). Today the vast majority of collectors of Coca-Cola artifacts collect within the comfortable 1886-to-1970 period. The definite sealing of an old era with the new 1970 program has not only reactivated the interest of long-time collectors, but has added many new collectors to the field. Additionally, collecting received the boost of literally millions of obsolete Coca-Cola advertising items.

For collectors of memorabilia it really isn't "the Pepsi generation" but rather "the Coke generation."

Eighteen-inch tall ceramic syrup dispenser first introduced in 1895. The dispensers were produced in high gloss. They were cream-colored, with embossed gold trim, and featured the embossed trademark "Coca-Cola" in red. Each dispenser was made in three pieces: a lid, a syrup bowl, and a base with a space for a glass. *(Archives, The Coca-Cola Company, Atlanta, Georgia)*

An unidentified scene featuring six ladies and an abundance of advertising memorabilia from around the turn of the century. Several collectors have dubbed this scene "Too Good to Be True." *(Archives, The Coca-Cola Company, Atlanta, Georgia)*

Left to right: "Man on the Grass" cutout issued in 1909 that ". . . costs less than thirty cents, looks like a dollar and a half"; 1956 national magazine advertisement featuring the grandsons of the "Man on the Grass"; 1958 poster with still another relative of the "Man on the Grass" *(Archives, The Coca-Cola Company, Atlanta, Georgia)*

Circular stained-glass leaded Tiffany-type chandelier issued by The Coca-Cola Company between 1905 and 1920. The originals measure 15¼ by 12½ inches. "Property of The Coca-Cola Company/To Be Returned on Demand" is debossed in the ornate metal band near the top. The dome panels are white opaque glass, the strips above and below the trademark panel are green opaque glass, the trademark panel is ruby-red granite-patterned stained glass, and the trademark is white opaque glass.

Milk-glass light globe produced in the 1920's and used in both bottling plants and retail outlets. These fourteen-inch-wide globes feature the trademark "Coca-Cola" in red and have a metal tassel pull string.

Rectangular stained-glass and leaded Tiffany-type chandelier issued by The Coca-Cola Company between 1905 and 1915. These chandeliers are 22 inches long, 11 inches wide, and 7½ inches high and are marked on one side with the words "Pittsburgh Mosaic Glass Co., Inc., Pittsburgh, Pa." The slanting part of the shade is made of green and white opaque glass; the ends are green and white opaque glass. All lettering is white opaque glass. *(Dr. Burton Spiller, Rochester, New York; photograph by Richard P. Daley, Rochester, New York)*

Circa 1920 stained-glass three-foot replica of the classic hobble-skirt bottle. These illuminated bottles were little used by bottlers because of their initial cost. Today less than a dozen are known to exist, and when available, each would cost approximately $2,000.

1910 metal sign

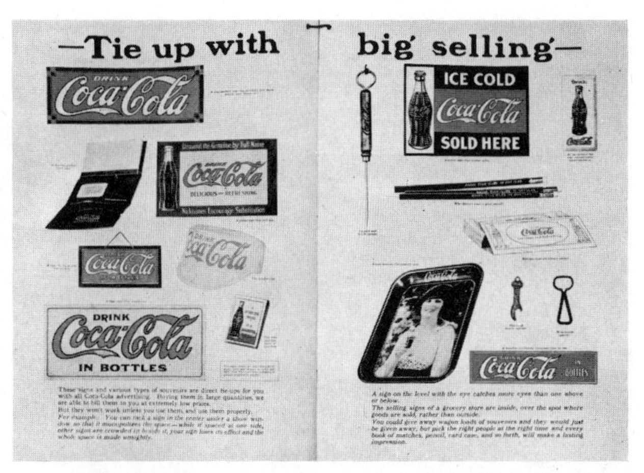

Two pages of *Coca-Cola Opens the Door*, illustrating some of the advertising materials available to Coca-Cola bottlers in 1922

One of the first separate price lists of advertising materials. This publication featured illustrations of thirty-five of the items (most in full color) available to bottlers during 1925 (*Archives, The Coca-Cola Company, Atlanta, Georgia*)

The February 15, 1929, issue of *The Red Barrel*, a periodical published by The Coca-Cola Company and distributed to bottlers. These periodicals are not only collectors' items but are also valuable sources of historical data. (*Archives, The Coca-Cola Company, Atlanta, Georgia*)

A miscellaneous selection of *The Red Barrel*. This grouping belongs to a collector interested in movie-star memorabilia.

The 1934 price list of advertising items available to bottlers (*Archives, The Coca-Cola Company, Atlanta, Georgia*)

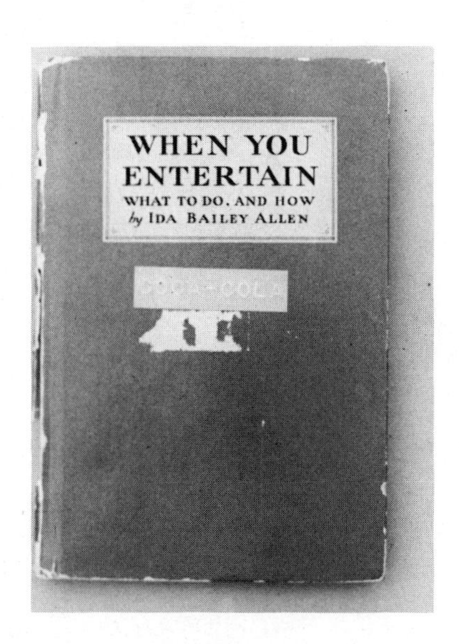

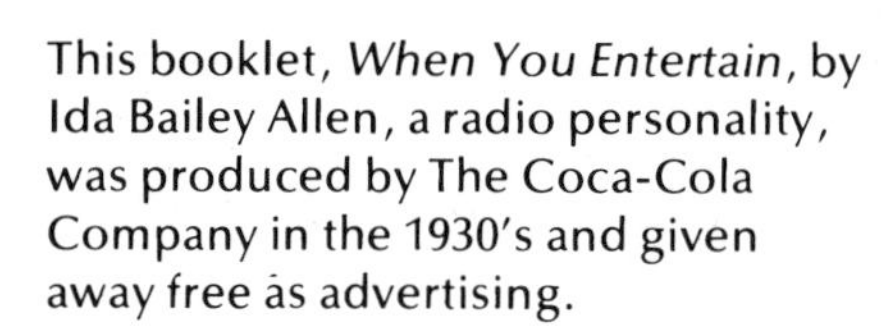

This booklet, *When You Entertain*, by Ida Bailey Allen, a radio personality, was produced by The Coca-Cola Company in the 1930's and given away free as advertising.

MRS. IDA BAILEY ALLEN

IDA BAILEY ALLEN

Tells how this Book came to be written

During the three years it has been my happy privilege to broadcast, almost daily, to the home-makers of America, hundreds of thousands of letters have come in, asking such questions as: Where are butter plates placed? When are finger-bowls used? Is colored linen smart? And so forth, ad infinitum.

It was so apparent that some way was needed to answer them other than by letter, that I finally decided to write a book covering the essentials of entertaining. At first, I expected to bring it out through my publishers, but that would have made it too expensive for many. I wanted it to have wide distribution, and help millions to make their entertaining gay and easy.

About that time I met an officer of The Coca-Cola Company. An idea flashed through my mind. What more suitable way to bring out this book than under the sponsorship of Coca-Cola, the great beverage of American hospitality!

I revealed the letters and the plan I had made for the book. "Can you get it ready for spring?" he asked. And gladly I assented. The task has been one of joy, for I have mentally lived through all the parties described, and in my mind's eye have seen you planning your own gay times. I hope the book will encourage you to entertain easily and often.

You will find that the rules to be followed in entertaining are few; in fact, there is only one that is really important. Wherever you live, whatever your status in life may be, you can entertain charmingly if you will remember, that success comes from the dispensing of true hospitality, and that hospitality is simply consideration for others.

Ida Bailey Allen

Pages 6 and 7 from *When You Entertain*, showing a photograph of the author and explaining why the book was written specifically for The Coca-Cola Company

CHAPTER 18

CALENDARS

Of the hundreds and hundreds of advertising items used over the years by The Coca-Cola Company to promote Coca-Cola, certainly the numerous calendars are among the most popular with collectors. As early as 1891, the year Asa Griggs Candler began to deal exclusively in the development of Coca-Cola, the first calendar advertising Coca-Cola was issued. Almost every year since 1891 The Coca-Cola Company has issued at least one calendar.

The most popular calendars display pretty girls. Unlike some calendar art, the girls used on the calendars created by The Coca-Cola Company have always been pretty and wholesome and tastefully posed. As has been the case in other areas of advertising for Coca-Cola, however, some of the calendars produced by individual bottlers without the guidance of the parent company have been in "questionable" taste. Such unsanctioned calendars are extremely popular collectors' items today and command high prices. A study of calendar girls is truly an excellent opportunity to learn about fashions of the past. Much can be learned about the garb and equipment used in tennis and golf around the turn of the century.

An examination of any representative collection of calendars shows that more bottles of Coca-Cola than glasses have been featured over the years. Perhaps this is because calendars were a give-away item from those who sold bottled Coca-Cola. Of course, in some cases both bottles and glasses were featured together. Another interesting observation is that no calendar has been located that featured the amber bottles used in the Thomas territory before 1916.

Advances in graphic arts in the 1870's, specifically the perfecting of inexpensive methods of color lithography, made the use of calendars in full color a practical advertising medium for The Coca-Cola Company. The majority of Coca-Cola calendars are in full color and truly a credit to the printing industry.

The Coca-Cola Company has issued at least one calendar annually since 1891, with few exceptions. Serious collecting of the artifacts of The Coca-Cola Company is a recent activity, and the company itself was not concerned with its own history until the late 1930's. No specimens are known to exist for 1905 and 1906. It seems logical to assume that even though no examples are currently known, some do exist. For example, it is difficult to believe that the very popular tray models of 1909 and 1912 were not featured on calendars as they were on various other advertising items. As the hobby grows, more and more of the early and scarce items will come to light.

For approximately the first ten years, calendars were issued featuring girls who posed anonymously. Around the turn of the century The Coca-Cola Company was large enough and respected enough to entice two well-known personalities to pose for calendars and other point-of-sale advertising. In 1900 the famous singer and actress Hilda Clark posed for the 1901 calendar. In 1903 and again in 1904 Lillian Norton (1859–1914), better known and more famous as the great Metropolitan Opera star Lillian Nordica, posed for lithographic art that appeared on a variety of point-of-sale advertising, including calendars. The Nordica lithography is considered a classic among collectors.

After using these two famous ladies, The Coca-Cola Company returned to using unnamed girls. In 1916 the company issued two calendars. One calendar featured "The Moving Picture Star" Pearl White, and the other, the customary anonymous model. Again in 1919 two calendars were released. Along with the one featuring the usual anonymous model was one with Marion Davies, the film star.

Between 1920 and 1930 The Coca-Cola Company returned to the use of anonymous models for its calendar art. It is difficult to state with certainty, but it appears that in some cases the same model was used in successive years. In 1931 and lasting through 1937 the company selected calendar illustrations with human interest. The subjects were sometimes presented individually and sometimes in groups. During the years of World War II a great emphasis was placed on the women working in war plants and serving overseas. After the war, groups of teen-agers became a favorite subject for calendars. In 1954 the large store calendar was joined by a smaller size that was more appropriate for home use. The smaller calendar featured paintings of dogs, flower prints, bird illustrations, and table decorations. It was known as the Home Calendar.

Dating calendars is often tricky since many are not saved in their entirety; the calendar portion has often been cut off. Art found on some items may have been used in previous years or during the following year. It is not wise to take dates on calendars (and other items, for that matter) as indications of the year the calendar (item) was issued. In some cases such dates indicate the year the art was created.

Calendar illustrations were often painted either in oil or pastel, but in some instances direct color photography was used. Many fine commercial artists have been employed by The Coca-Cola Company to execute the art used on calendars. The list of artists used to produce the many fine calendars of The Coca-Cola Company and other advertising art is incomplete at this time because of the missing calendars. Much of the work is unsigned, and records are incomplete. A partial list of the artists who have worked for The Coca-Cola Company is included in Appendix C.

Calendars are among the most perishable of

the advertising items used by The Coca-Cola Company. As a result, few early examples have survived; those that have bring surprisingly high prices. It is safe to state that calendars advertising Coca-Cola generally command twice the price of other collectible calendars and range from several dollars to well over one hundred dollars.

The 1892 calendar of Asa G. Candler & Co. Although the 1891 calendar advertised a liquid dentifrice and Coca-Cola, this one promotes only Coca-Cola. (*Archives, The Coca-Cola Company, Atlanta, Georgia*)

Above: The first calendar (1891) advertising Coca-Cola, printed by the Calvert Lithography Company, of Atlanta (*Archives, The Coca-Cola Company, Atlanta, Georgia*)

Circa 1893–1896 calendar of The Coca-Cola Company. The glass held by the model is the first designed for Coca-Cola. No known specimens of either the glass or its holder exist. (*Archives, The Coca-Cola Company, Atlanta, Georgia*)

The 1897 calendar, in addition to featuring the first glass and holder designed for Coca-Cola, depicts a card like those issued around the turn of the century, offering a free Coca-Cola. The model is often called the Victorian Girl by collectors and company officials. (*Archives, The Coca-Cola Company, Atlanta, Georgia*)

The 1899 calendar (*Archives, The Coca-Cola Company, Atlanta, Georgia*)

This calendar for 1900 features the famous entertainer Hilda Clark. (*Archives, The Coca-Cola Company, Atlanta, Georgia*)

The illustration used on the 1898 calendar. The calendar has been cut away. Cola nuts around the border are inscribed "Coca-Cola."

One of the calendars for 1901 (*Archives, The Coca-Cola Company, Atlanta, Georgia*)

1901			OCTOBER			1901
SUN.	MON.	TUES.	WED.	THUR.	FRI.	SAT.
		1	2	3	4	5
6	7	8	9	10	11	12
13	14	15	16	17	18	19
20	21	22	23	24	25	26
27	28	29	30	31		

The 1901 calendar of The Coca-Cola Company, featuring Hilda Clark. Miss Clark was used in other poses in subsequent years in advertising for Coca-Cola. The oval metal-framed glass sign pictured is a very rare collectors' item. The photograph used for the calendar was copyrighted in 1900 by Morrison of Chicago. The actual calendar was printed by Wolf and Company, of Philadelphia. (*Archives, The Coca-Cola Company, Atlanta, Georgia*)

1902			JANUARY			1902
Sun.	Mon.	Tues.	Wed.	Thur.	Fri.	Sat.
· ·	· ·	· ·	1	2	3	4
5	6	7	8	9	10	11
12	13	14	15	16	17	18
19	20	21	22	23	24	25
26	27	28	29	30	31	· ·
· ·	· ·	· ·				

The 1902 calendar features an unidentified model and the same glass-holder and oval metal-framed glass sign (with a slightly different stand) as pictured on the 1901 calendar. The photograph was copyrighted in 1901 by The Coca-Cola Company. The calendar was printed by Wolf and Company, of Philadelphia. (*Archives, The Coca-Cola Company, Atlanta, Georgia*)

The 1904 calendar, featuring Lillian Nordica (*Archives, The Coca-Cola Company, Atlanta, Georgia*)

The 1903 calendar features the famous opera star Lillian Nordica.

The 1907 calendar. The model is holding a glass that became standardized. (*Archives, The Coca-Cola Company, Atlanta, Georgia*)

The calendar for 1908. Note the slogan "Good to the last Drop," which was later adopted and made more famous by the Maxwell House Coffee Company. (*Archives, The Coca-Cola Company, Atlanta, Georgia*)

One of the 1909 calendars advertising Coca-Cola. The same picture was used on the 1904 calendar. (*Archives, The Coca-Cola Company, Atlanta, Georgia*)

The illustration used on the 1909 Coca-Cola calendar. The clear glass bottle, embossed around the base, was used in the Whitehead/Lupton territory before 1916. (*Archives, The Coca-Cola Company, Atlanta, Georgia*)

One of the three calendars issued for 1910. The glass lacks a syrup line. (*Archives, The Coca-Cola Company, Atlanta, Georgia*)

The calendar illustration of 1911. This is the first illustration of a model drinking from a bottle with two straws. (*Archives, The Coca-Cola Company, Atlanta, Georgia*)

One of the three calendars offered to bottlers by The Coca-Cola Company in 1910 (*Archives, The Coca-Cola Company, Atlanta, Georgia*)

The illustration from the 1912 calendar. This was the first calendar featuring two models. (*Archives, The Coca-Cola Company, Atlanta, Georgia*)

"Betty," the model for the 1914 calendar. She was featured on almost all of the company's advertising items for 1914. Because of the large metal signs, change and serving trays, and the calendars, "Betty" is one of the most remembered Coca-Cola girls. (*Archives, The Coca-Cola Company, Atlanta, Georgia*)

The 1913 calendar, with an unidentified brunette model (*Archives, The Coca-Cola Company, Atlanta, Georgia*)

The 1915 calendar illustration. Because of the popularity of "Betty," this calendar is difficult to find; 1915 calendars were not saved. (*Archives, The Coca-Cola Company, Atlanta, Georgia*)

Miss Pearl White, "The Moving Picture Star," was featured on one of the calendars for 1916. (*Archives, The Coca-Cola Company, Atlanta, Georgia*)

"Constance" was featured on one of the 1916 calendars. Not since "Betty" in 1914 had The Coca-Cola Company named a calendar girl. (*Archives, The Coca-Cola Company, Atlanta, Georgia*)

The 1918 calendar models (*Archives, The Coca-Cola Company, Atlanta, Georgia*)

The 1917 calendar featuring the "World War I Girl." This model was featured in the same pose on the serving and change trays of 1917. (*Archives, The Coca-Cola Company, Atlanta, Georgia*)

1919 calendar (*Archives, The Coca-Cola Company, Atlanta, Georgia*)

The 1919 "Knitting Girl" (*Archives, The Coca-Cola Company, Atlanta, Georgia*)

The "Garden Girl" of the 1920 calendar. The girl is actually on a golf course. (*Archives, The Coca-Cola Company, Atlanta, Georgia*)

The 1921 calendar model (*Archives, The Coca-Cola Company, Atlanta, Georgia*)

The 1922 "Autumn Girl" calendar (*Archives, The Coca-Cola Company, Atlanta, Georgia*)

The 1923 calendar featured the "Flapper Girl." (*Archives, The Coca-Cola Company, Atlanta, Georgia*)

The "Smiling Girl" of 1924 (*Archives, The Coca-Cola Company, Atlanta, Georgia*)

The "Girl at Party" appeared on the 1925 calendar. (*Archives, The Coca-Cola Company, Atlanta, Georgia*)

The 1926 calendar model (*Archives, The Coca-Cola Company, Atlanta, Georgia*)

The 1927 calendar model, with framed bottle (*Archives, The Coca-Cola Company, Atlanta, Georgia*)

The 1928 calendar model (*Archives, The Coca-Cola Company, Atlanta, Georgia*)

The 1929 calendar model (*Archives, The Coca-Cola Company, Atlanta, Georgia*)

1930 MARCH 1930

It Had to Be Good to Get Where It Is

Sunday	Monday	Tuesday	Wednesday	Thursday	Friday	Saturday
						1
2	3	4	5	6	7	8
9	10	11	12	13	14	15
16	17	18	19	20	21	22
23/30	24/31	25	26	27	28	29

The 1930 bathing beauty. Although the illustration features the traditional slogan "Delicious and Refreshing," the actual calendar used "It Had to Be Good to Get Where It Is." (*Archives, The Coca-Cola Company, Atlanta, Georgia*)

In 1931 Norman Rockwell created the illustration used on the calendar and tray. This scene is called "Tom Sawyer" by collectors and "Farm Boy with Dog" by officials of The Coca-Cola Company. (*Archives, The Coca-Cola Company, Atlanta, Georgia*)

Another Norman Rockwell creation for 1932. This illustration is called "Huckleberry Finn" by collectors. (*Archives, The Coca-Cola Company, Atlanta, Georgia*)

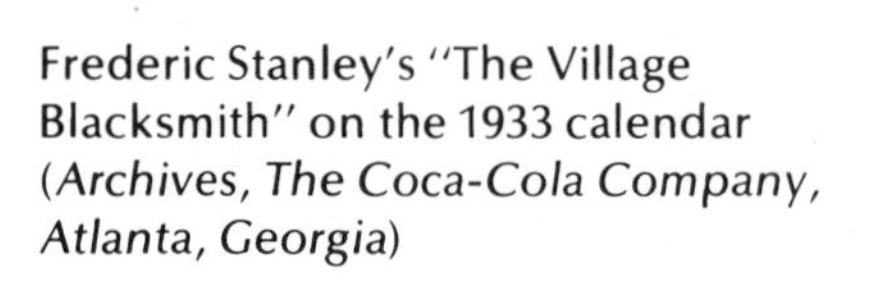
Frederic Stanley's "The Village Blacksmith" on the 1933 calendar (*Archives, The Coca-Cola Company, Atlanta, Georgia*)

The 1935 Norman Rockwell creation (*Archives, The Coca-Cola Company, Atlanta, Georgia*)

N. C. Wyeth produced this boy and dog for the 1937 calendar. (*Archives, The Coca-Cola Company, Atlanta, Georgia*)

Artist N. C. Wyeth drew the 1936 calendar. (*Archives, The Coca-Cola Company, Atlanta, Georgia*)

Left: In 1934 Norman Rockwell again illustrated the calendar. (*Archives, The Coca-Cola Company, Atlanta, Georgia*)

Bradshaw Crandall created the 1938 calendar. (*Archives, The Coca-Cola Company, Atlanta, Georgia*)

An interesting feature of this 1939 calendar is the unmarked glass. The lithography was done by Forbes of Boston. (*Archives, The Coca-Cola Company, Atlanta, Georgia*)

The 1940 calendar model (*Archives, The Coca-Cola Company, Atlanta, Georgia*)

The 1941 calendar (*Archives, The Coca-Cola Company, Atlanta, Georgia*)

The second page of the 1942 calendar (*Archives, The Coca-Cola Company, Atlanta, Georgia*)

The 1943 calendar honored the U.S. Army Nurse Corps.

Two pages from the 1943 calendar. Much advertising during World War II featured war-oriented scenes. (*Archives, The Coca-Cola Company, Atlanta, Georgia*)

The second page of the 1946 calendar (*Archives, The Coca-Cola Company, Atlanta, Georgia*)

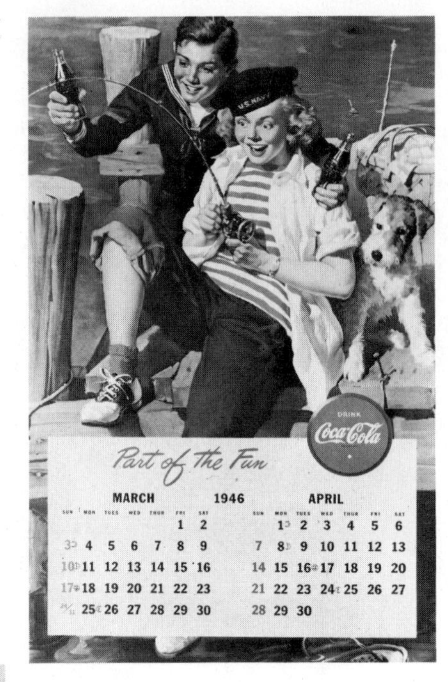

Above: The 1947 calendar (*Archives, The Coca-Cola Company, Atlanta, Georgia*)

A page from the 1944 calendar (*Archives, The Coca-Cola Company, Atlanta, Georgia*)

The first page of the calendar for 1945 (*Archives, The Coca-Cola Company, Atlanta, Georgia*)

The 1947 calendar (*Archives, The Coca-Cola Company, Atlanta, Georgia*)

The 1948 calendar (*Archives, The Coca-Cola Company, Atlanta, Georgia*)

The 1949 calendar (*Archives, The Coca-Cola Company, Atlanta, Georgia*)

The 1950 calendar (*Archives, The Coca-Cola Company, Atlanta, Georgia*)

The 1951 calendar (*Archives, The Coca-Cola Company, Atlanta, Georgia*)

The 1955 calendar (*Archives, The Coca-Cola Company, Atlanta, Georgia*)

The 1953 calendar (*Archives, The Coca-Cola Company, Atlanta, Georgia*)

The 1954 calendar (*Archives, The Coca-Cola Company, Atlanta, Georgia*)

The 1956 calendar (*Archives, The Coca-Cola Company, Atlanta, Georgia*)

The next to the last page of the 1957 calendar (*Archives, The Coca-Cola Company, Atlanta, Georgia*)

The 1958 calendar (*Archives, The Coca-Cola Company, Atlanta, Georgia*)

The first page of the 1957 calendar (*Archives, The Coca-Cola Company, Atlanta, Georgia*)

Famed artist Athos Menaboni illustrated a 1959 calendar.

The 1959 calendar (*Archives, The Coca-Cola Company, Atlanta, Georgia*)

The calendar for 1960 (*Archives, The Coca-Cola Company, Atlanta, Georgia*)

The 1961 calendar (*Archives, The Coca-Cola Company, Atlanta, Georgia*)

The 1962 calendar (*Archives, The Coca-Cola Company, Atlanta, Georgia*)

The 1963 calendar (*Archives, The Coca-Cola Company, Atlanta, Georgia*)

The 1964 calendar (*Archives, The Coca-Cola Company, Atlanta, Georgia*)

The 1965 calendar (*Archives, The Coca-Cola Company, Atlanta, Georgia*)

The 1966 calendar (*Archives, The Coca-Cola Company, Atlanta, Georgia*)

The 1967 calendar (*Archives, The Coca-Cola Company, Atlanta, Georgia*)

The 1969 calendar (*Archives, The Coca-Cola Company, Atlanta, Georgia*)

The 1968 calendar (*Archives, The Coca-Cola Company, Atlanta, Georgia*)

In 1970 The Coca-Cola Company presented its first calendar featuring the "new" image. Most collectors do not seek memorabilia from the 1970's because they consider the "new" image as a cutoff point. (*Archives, The Coca-Cola Company, Atlanta, Georgia*)

CHAPTER 19

METAL SERVING AND CHANGE TRAYS

If any one group of Coca-Cola advertising collectibles is more popular than the others, it is trays. Starting just before the turn of the century, The Coca-Cola Company spent a portion of its advertising budget on metal trays bearing advertisements. Like much of the early history of The Coca-Cola Company, the history of these trays is sketchy. While records as early as 1896 mention expenditures for "metal serving trays," known collections do not contain any Coca-Cola trays made earlier than 1898. It can probably be expected that as interest continues to grow and more trays are rediscovered, trays from the period before 1898 will emerge.

Metal trays advertising Coca-Cola were made of tin plate and were of two types: serving trays and change trays. They were round, oval, or rectangular. All known metal trays were made of tin plate from 1898 through 1949. The serving trays have been a standard item from the 1890's to the present, but the change trays were issued intermittently from 1899 to 1920. Round and oval trays were used exclusively from the 1890's to 1910. In 1910 The Coca-Cola Company issued its first rectangular metal tray. The last known round tray used in this country was produced in 1905. From 1910 until the present, most trays advertising Coca-Cola have been rectangular, but some oval trays were used as late as 1920.

Not much is known about the metal serving and change trays produced for and used in foreign countries. Metal trays from foreign countries have not attracted much American collector attention until recent years for several reasons:

(1) They are not easily accessible because of their geographical use; (2) many American collectors (the bulk of the collector population) have had little interest in foreign items; and (3) there has been, until recently, an adequate supply of domestic trays to satisfy the demand.

Interest in foreign trays centers on those produced in Mexico. Coca-Cola was introduced to Mexico in 1903. Knowledge of Mexican trays is sparse, and the earliest known Mexican tray is a small, round, 4½-inch change tray. Although some trays designed for Mexican use were merely duplicates of those used in the United States, a great number are unique to Mexico.

Since trays advertising Coca-Cola were not as popular an advertising medium in Mexico, only a few change trays were utilized, and the variety in trays available today is not as great. Trays of the United States are predominantly rectangular, whereas trays of Mexico were mostly round.

The most popular subject of trays over the years has been young women; in fact, female models were exclusively used until 1926. In 1926 a man and a woman were used. From 1926 to 1934 men were pictured on trays intermittently. The last male to appear on a tray advertising Coca-Cola was (in 1934) the famous movie Tarzan, Johnny Weissmuller. For one year (1931) a boy model was featured. Beginning in 1950 miscellaneous designs, scenes, and the Coca-Cola trademark were featured on metal and plastic trays.

During the early years until 1920, trays were produced in mostly one, sometimes two, and occasionally three sizes. A collection of trays of one type in all existing sizes is worth much more than the same trays would be individually.

Metal trays advertising Coca-Cola are expensive, and the oldest and rarest are valued at more than several hundred dollars. Other advertising memorabilia of the same age and rarity do not command nearly the price, in general, that metal trays do. The explanation seems to be twofold: (1) Metal trays have long enjoyed popularity among collectors; (2) tray collecting in itself is a hobby, and as a result there seems to be about twice the market for trays.

The Coca-Cola Company never used manufacturer's stock designs on its trays. Yet an examination of tray collecting readily reveals that numerous companies using metal trays to advertise their products purchased manufacturer's stock designs and had a slogan, trademark, and/or some personal message printed on them.

Tray subjects were often the same ones used on calendars, pocket mirrors, and other items of the same period. It is worthy for collectors to note that tray subjects were sometimes used on calendars and other advertising items of the preceding or succeeding year. Too often collectors overlook this fact and inaccurately date their finds as a result.

Although various methods must be used to date the early trays, it is helpful to know that most trays of the 1920's had green and brown borders and that trays of the 1930's had red borders.

Other identifying characteristics for Coca-Cola trays include signed art and manufacturer names. Some artists whose signatures appear on trays include Hamilton King, Hayden Hayden (Howard Renwick), and Haddon Sundblom. The seven notable manufacturers of trays are Standard Advertising Company, Coshoctin, Ohio; Charles W. Shonk Lithograph Company, Chicago, Illinois; American Art Works, Inc. (successors to Meek Company), Coshoctin, Ohio; Wolf and Company; Stelad Signs, Passaic Metal Ware Company, Passaic, New Jersey; H. D. Beach Company, Coshoctin, Ohio; and a firm identified only as Tendeco. Further information about some of the firms that did chromolithographic printing on metal trays and signs can be found in Appendix D.

Finally, it should be noted that on occasion individual Coca-Cola bottlers have produced (with, but most often without, the parent company's knowledge) their own trays. Such trays are considered an integral part of collectible memorabilia. Sometimes such individually produced trays are considered of "questionable" taste by The Coca-Cola Company. As might be expected, such advertising "step-children" are considered choice items by collectors, and consequently the value of these trays is enhanced. Another factor related to the value of such items is their scarcity: Because of their localized nature they were produced in limited quantities.

Although metal serving trays were used to advertise Coca-Cola as early as 1896, this 1898 specimen (9½ inches in diameter) is the oldest known to exist. (*A.N. Shpil, Castro Valley, California*)

Hilda Clark posed for advertising around the turn of the century. This small (5½ inches in diameter) metal change tray was the first of several featuring Hilda Clark. The tray was made in 1899 by the Standard Advertising Company, of Coshoctin, Ohio.

This 1901 serving tray measures 9¾ inches. The model is Hilda Clark. (*Jim Cope, Orange, Texas*)

The 1904 change tray

These three oval trays were produced in 1904 to commemorate the St. Louis Exposition. Left to right: 13½ by 16½ inches, 4½ by 6¼ inches, 10¾ by 13 inches.

Nine trays were produced in 1904. This oval serving tray, 15 by 18½ inches, is the largest. (*Archives, The Coca-Cola Company, Atlanta, Georgia*)

1904 metal serving tray, 10½ by 13 inches, featuring Lillian Nordica (*Jim Cope, Orange, Texas*)

This 9¾-inch metal serving tray was issued in 1905 with the slogan "THE MOST REFRESHING DRINK IN THE WORLD." (*Jim Cope, Orange, Texas*)

1905 metal serving tray, 10½ by 13¼ inches

1905 metal change tray, 4½ inches in diameter

1906 serving tray, measuring 13¼ by 10½ inches

1906 change tray, measuring 4⅜ by 6 inches

Occasionally, individual bottlers issued trays without the sanction of The Coca-Cola Company. This tray was issued by the Western Coca-Cola Bottling Company, of Chicago, Illinois. The tray, released between 1905 and 1912, measures 12½ inches in diameter.

In 1909 The Coca-Cola Company issued its first rectangular tray, 10½ by 13¼ inches. The tray features "The Coca-Cola Girl" painted by artist Hamilton King. The tray was manufactured by the American Art Works, Inc., of Coshoctin, Ohio. Collectors should note that in 1971–1972 an exact reproduction of this tray was made. Over one million of the reproductions were used as promotional items. Since they are common, they are not worth more than several dollars.

The 1912 rectangular tray, 10½ by 13¼ inches, features a model painted by artist Hamilton King. This tray was manufactured by Wolf and Co.

This is one of three trays issued in 1914 featuring "Betty." It measures 10½ by 13¼ inches. The manufacturer was Stelad Signs, Passaic Metal Ware Company, of Passaic, New Jersey.

1912 change tray, measuring 4⅜ by 6⅛ inches, painted by Hamilton King. A similar tray measuring 12½ by 15¼ inches was also produced in 1912.

This 1909 change tray measures 4⅜ by 6⅛ inches. A large oval tray, 12½ by 15¼ inches, was also issued in 1909.

1914 change tray featuring "Betty." A large oval serving tray, 12½ by 15¼ inches, was also issued in 1914.

This 1917 tray measures 8½ by 19 inches. The model is the "World War I Girl." The tray was produced by Stelad Signs, Passaic Metal Ware Company, of Passaic, New Jersey.

1917 change tray, 4⅜ by 6⅛ inches, featuring the "World War I Girl"

1920 serving tray, measuring 10½ by 13¼ inches

1920 change tray measuring 4⅜ by 6⅛ inches. A large oval serving tray measuring 13¾ by 16½ inches and featuring the same model was also issued in 1920. This was the last change tray issued in the United States.

"Summer Girl" is featured on this 1921 serving tray measuring 10½ by 15¼ inches. The tray was manufactured by the H.D. Beach Company, of Coshoctin, Ohio.

The 1922 tray, measuring 10½ by 13¼ inches, was manufactured by American Art Works, Inc., of Coshoctin, Ohio.

1923 serving tray, 10½ by 13¼ inches

1924 serving tray, 10½ by 13¼ inches

1925 serving tray, 10½ by 13¼ inches

1926 serving tray, 10½ by 13¼ inches

One of two serving trays issued in 1927

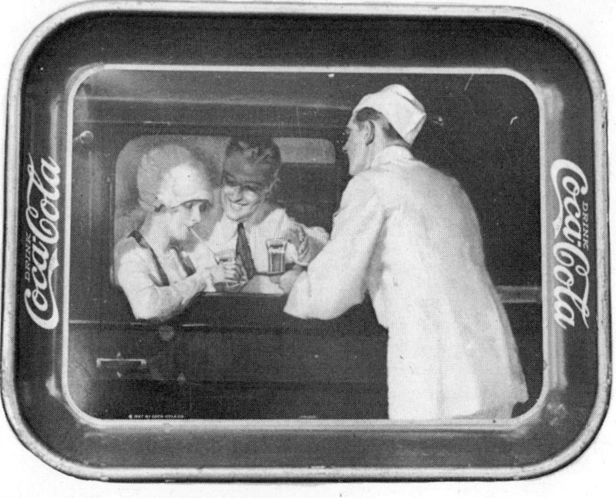

One of the two 1927 serving trays

1928 serving tray

1929 tray, manufactured by a company called Tindeco

Another 1929 tray, produced by the American Art Works, Inc., of Coshoctin, Ohio

1930 serving tray, manufactured by the American Art Works, Inc., of Coshoctin, Ohio

1930 serving tray, manufactured by the American Art Works, Inc., of Coshoctin, Ohio

1931 serving tray by Norman Rockwell

Movie star Frances Dee on the 1933 serving tray

The 1934 tray, featuring Johnny Weismuller and Maureen O'Sullivan. Produced by the American Art Works, Inc., of Coshoctin, Ohio.

1932 serving tray by artist Hayden Hayden

1935 serving tray with movie star Madge Evans. American Art Works, Inc., Coshoctin, Ohio.

1936 serving tray. American Art Works, Inc., Coshoctin, Ohio.

1937 serving tray. American Art Works, Inc., Coshoctin, Ohio.

1938 serving tray. American Art Works, Inc., Coshoctin, Ohio.

1939 serving tray by Haddon Sundblom. American Art Works, Inc., Coshoctin, Ohio.

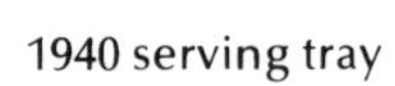

1940 serving tray

1941 serving tray

1942 serving tray. This was the last tray produced until after World War II. The metal involved in such productions was needed for the war effort.

1948 serving tray

One tray produced in 1950

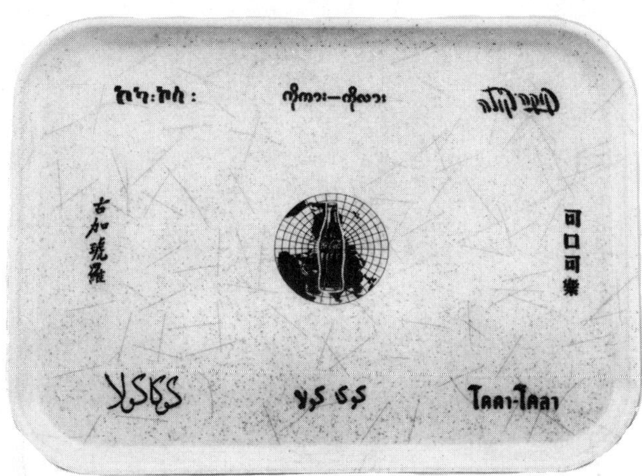

Plastic serving tray measuring 12 by 16½ inches was given away at a circa 1950 bottlers' convention. "Coca-Cola" is printed in eight different languages.

1956 TV tray, measuring 13½ by 18¾ inches

1958 TV tray

1958 serving tray, measuring 10½ by 11¼ inches

1960 TV serving tray, measuring 13¼ by 18½ inches. Produced by Agosta.

Serving tray for 1961

Serving tray for 1961

One of three 1961 serving trays

1961 TV tray, measuring 13½ by 18¾ inches

Serving tray produced in Mexico circa 1940-1945

1941 serving tray. One of two similar trays issued for several years. "TRADE MARK REG. U.S. PAT. OFF." in black. *(Archives, The Coca-Cola Company, Atlanta, Georgia)*

1941 serving tray. "REG. U.S. PAT. OFF." in white. *(Archives, The Coca-Cola Company, Atlanta, Georgia)*

1968 serving tray featuring Lillian Nordica. This tray was made in Canada to commemorate the early advertising of Coca-Cola.

1968 serving tray made in Canada. Identical to the other 1968 tray except that the slogan is printed in French.

1969 tray featuring Lillian Nordica, who originally posed in 1905. Commemorative tray made in Canada.

CHAPTER 20

CHANGE RECEIVERS, DISHES, AND COASTERS

The various objects on which advertisements for Coca-Cola have been placed throughout the years include such unusual receptacles as change receivers, plates, bowls, and coasters.

Almost out of date are advertising change receivers, objects found near the cash registers of almost all turn-of-the-century stores. Change receivers have not historically made up a major portion of the items used to advertise Coca-Cola, and therefore few examples remain. The earliest known change receiver advertising Coca-Cola can be dated 1892. The most valuable example, however, is one produced in 1901. Its value is attributed to the beautiful art work involved. Later examples are certainly collectible but are not as interesting or valuable as the early specimens.

Plates advertising Coca-Cola seem to be a post-World War I inspiration. Both Hire's Root Beer and Moxie, which were big competitors of Coca-Cola, experienced a great deal of advertising success with ceramic bowls, mugs, cups, saucers, and plates during the early 1900's, especially during the 1920's. The Coca-Cola Company failed to produce as many plates as their soft drink competitors because so much competition existed already in this area. The few plates produced lack variety but nevertheless are very much sought after.

The fiftieth anniversary celebration of The Coca-Cola Company in 1936 resulted in an exceptionally large and varied issue of advertising items, of which the aluminum pretzel dish made in 1935 for the 1936 celebration is probably the most popular with collectors. Three replicated Coke bottles serve as legs for this dish and account for part of the appeal of this piece.

Coasters are a natural accessory to a product like Coca-Cola which is marketed in bottles and served in glasses. While collectors can expect to locate quite a variety of these disk- and saucer-like bottle or glass protectors, they do not date much before the 1930's and most are of a post-World War II era. Coasters are not necessarily a new invention, but their popularity is recent.

Change receivers, dishes, and coasters make an interesting collecting combination. The range in collector-paid prices for these items is from less than a dollar to over one thousand dollars.

White ceramic change receiver, with red lettering, 10½ inches in diameter. Made by Charles Lippincott & Co., of Philadelphia. It has sold for several hundred dollars but is not the most valuable change receiver. (*Dr. Burton Spiller, Rochester, New York; photograph by Richard P. Daley*)

1901 glass change receiver, 8¼ inches in diameter, featuring Hilda Clark. Illustration copyrighted in 1900 by "Morrison of Chicago." The lithography was produced by Wolf & Co., of Philadelphia. Most valuable change receiver. One sold for over $1,000.

1969 aqua plastic change receiver, measuring 6¼ by 7¾ inches, made by a Montreal, Canada, firm, "Ornamin by Ornamold"

1924 cream-colored plate with red and yellow lettering, 7¼ inches in diameter

Ad from *The Coca-Cola Bottler*, 1959, for plate with picture of the home of the inventor of Coke. Made by the Balfour Company, of Attleboro, Massachusetts.

1967 amber glass plate with gold lettering, 7¼ inches in diameter

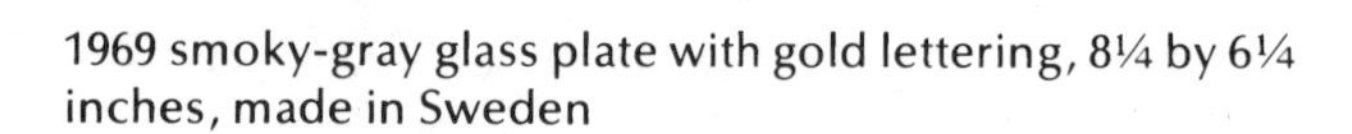
1969 smoky-gray glass plate with gold lettering, 8¼ by 6¼ inches, made in Sweden

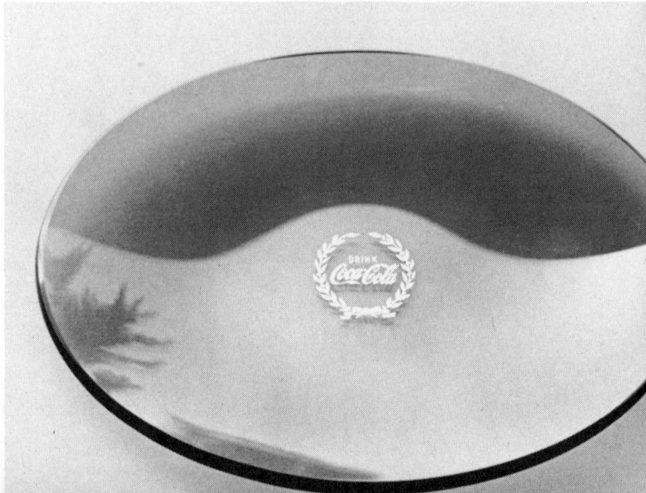

8¼-inch aluminum pretzel dish, made by "Brunhoff Mfg. Co." for the fiftieth anniversary celebration held in 1936

Solid brass coaster commemorating the fiftieth anniversary of The Coca-Cola Bottling Company

3½-inch foil-covered cardboard drink coasters issued in 1957

1969 white coaster, three inches in diameter. These are readily available to collectors.

CHAPTER 21

POCKET MIRRORS

Pocket mirrors that were officially produced for and used by The Coca-Cola Company, according to current information, were produced in two shapes, oval and rectangular. The oval-shaped examples are in the majority. Extensive research has revealed that there were eleven different oval mirrors made between 1904 and 1920. It is not impossible that others will be discovered in the future. In a rectangular shape only one type is currently known to exist, but records indicate that others were made. It is also possible that individual domestic bottlers and/or foreign bottlers have issued pocket mirrors at one time or another, but none have been noted as yet.

The first of the classic and most popular oval pocket mirrors was issued in 1904. The mirror features an illustration identical to the one that appeared on the 1904 metal serving and change trays issued to commemorate the St. Louis Exposition. A second oval mirror was produced in 1905; again, the illustration is identical to the one that appears on the 1905 metal serving and change trays. Like all the oval pocket mirrors, it measures 1¾ by 2¾ inches. The attractive model is shown drinking a glass of Coca-Cola; she is also wearing a distinctive corsage of violets and a locket with "CC" engraved on it.

The next mirror was produced in 1906, and like its two predecessors it is an imitation of a metal serving and change tray. The young girl pictured is wearing a rather low-cut dress, and she is holding a glass marked "Coca-Cola." The same scene was used on the 1907 calendar.

Fourth in the series of pocket mirrors is the

one issued in 1907. This mirror features a young woman dressed in pink sitting in a drugstore sipping a glass of Coca-Cola. The pink roses in her hat match those on the table. The same model and pose is featured on the calendar for 1908. This mirror is often mistakenly dated 1903; this is easily refuted when one notices that on the table in front of the young woman is a small piece of paper with the slogan "Good to the last drop," first used by The Coca-Cola Company in 1908. (See Appendix B.)

The fifth and sixth oval pocket mirrors were made in 1909 and 1912, respectively, and feature illustrations by the famous artist Hamilton King. The 1909 mirror is illustrated with "The Coca-Cola Girl," Mr. King's version of "The American Girl," and the 1912 mirror has a similar but unnamed girl on it. Both illustrations are identical to their 1909 and 1912 serving and change tray counterparts. The 1912 mirror is often incorrectly dated. Some authorities claim that the 1912 mirror was manufactured in 1911. It can be proved, however, that the illustration was copyrighted in 1912, which indicates that 1911 is not correct.

Next in the series of pocket mirrors is one dated 1913. This mirror is unusual in that the featured illustration was not used on any other major advertising items but was used in magazine advertisements. The illustration is of an auburn-haired girl with a lace-trimmed dress holding a glass of Coca-Cola in her right hand; unlike the other mirrors, this one has an olive-colored background.

Number eight in the series featured "Betty." This mirror was issued in 1914 along with a calendar, metal serving and change trays, a large metal sign, and other items featuring "Betty," the Coca-Cola girl of 1914. Although Betty was one of the most heavily advertised subjects, only one pocket mirror with her picture is currently known to exist.

In 1917 the ninth oval pocket mirror was produced; it features the "World War I Girl." The same illustration was used on the 1916 calendar; almost the same illustration was used on 1917 serving and change trays—the one difference is that on the trays that the girl is holding, there is a glass instead of a bottle.

The tenth known oval pocket mirror was issued in 1918 and features a girl on the beach dressed in a black bathing costume with long black beach stockings. The girl is holding a bottle of Coca-Cola in her right hand; she is shown standing and facing left, posed in front of a large red beach umbrella. In the lower left of the scene is an oval white sign with the trademark "Coca-Cola" in red. The featured scene of the 1918 mirror is not known to have been used in other advertising; similar beach scenes are known, however.

The last of the oval pocket mirrors is one produced in 1920. The scene on this mirror is the same one appearing on the 1920 calendar—the "Garden Girl." On the mirror and trays the bottle has been replaced by a glass, but the picture is otherwise identical to the 1920 calendar.

After the oval pocket mirrors came the rectangular ones. Although several types had been produced over the years, they were apparently not saved. The only known example is one measuring 2 by 3 inches. This one was made in 1923 and featured no picture or scene, only the statement "Enjoy thirst—5¢ gives you the beverage that delights taste and truly quenches thirst pure and wholesome—sold everywhere—glass or bottle. Drink *Coca-Cola* Delicious and Refreshing."

First known pocket mirror, commemorating the 1904 St. Louis Exposition

1906 pocket mirror

1909 pocket mirror

1912 pocket mirror

1913 pocket mirror

1914 pocket mirror, with "Betty"

1917 pocket mirror

CHAPTER 22

ADVERTISING CLOCKS

Clocks advertising a product or service were not an innovative advertising item in the mid-1890's when The Coca-Cola Company first began using them. When it was first suggested that clocks would be a good method of promoting Coca-Cola, Asa Candler argued that clocks were a rather expensive form of advertising. Although clocks are more expensive initially, they have a long life and outlast many less expensive advertising items. Retailers and customers would keep and display such a practical and utilitarian item as a clock much longer than they would items that were less useful.

In the 1890's a leader in the field of advertising clocks was the Baird Clock Company of Plattsburgh, New York. This firm offered customers a wind-up pendulum clock of a standard design. The machinery was housed in a wooden case, and the face of the clock and the pendulum were protected by circular plaster-of-paris frames covered with glass. The frames were attached to the wooden case with hinges so that when opened the hands could be moved, the clock wound, and the pendulum adjusted. On the circular plaster-of-paris frames the advertiser's message was embossed. It was in 1893 that The Coca-Cola Company used Baird clocks to advertise Coca-Cola. They were offered to dealers who bought and dispensed a minimum of one hundred gallons of Coca-Cola annually.

It is reasonable to assume from present evidence that the 1893 Baird clock was the first clock to have been purchased to promote the beverage.

The 1893 Baird clock features the trademark "Coca-Cola" and four slogans. Very quickly The Coca-Cola Company realized that four slogans were too many and that the use of no more than two would be more effective. It was quickly decided that the slogans which appeared on the more expensive advertising items should be as simple as possible and not reflect current campaigns of the company, so that such items would have lasting advertising value. Clocks advertising Coca-Cola that were purchased subsequently to those manufactured by Baird illustrate such a policy. The slogan and trademark were then combined to read, "Drink Coca-Cola." Another advantage was that any clock company could supply the needed clocks by merely modifying the face.

Until 1920 The Coca-Cola Company advertised with two types of clocks: wall clocks with pendulums powered by a spring, and small leather-covered boudoir clocks powered by a spring. The larger wall clocks suggested, "Drink Coca-Cola" in any form, and the smaller boudoir timepieces, because they were designed for home use, advocated the drinking of bottled Coca-Cola.

After World War II, when electric wall clocks became a practical reality, The Coca-Cola Company stopped purchasing the large spring-operated pendulum clocks in favor of the less bulky, less expensive, and more reliable electric clocks.

Clocks advertising Coca-Cola are among the most sought-after and expensive of advertising clocks. Early spring-operated pendulum wall clocks lead in prices, ranging up to several hundred dollars. Because of current demand, reproduced clock faces advertising Coca-Cola are regularly being added to old clocks and sold as original clocks.

Clocks advertising Coca-Cola that were manufactured prior to World War I are scarce. Although many have survived the years, they were not especially plentiful in the first place. Post-World War I clocks are more easily obtainable and less expensive. The Coca-Cola Company was large enough by then to make mass purchases and to widely distribute its advertising timepieces.

1893 spring-powered pendulum wall clock. This two-foot-tall clock was manufactured by the Baird Clock Company, of Plattsburgh, New York.

Walnut-finished spring-operated wall clock with a brass pendulum, 39 by 17 inches, circa 1905. The faded red lettering on the white face reads "COCA-COLA DELICIOUS REFRESHING DRINK Coca-Cola."

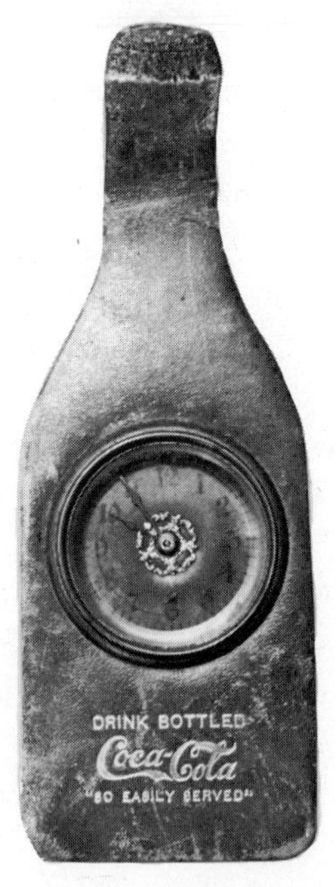

Brown leather boudoir table clock measuring 3 by 8 inches, circa 1910

Walnut-stained wall clock, measuring 40 by 18 inches (*Ray Klug, Akron, Ohio*)

1910 table clock, measuring 4½ by 6 inches.

1915 boudoir clock, 3½ by 3½ inches

1951 circular electric wall clock, 17½ inches in diameter

A brass mantel clock with a glass dome. The four balls near the base circle clockwise, reverse, and then move clockwise once again. These clocks were popular during the 1950's.

Circa 1915 wall clock in walnut, measuring 34½ by 14½ inches

Circa 1960 electric brass wall clock, measuring 18 by 24 inches

CHAPTER 23

PERIODICAL ADVERTISING

The term "periodical advertising" can be defined as both newspaper and magazine advertising. Although in many situations newspaper and magazine materials are considered as two distinctive types, collectors of Coca-Cola advertising generally consider them as one type of paper artifact. Newspaper and magazine advertisements are often kept in the same album in chronological order.

There are some basic differences in newspaper and magazine advertisements, even though collectors generally consider them both as periodical material. Collectors feel that magazine advertisements are worth several times what equivalent newspaper advertisements are, but they seem to search for both with equal enthusiasm.

One of the most important differences is that newspapers are published more frequently than magazines, and consequently more newspaper advertisements were available. But because of the inferior grade of paper, newspaper advertisements are not durable and few survive to be collected. In addition to being small and having few illustrations, newspaper advertisements are usually produced in black and white. Magazine advertisements, on the other hand, are more often than not relatively large and in full color. Newspaper advertisements, however, do have at least one advantage, from a collecting standpoint. They were, in the early years at least, often locally inspired and more apt to contain the errors and inconsistencies that delight collectors.

Both types do, however, lend themselves to the

same methods of storage and/or display—usually in an album or scrapbook. In general, newspaper and magazine advertisements for Coca-Cola feature the same type of copy, because they reflect the same advertising campaigns.

A. NEWSPAPER ADVERTISING

Beginning with John S. Pemberton's first newspaper advertisement in the May 29, 1886, issue of *The* (Atlanta) *Daily Journal* and running consistently to the present, Coca-Cola has been religiously advertised in newspapers.

In the early years, probably from 1886 until about 1900, newspaper advertising was largely an individual bottler's responsibility. It is safe to assume that some company advice was offered during the final years of the nineteenth century. For the most part, however, newspaper advertisements were left up to local bottlers.

When W. C. D'Arcy began to create advertising copy for The Coca-Cola Company in 1906, newspaper advertisements became more standardized and professional—a fact that any good collection of early newspaper advertising for Coca-Cola will demonstrate.

Of all the newspaper advertisements used over the years by Coca-Cola, the early ones produced by the D'Arcy Company are among the most sought after by collectors. These early D'Arcy advertisements are popular because they featured testimonials for Coca-Cola by prominent baseball players. Among these baseball advertisements, one big favorite was produced in 1906, featuring a twenty-two-year-old player who led the American League in batting in 1908 and 1909: Ty Cobb.

In 1911, the first year The Coca-Cola Company spent over a million dollars on advertising, D'Arcy developed a baseball advertisement for newspapers, featuring the National League batting champion, Honus Wagner.

Shortly before World War I, proof books of sample newspaper advertisements were sent to bottlers by The Coca-Cola Company. Upon request bottlers could get electrotypes or mats of the sample advertisements from the company and use them in the local press at their own expense. In 1916 The Coca-Cola Company made its first known appeal to bottlers to use standardized advertising copy prepared by its advertising agency. The appeal concluded with the assurance that such copy would be supplied free of charge by the company.

Obviously bottlers did not generally heed the 1916 appeal or another in 1922, for in the April, 1927, issue of *The Coca-Cola Bottler* still another appeal for the use of standardized advertising copy was made. The article reported on a survey of newspaper advertising that was conducted by the company on advertisements run in newspapers during the last six months of 1926. The survey revealed that 357 bottlers in thirty-six states purchased over 1,140,000 lines (approximately 82,000 column inches) of newspaper space during the second half of 1926. Further analysis showed that only 200 of the 357 bottlers used company material and that 29 percent of the purchased line space (1,140,000 lines) consisted of local advertisements. Supplementing the article was a collection of bottler newspaper advertisements which graphically showed the need for standardized and professionally produced material.

From a collector's point of view, this lack of uniformity means that literally hundreds of nonprofessionally prepared advertisements are a collecting possibility. A large number of collectors specialize in gathering bottler-produced newspaper copy. Company-provided advertisements are, of course, worthy of collecting. All Coca-Cola newspaper advertisements are very desirable collectors' items. In addition to being collectible, newspaper advertisements are excellent tools for dating other artifacts. The slogans, illustrations, and so forth are all excellent reference materials.

The standardized copy offered by the parent company, records reveal, came out twice annually in a spring/summer and fall/winter proof book. (It is a proud and lucky collector who has managed to obtain one or more of these books.)

In 1939 the company initiated a program of cooperative advertising. In areas where per-capita consumption of Coca-Cola was ten bottles or less, the company assumed 80 percent of the newspaper advertising costs. In more developed areas more of the costs were assumed by the bottler. The most any bottler had to pay, however, was 50 percent. The cooperative plan virtually stopped dealer-created advertisements for obvious reasons. Thus, from 1939 on, collectors can expect to locate very few of the interesting and unusual advertisements produced at the local level.

A source of newspaper advertisements for Coca-Cola often overlooked by collectors is college publications. Coca-Cola was advertised sporadically in college newspapers during the 1920's and 1930's. From 1940 on, the beverage was regularly advertised in college periodicals.

One final thought about collecting newspaper advertisements for Coca-Cola: Since newspaper advertising was used practically from the birth of Coca-Cola, it is obviously one of the few artifacts that a collector can expect to obtain on at least a year-to-year basis from 1886 to the present.

B. MAGAZINE ADVERTISING

Magazine advertising is more expensive than newspaper advertising because of its superior quality. The Coca-Cola Company did not fully indulge itself in the services of this medium until about the turn of the century.

In the early years of the twentieth century, advertisements promoting Coca-Cola began to appear in the nation's leading magazines. The majority of the magazine advertisements of that early period and those that followed were presented in full color. The subjects of the early magazine advertisements included people of all ages (with the traditional stress on pretty young girls) at soda "founts," on the golf course, in horse and buggies, in automobiles, at the theater, and at the seashore.

Both the Massengale Advertising Agency and the D'Arcy Company were responsible for early magazine advertising. It will be of value to collectors to note that the work of these two advertising firms can easily be distinguished. Almost without exception, material from Massengale is clearly marked at the bottom with "MASSENGALE, ATLANTA."

By 1917, magazine advertising for Coca-Cola stressed the trademark "Coca-Cola," the bottle, and/or a glass and was getting away from the elaborate scenes of previous years. There is also a stress on lengthy copy in this period.

The subjects of magazine advertisements were frequently the same ones used on the popular metal serving and change trays, pocket mirrors, and calendars. Often these generally undated items can be assigned a year according to a magazine advertisement. Such a valuable dating tool should not be overlooked by collectors.

Recognizing and promoting great slogans was of particular interest to Robert W. Woodruff. The classic slogan "The pause that refreshes" was introduced in its complete concept for the first time in 1929 and was effectively promoted when Woodruff became personally involved. The slogan, which had its genesis as early as 1914, was originally guided and nurtured by Archie Lee, of the D'Arcy Company.

In 1924 the word "pause" was included in an advertisement that was titled "4 o'clock in the Afternoon." The 1924 advertisement cited the various methods of taking a break from work throughout the world. It went on to prove that Americans paused during the work day to drink Coca-Cola. The advertisement concluded with more statements about how the idea of pausing during the work day was borrowed from people in other lands. That advertisement is a fine example of the type of magazine advertising that uses a rather long textual message quite effectively.

Four years later, in 1928, the word "pause" was used again in several advertisements. One, featuring the traditional red sign with the Coca-Cola trademark, read, "A good sign to pause and refresh yourself."

In the February 9, 1929, issue of *The Saturday Evening Post* an advertisement was headed, "All think alike about the pause that refreshes." While all previous references to "pause" were directed at Coca-Cola in glasses, in September, 1929, the now very famous slogan was used in connection with bottled Coca-Cola for the first time. Knowledgeable collectors have long considered this advertisement a prized item.

Another Woodruff-guided advertising promotion was the 1927 $30,000 cash-prize contest. The contest was announced in May of that year in *The Saturday Evening Post.* (That particular issue has long been a magazine must for collectors of the memorabilia of Coca-Cola.) Other magazines were also used to promote the contest, including *Collier's, The Literary Digest, Liberty,* and *Life.* A complete set of the five magazines and all of the issues involved is an interesting as well as valuable collection. The contest requirements were (1) to find the six keys to the popularity of Coca-Cola as preached in various advertisements, (2) to select *the one* that appealed most and write one paragraph telling why that key was a good reason for the popularity of Coca-Cola, and (3) to ". . . write an answer (in one paragraph) to the following question: What advertisement (painted wall, bulletin, poster, red sign, show-window display, soda-fountain or refreshment-stand decoration) best illustrates or presents to you one or more of the six keys? Tell why and also where you saw the advertisement." Thousands of people correctly identified the six keys (taste, purity, refreshing, sociability, the nickel, and thirst) found in the magazine advertisements, and 635 of those people were awarded cash prizes. The first prize of ten thousand dollars was won by Miss Mabel Millspaugh, of Anderson, Indiana.

The Coca-Cola Company fought hard to maintain and retain its registered trademark "Coca-Cola." Only after realizing that in the case of "Coke" as an abbreviation they were fighting a losing battle, did the company adopt the "if you can't beat 'em, join 'em" attitude. Early in 1940 it was decided that the company would henceforth actively use "Coke" as a sanctioned abbreviation for "Coca-Cola." So in the June 9, 1941, issue of *Newsweek* magazine, the June, 1941, issue of *Fortune Magazine,* and in several business periodicals, The Coca-Cola Company published its first advertising stressing the abbreviation "Coke." The historic advertisement was headed, "The once idle minute now does its job, too." Once again the company used the lengthy approach and began with a paragraph justifying the busy lives Americans live and telling how fortunate they are to have such a refreshment as Coca-Cola. The next portion of the advertisement discusses how "People long ago discovered that ice-cold Coca-Cola made any pause *the pause that refreshes.*" The next section expounds on the virtue of the small cost of the beverage. Finally they publicly admit the adoption of the abbreviation with ". . . when such phrases as 'Give me a "Coca-Cola"' and 'Make mine a "Coke" too' have become familiar expressions. . . ."

Subsequently, under the guidance of Archie Lee, both "Coca-Cola" and "Coke" were used interchangeably. Late in the summer of 1941, Lee had Haddon Sundblom create the Coca-Cola Sprite sporting a bottle cap for a hat. In this advertisement and the many others that followed over the years featuring the Sprite, "Coca-Cola" and "Coke" were promoted as being synonymous.

Following Coca-Cola magazine advertisements

is like turning the pages of a history book. Careful reading of the advertising copy itself, and study of the models, their clothing, and the settings gives a fairly accurate history of the United States. The Coca-Cola Company is very sensitive to current issues and quite regularly points its magazine (and other) advertising in the popular direction.

Over the years, national issues such as wars, dress fashions, hair styles, and sexual mores have been reflected in the promotion of Coca-Cola. The 1930's, for example, were the glamorous years of the movie industry, and The Coca-Cola Company used numerous stars in its advertisements. The 1940's were the years of World War II, and The Coca-Cola Company promoted its beverage through the use of service men and women and defense plant workers. The 1950's were devoted, at least in part, to an after-the-war, relax-and-enjoy-the-victory atmosphere. The 1960's were involved with social issues; Coca-Cola advertising was filled with racial and ecological concerns.

Right: An 1890 magazine advertisement for Coca-Cola syrup and another proprietary product owned by Asa G. Candler before he formed The Coca-Cola Company (*Archives, The Coca-Cola Company, Atlanta, Georgia*)

M. M. MAUCK,
DEALER IN
WALL AND BUILDING PAPER
PAINTERS' SUPPLIES, ROOM MOLDING, ETC.
27 E. HUNTER STREET,
ATLANTA, GA.

36 INCHES WIDE.

KEELY COMPANY
LEADERS OF LOW PRICES.
THE KEELY "LEADER" $2.00 SHOE.
ZIEGLER BROTHERS' SHOES
SPRING-HEEL SHOES.
KEELY COMPANY

DE-LEC-TA-LAVE
DE-LEC-TA-LAVE WILL
THE WONDERFUL NERVE AND BRAIN TONIC
REMARKABLE THERAPEUTIC AGENT
Coca-Cola
ASA G. CANDLER & CO. 47 PEACHTREE STREET ATLANTA, GA.

DOBBS, WEY & CO.
No. 45 PEACHTREE STREET, ATLANTA, GA.
Fine White and Decorated China
CRYSTAL GLASSWARE
LAMPS OF ALL KINDS

1794 THE OLDEST INSURANCE COMPANY IN HARTFORD. 1890
HARTFORD
FIRE INSURANCE COMPANY.
CAPITAL, $1,250,000. ASSETS, $6,142,454.49
GEO. L. CHASE, Pres't. P. C. ROYCE, Sec'y. THOS. TURNBULL, Ass't Sec'y.

$5,000 worth of Straw Hats, and they MUST go.

POPE, THE HATTER.

$5,000 worth of Straw Hats, and they MUST go.

Tel. 47, Warlick & Wingate, for Plumbing and Gas Fitting.

W. S. Webster

23 E. Alabama St.

Now is your chance to test the virtue of Moxie Nerve Food, on draught at H. C. Beerman's Soda Water Palace

POPE, THE HATTER.

$5,000 worth of Straw Hats, and they MUST go.

Get estimates on Galvanized Iron Work. Warlick & Wingate, 19 and 21 Collins street.

JUST RECEIVED,
One case new style Seersuckers. See them this week.
Chamberlin, Johnson & Co.

FRENCH AND GERMAN LINENS
Table Linen in the most exquisite designs, Imported Goods, with Napkins, D'Oyles, etc., to match. Prices and quality guaranteed.
Chamberlin, Johnson & Co.

SEE THE NEW CARPETS!
English Goods, all wid hs.

POPE, THE HATTER.

$5,000 worth of Straw Hats, and they MUST go

Try Stewart's premium corn beef, corned in his fine cooler, Washington Market, 110 Peachtree street. Telephone 784

FRESH VEGETABLES,
Spring Chickens, Eggs, Butter, etc, at the lowest prices.
J. B. JACKSON,
140 Marietta St

POPE, THE HATTER.

$5,000 worth of Straw Hats, and they MUST go.

IVIE,
The Photographer.

COCA-COLA.

NATIONAL DECORATION DAY

Monday, May 31st, at 9:30 A. M.

BREAD.
BREAD.
JACK'S
NEW PROCESS BREAD
STEAM-MADE.

68 and 70 Alabama St.,
Cor. Loyd.
W. G. ROBERTS,
55 Peachtree Street.

HO! FOR WHITE PATH SPRINGS!
At Auction Tuesday, June 15, '86
Special Train from Atlanta Over the W. & A. and Marietta & North Georgia Railroads,
ROUND TRIP TICKETS, ONLY $2!

A page from *The Daily Journal* (Atlanta) of Saturday, May 29, 1886, featuring the first known newspaper advertisement for Coca-Cola (*Archives, The Coca-Cola Company, Atlanta, Georgia*)

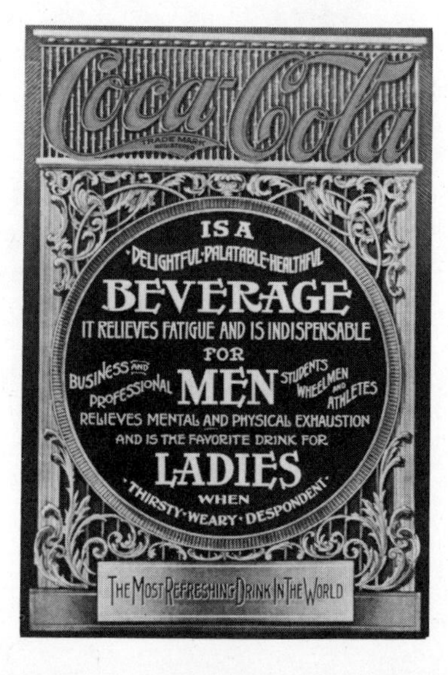

1904 magazine advertisement in red, white, and green

1905 magazine advertisement from the Massengale Advertising Agency (*Archives, The Coca-Cola Company, Atlanta, Georgia*)

June 3, 1905, *Saturday Evening Post* advertisement

1906 newspaper advertisement featuring the famous baseball player Ty Cobb. This was one of a long series of sports advertisements inspired by W.C. D'Arcy. (*Archives, The Coca-Cola Company, Atlanta, Georgia*)

Full-color magazine advertisement appearing on the back cover of *The Housekeeper* of May, 1906

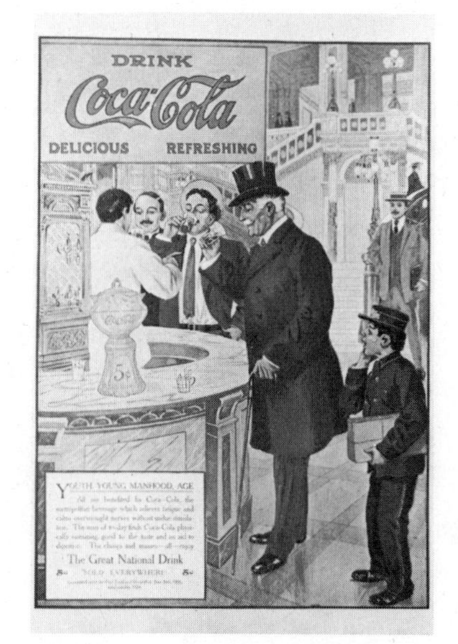

Full-color advertisement on the back cover of *Success* magazine, September, 1907

Early 1900–1910 newspaper advertisement

1908 Massengale advertisement

1905 Massengale magazine advertisement

Advertisement on the back cover of *The Coca-Cola Bottler* of April, 1909

Below: A very rare magazine advertisement that appeared on the cover of *The Housewife* of June, 1910

1911 magazine advertisement

1912 magazine advertisement

Advertisement featuring "Betty," from the *Farm and Home* magazine of December 1, 1914

1914 magazine advertisement

Advertisement from a *Pictorial Review* magazine of 1914

Advertisement from the July, 1915, *Woman's Home Companion*

Advertisement from *The Delineator* of July, 1916

1916 magazine advertisement

Advertisement from the June, 1917, *Woman's Home Companion*

Advertisement from the *Pictorial Review* of August, 1917

1919 advertisement from *Sunset, the Pacific Monthly*

Advertisement from the June, 1919, issue of *Woman's Home Companion*, featuring movie star Marion Davies

Magazine advertisement of 1921

A June, 1920, magazine advertisement

Advertisement from the May, 1919, issue of *Pictorial Review* (*Archives, The Coca-Cola Company, Atlanta, Georgia*)

1922 magazine advertisement (*Archives, The Coca-Cola Company, Atlanta, Georgia*)

1922 magazine advertisement (*Archives, The Coca-Cola Company, Atlanta, Georgia*)

Advertisement from the December, 1922, issue of *The Ladies' Home Journal*

From the October, 1923, issue of *The Ladies' Home Journal*

From the December, 1923, issue of *The Ladies' Home Journal*

From the August, 1924, issue of *The Ladies' Home Journal (Archives, The Coca-Cola Company, Atlanta, Georgia)*

June, 1923, advertisement from the *Woman's Home Companion*

Advertisement from the May, 1924, issue of *The Red Book Magazine*, using the word "pause." This is a piece much desired by collectors. *(Archives, The Coca-Cola Company, Atlanta, Georgia)*

From *The Ladies' Home Journal* of August, 1925

From the December, 1924, issue of *The Ladies' Home Journal*

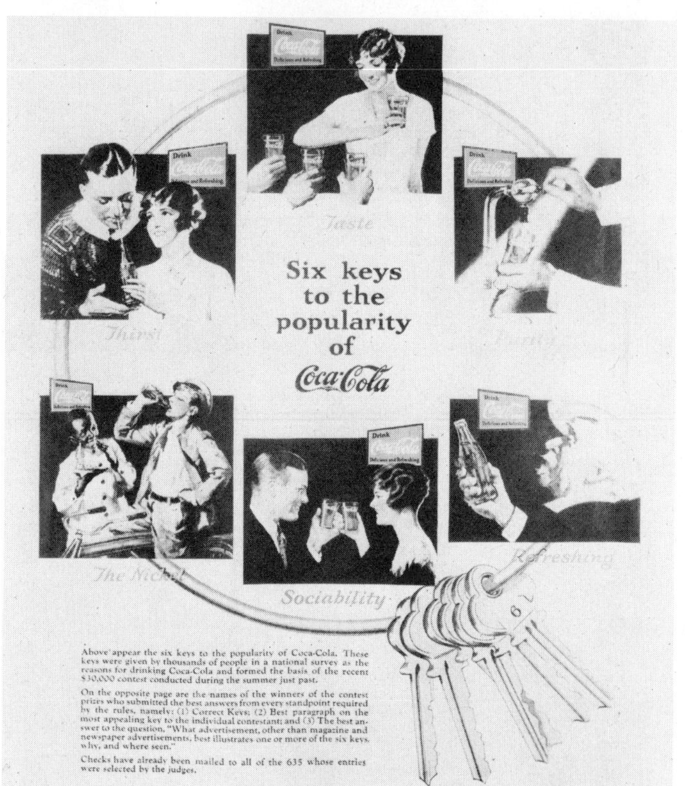

1927 advertisement (*Archives, The Coca-Cola Company, Atlanta, Georgia*)

Advertisement from *The Saturday Evening Post*, February 9, 1929, featuring the first use of the classic slogan, "the pause that refreshes" (*Archives, The Coca-Cola Company, Atlanta, Georgia*)

Advertisement from the June 15, 1929, issue of *The Literary Digest*

THE SATURDAY EVENING POST

Drink
Coca-Cola
Delicious and Refreshing

The opening ceremonial at the famous la plaza de toros (the bull ring) in Barcelona, Spain.

K OR BULL RING . . . THE SAME RED SIGN
SIGNALS: *Pause and refresh yourself*

A 1934 magazine advertisement featuring Martin and Osa Johnson. The Johnsons were famous for their feature-length film travelogues. (*Archives, The Coca-Cola Company, Atlanta, Georgia*)

Above: 1931 advertisement from *The Saturday Evening Post* (*Archives, The Coca-Cola Company, Atlanta, Georgia*)

1939 advertisement from *The Ladies' Home Journal* (*Archives, The Coca-Cola Company, Atlanta, Georgia*)

Below: A 1939 magazine advertisement drawn by N. C. Wyeth. By 1939, Coke had earned the Good Housekeeping Seal of Approval. (*Archives, The Coca-Cola Company, Atlanta, Georgia*)

June, 1941, magazine advertisement in which the abbreviation "Coke" was used for the first time. (*Archives, The Coca-Cola Company, Atlanta, Georgia*)

1942 magazine advertisement (*Archives, The Coca-Cola Company, Atlanta, Georgia*)

1943 magazine advertisement drawn by Frank Godwin (*Archives, The Coca-Cola Company, Atlanta, Georgia*)

1944 advertisement directed at retailers (*Archives, The Coca-Cola Company, Atlanta, Georgia*)

1944 magazine advertisement (*Archives, The Coca-Cola Company, Atlanta, Georgia*)

1945 magazine advertisement drawn by James Montgomery Flagg (*Archives, The Coca-Cola Company, Atlanta, Georgia*)

1946 magazine advertisement promoting both Coca-Cola and savings bonds (*Archives, The Coca-Cola Company, Atlanta, Georgia*)

Advertisement from the back cover of *National Geographic* magazine, June, 1949

1953 magazine advertisement (*Archives, The Coca-Cola Company, Atlanta, Georgia*)

1959 advertisement published in *Life, Saturday Evening Post, Better Homes & Gardens, Holiday, McCall's, Ladies' Home Journal, Seventeen, Good Housekeeping, Sports Illustrated,* and *National Geographic* (*Archives, The Coca-Cola Company, Atlanta, Georgia*)

Magazine advertisement used during April of 1959 (*Archives, The Coca-Cola Company, Atlanta, Georgia*)

1962 magazine advertisement used in Europe (*Archives, The Coca-Cola Company, Atlanta, Georgia*)

1965 advertisement used in *Boys' Life, American Girl, Scholastic Magazine, Co-Ed, Sports Illustrated, Motor Trend, Sports Car Graphic, Hot Rod, Car Craft,* and *Scholastic Roto* (*Archives, The Coca-Cola Company, Atlanta, Georgia*)

1968 advertisement that appeared in the March 8 issue of *Life*, the April *Motor Trend*, and the April *Sports Car Graphic* (*Archives, The Coca-Cola Company, Atlanta, Georgia*)

1969 advertisement in the February issues of *Hot Rod, Car Craft,* and *Boys' Life*

Advertisement in the March, 1969, issues of *Sports Car Graphic, Car Craft,* and *Hot Rod*

Left: Advertisement in the May, 1969, issues of *Hot Rod* and *Scholastic* and the June issues of *Car Craft, American Girl, Boys' Life*, and *Seventeen*

Advertisement in the July, 1969, issues of *American Girl* and *Seventeen* and the August issues of *Boys' Life, Hot Rod*, and *Car Craft*

Advertisement in the August, 1969, issues of *Boys' Life* and *Seventeen* and the September issues of *American Girl, Car Craft, Hot Rod*, and *Scholastic*

CHAPTER 24

DISPLAY POSTERS

Display posters promoting Coca-Cola were used mostly in soda fountains during the early years, but in the late 1920's and thereafter they were extensively used to advertise bottled Coca-Cola.

Display posters, billboard posters, and display cutouts are often confused. It should be noted that display posters are generally heavy-duty paper posters (sometimes cardboard) usually several feet square, whereas billboard posters are exceptionally large paper posters, made in several sections and used in outdoor advertising on highway billboards. Display cutouts are cardboard figures that were precut and free-standing, or hanging. Separate chapters have been devoted to both billboard posters and display cutouts.

The subject feature of a poster is frequently the same one used on a calendar, tray, or other item. For that reason no great emphasis will be placed on subjects or dates in this chapter. Such information can be found in other chapters throughout the book.

Posters, as well as calendars, periodical advertisements, and other not very durable advertising pieces, are relatively scarce. Although they were issued and used in great quantity, most were destroyed after use, and as a result, few examples survive. Prices of display posters, however, are not extreme. Collectors can expect to pay less than one hundred dollars for many of the better examples.

Display posters that are known to exist date only as far back as the late 1890's. Records, however, indicate that such advertising pieces were used as early as the late 1880's.

This unusual poster was used in soda fountains and other retail outlets in 1900 (*Archives, The Coca-Cola Company, Atlanta, Georgia*)

One of the first display posters, made in the early 1890's (*Archives, The Coca-Cola Company, Atlanta, Georgia*)

In 1901 Cuba began to produce Coca-Cola; Hilda Clark and a Spanish slogan were used on this poster. (*Archives, The Coca-Cola Company, Atlanta, Georgia*)

1909 poster painted by Hamilton King (*Archives, The Coca-Cola Company, Atlanta, Georgia*)

1913 poster (*Archives, The Coca-Cola Company, Atlanta, Georgia*)

1914 poster, with "Betty" (*Archives, The Coca-Cola Company, Atlanta, Georgia*)

1918 poster (*Archives, The Coca-Cola Company, Atlanta, Georgia*)

1923 poster painted by John Newton Howitt (*Archives, The Coca-Cola Company, Atlanta, Georgia*)

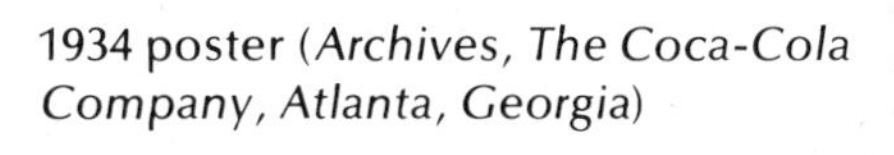
1934 poster (*Archives, The Coca-Cola Company, Atlanta, Georgia*)

1924 poster (*Archives, The Coca-Cola Company, Atlanta, Georgia*)

1929 poster (*Archives, The Coca-Cola Company, Atlanta, Georgia*)

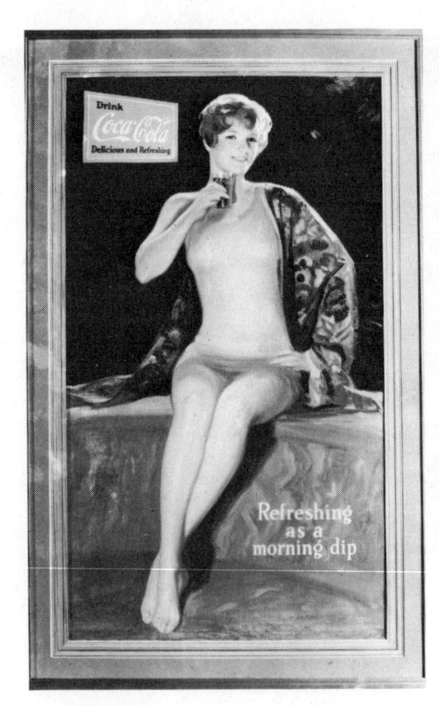

1935 poster (*Archives, The Coca-Cola Company, Atlanta, Georgia*)

1936 poster of actress Florine McKinney (*Archives, The Coca-Cola Company, Atlanta, Georgia*)

1943 poster (*Archives, The Coca-Cola Company, Atlanta, Georgia*)

1948 poster featuring the Sprite (*Archives, The Coca-Cola Company, Atlanta, Georgia*)

CHAPTER 25

CARDBOARD CUTOUTS

The advertising needs of soda fountains, drugstores, grocery stores, and other retail outlets for Coca-Cola in glasses and/or bottles caused the development of a number of unusual advertising items. Among those items are the cardboard cutout display pieces.

Cardboard cutouts are relatively scarce. These figural artifacts are generally two to several feet in height and width and are bulky. Because these cardboard cutouts were so easily damaged or soiled and because they were fairly large, most were discarded. Most collections of Coca-Cola memorabilia do not contain many of these cutout display pieces. Of the few that are occasionally located, most have frayed edges and are wrinkled. These cutouts were most popularly utilized as window displays and often faded in the sunlight.

In the early years cutout display units promoted Coca-Cola in glasses. Later examples reflect The Coca-Cola Company's relatively late interest in their product as a bottled drink. In fact, it wasn't until the 1930's that bottled Coca-Cola became a favorite cardboard cutout display subject.

In general it can be noted that although cardboard cutout display pieces featured typical subjects, they seldom pictured the same art simultaneously found in tray, calendar, poster, billboard, and magazine advertising. This makes cardboard cutouts unusual and very desirable to collectors. Gibson-type girls and beach scenes were popular subjects for the early years.

"Lady on the Grass," first issued in 1910, and "Man on the Grass," first produced and distributed in 1909 (*Archives, The Coca-Cola Company, Atlanta, Georgia*)

1911 cutout (*Archives, The Coca-Cola Company, Atlanta, Georgia*)

1915 cardboard cutout display (*Archives, The Coca-Cola Company, Atlanta, Georgia*)

1918 cardboard cut-out display (*Archives, The Coca-Cola Company, Atlanta, Georgia*)

1919 cardboard cutout (*Archives, The Coca-Cola Company, Atlanta, Georgia*)

1920 cardboard cutout display (*Archives, The Coca-Cola Company, Atlanta, Georgia*)

1921 cardboard cutout

1922 cardboard cutout display (*Archives, The Coca-Cola Company, Atlanta, Georgia*)

1923 cardboard display (*Archives, The Coca-Cola Company, Atlanta, Georgia*)

1925 cardboard cut out

Display units used during the 1920's (*Archives, The Coca-Cola Company, Atlanta, Georgia*)

1928 cardboard amusement park (*Archives, The Coca-Cola Company, Atlanta, Georgia*)

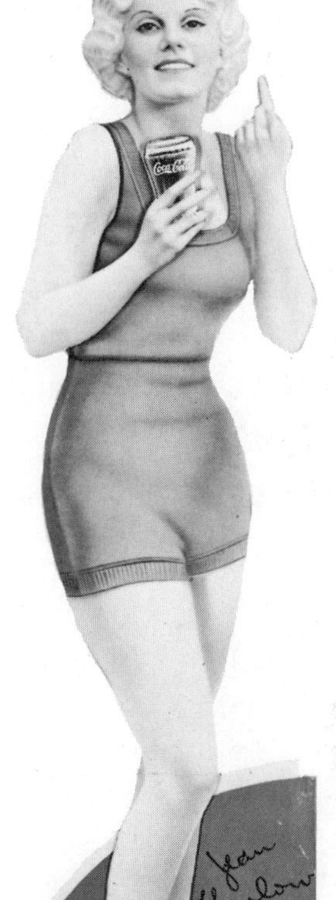

1931 display with Jean Harlow (*Archives, The Coca-Cola Company, Atlanta, Georgia*)

Cardboard displays of 1930's, featuring, left to right: Wynne Gibson and Randolph Scott, Claudette Colbert, Sari Maritza and Cary Grant (*Archives, The Coca-Cola Company, Atlanta, Georgia*)

1932 cardboard circus (*Archives, The Coca-Cola Company, Atlanta, Georgia*)

1933 three-dimensional display (*Archives, The Coca-Cola Company, Atlanta, Georgia*)

1935 cardboard cutout by Norman Rockwell (*Archives, The Coca-Cola Company, Atlanta, Georgia*)

1936 (fiftieth anniversary year) hanging cardboard cutout display

1938 display

1961 display

CHAPTER 26

SIGNS

The Coca-Cola Company has used small metal signs to advertise its product since before the turn of the century, and large outdoor metal signs became popular about 1910.

The most popular of the earliest known specimens of the small metal signs used to advertise Coca-Cola is the $16\frac{1}{2}$-by-$19\frac{3}{4}$-inch oval metal sign made by the Charles W. Shonk Manufacturing and Lithograph Company, of Chicago, Illinois (see Appendix D for further information on this firm). This classic sign featured the famous singer Hilda Clark and was produced in 1901.

In 1910 ten thousand dollars was spent to produce hundreds of $7\frac{1}{2}$-by-8-foot metal signs for outdoor advertising. These signs broadcast the information "Ice Cold Coca-Cola Sold Here" to the right of a panel picturing a straight-sided and paper-labeled full bottle of Coca-Cola. This particular design was used from 1910 until approximately 1917.

The acceptance of metal signs, which incidentally grace many collections today because of their durability, was cinched with the introduction in 1914 of the 31-by-41-inch pictorial sign featuring "Betty." These handsome signs were lithographed in fourteen colors and stamped from a single sheet of metal. The dies alone cost The Coca-Cola Company five thousand dollars. The company vigorously promoted the signs, claiming, "The price may seem high but it is about right in cost because this sign will be there when several times as much cheap stuff has disappeared." Records show that ten thousand metal "Betty" signs were produced in 1914. The original Betty, because of the metal sign, became a classic and was used in other advertising for several years after 1914. (Another model called Betty was introduced in 1941, but she was not nearly as popular as the original "Betty.")

Metal signs are very important in collecting today, especially pictorial ones. Following the success of the "Betty" sign, another was produced in 1917 featuring the "World War I Girl," the calendar model of that year. Although it is not as beautiful and not as large as the classic "Betty," it is a fine specimen, sought by almost all collectors. This 1917 pressed-metal sign was manufactured by Stelad Signs, Passaic Metal Ware Company, of Passaic, New Jersey.

In 1920, among others, a rather interesting diamond-shaped aluminum-celluloid sign was produced. This 7$^{1}/_{4}$-inch-wide sign was made by the New Jersey Aluminum Company, of Newark. The message was a simple "Drink Coca-Cola With Soda, 5¢." In the more common outdoor metal signs four different sizes were issued in 1920. These signs featured a large trademark with "Drink" above it and most often "Delicious and Refreshing" below.

During the early 1920's a "privilege panel" was added to the rectangular metal signs. The four-by-ten-foot panel was placed above the sign advertising Coca-Cola and provided space for a message by the retailer. Such individuality adds variety for the collector. During 1925 the company offered a good selection of metal signs, including a 12-by-36-inch flat sign which sold for $0.14, a 12-by-18-inch metal flange sign for $0.19, and the standard 4-by-10-foot sign with the accompanying privilege panel, which sold for $7.35. The catalogue of 1925 mentions that 2,045 4-by-10-foot metal signs with privilege panels, as compared to 2,471 without, were sold in 1924.

In 1926, among other signs, a very attractive 8-by-11-inch metal sign was offered. This advertising artifact featured a model holding a bottle of Coke, framed within a white oval, and standing in front of the trademark "Coca-Cola."

In 1927 the catalogue offered bottlers seven metal signs ranging in size from 8 by 11 inches to 4 by 10 feet. The 8-by-11-inch sign is very similar to the one marketed in 1926, but a different model was used.

By 1934 a change in the metal signs occurred. The standard designs were simplified and modernized. Color combinations, as well as the distribution of colors, were improved. A year of particular interest to collectors of metal signs is 1934; in that year 28 regular and 4 cooler signs were offered.

Another change in outdoor metal signs was made in 1938. The privilege panel was eliminated from the surface of the metal signs and were provided as a separate unit, because of their popularity. Some privilege panels with painted white embossed bottle units were produced for others. The familiar diamond-shaped sign was introduced in 1938 and retained for many years —until the 1950's.

In 1941, as previously mentioned, another "Betty" was introduced. She appeared in multicolor lithography on signs of several different sizes. During World War II metal signs were not produced in the manufacture of outdoor signs. After the war, in 1947, new materials were employed. Materials other than metal were also used in earlier years. In 1950 aluminum was introduced and has remained a popular outdoor sign material ever since.

In addition to metal signs, some very attractive signs have been painted on glass while others have been made of wood and fiberboard. In recent years plastic has become a popular material.

With the refurbishing of the image of Coca-Cola in 1970, most of the existing signs suddenly became obsolete. Each one, of course, is a potential collectors' item, and many of the two million outdoor metal signs will be saved on that basis.

1901 pressed-metal sign, 16½ by 19¾ inches, featuring Hilda Clark. Made by the Charles W. Shonk Manufacturing and Lithograph Company, of Chicago.

Metal sign used between 1910–1917, measuring 7½ by 8 feet (*Archives, The Coca-Cola Company, Atlanta, Georgia*)

1914 sign, with "Betty," measuring 31 by 41 inches. Worth several hundred dollars to collectors.

1917 metal sign, 20 by 30½ inches, featuring "World War I Girl." Made by Stelad Signs, Passaic Metal Ware Company, of Passaic, New Jersey.

1920 aluminum sign covered with celluloid, 7¼ inches wide. Made by the New Jersey Aluminum Company, of Newark.

1926 indoor metal sign, 8 by 11 inches

1927 sign

1916 metal sign, measuring 4 by 10 feet. Standard until 1934. (*Archives, The Coca-Cola Company, Atlanta, Georgia*)

1934 metal sign, 4 by 10 feet (*Archives, The Coca-Cola Company, Atlanta, Georgia*)

Metal sign, 12 by 36 inches, issued in the mid-1930's (*Archives, The Coca-Cola Company, Atlanta, Georgia*)

1938 metal sign, 4 by 10 feet, featuring the "privilege panel" upon which the retailer displayed a personal message (*Archives, The Coca-Cola Company, Atlanta, Georgia*)

1938 sign

Advertisement from April, 1959, issue of *The Coca-Cola Bottler* for signs made by Temco, Inc. of Nashville, Tennessee

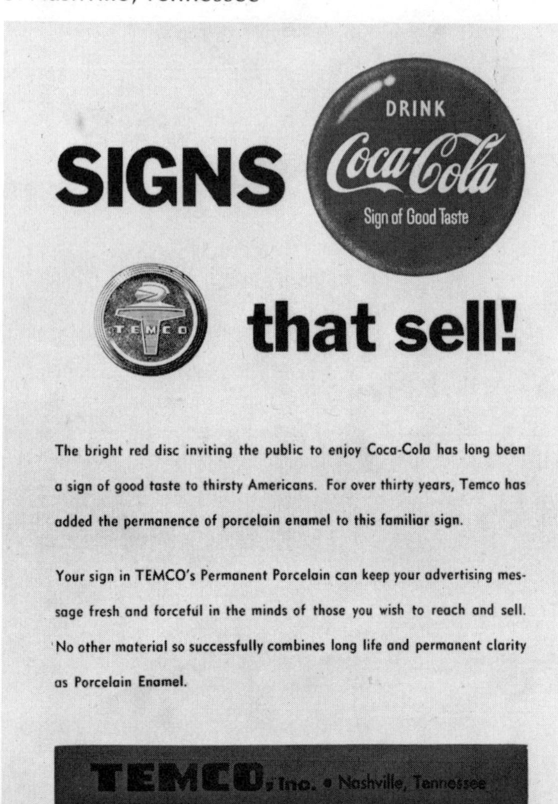

Metal sign of the late 1930's (*Archives, The Coca-Cola Company, Atlanta, Georgia*)

1941 catalog page featuring the new "Betty" (*Archives, The Coca-Cola Company, Atlanta, Georgia*)

Circa 1915 glass-covered signs. Top: maroon with silver lettering, 6¾ by 9 inches. Bottom: blue with gold lettering, 8 inches.

This fiberboard wall plaque (sign) was used circa 1915 to advertise Coca-Cola in soda fountains.

Wooden sign from the 1940's (*Archives, The Coca-Cola Company, Atlanta, Georgia*)

Twelve-inch glass sign

1950's electric sign

1936 sign promoting the fiftieth anniversary of Coca-Cola (*Archives, The Coca-Cola Company, Atlanta, Georgia*)

1950's electric sign with clock, 9 by 20 inches

CHAPTER 27

BLOTTERS, BOOKMARKS, CARDS, COUPONS, AND MENUS

Paper products have been a much favored advertising medium since the 1870's, when improvements in graphic arts allowed inexpensive printings in large quantities. Among the many paper products used by The Coca-Cola Company were blotters, bookmarks, cards, coupons, and menus.

Blotters were especially popular in the first several decades of the twentieth century when the fountain pen was a primary writing instrument. Whenever possible the company tried to advertise its product on items which would be appreciated and utilized by customers. The blotter was such an item. Blotters are found in basic oblong shapes but with numerous illustrations, slogans, and statements imprinted on them. Because of the various messages imprinted on blotters advertising Coca-Cola, they are not only excellent collectors' items but also fine sources of historical information.

Bookmarks in full color were popular turn-of-the-century advertising articles. Of the dozen or so bookmarks used in this century, those produced in the first decade are most valued by collectors. Specifically, the two bookmarks featuring Lillian Nordica are very popular. Both were published by Wolf & Co., of Philadelphia.

Cards of several types have been one of the paper products used effectively to advertise Coca-Cola. The most popular of the cards are the post cards. Only a few of the earliest examples are known to exist, and as a result collectors delight in any opportunity to add one to their collection.

Coupons good for one free drink of Coca-Cola were among the very first items used to promote the drink. From the very first year that Coca-Cola was placed on the market (1886), coupons were used to entice people to try the beverage. John S. Pemberton, the inventor of Coca-Cola, spent some of his advertising money on oilcloth signs and newspaper advertisements, but coupons that promised a free drink took a fair share of his advertising budget for Coca-Cola. In the field of advertising it has long been known that one of the most effective methods of obtaining customers for a new product is to give them a free sample. People are hesitant to spend money on a product that is new to them. Both Pemberton and Asa Candler effectively used coupons to get people to try, and eventually to buy, the new drink called Coca-Cola.

While records show that Pemberton used coupons to promote Coca-Cola, no examples of his coupons are currently known to exist. Asa G. Candler continued Pemberton's successful use of free drink coupons, and The Coca-Cola Company has used coupon promotions intermittently ever since. Unlike Pemberton's coupons, Candler's have not disappeared. Examples of those used before the founding of The Coca-Cola Company in 1892 do exist and are occasionally found in sophisticated collections. The more professional coupons used after 1892 are also occasionally available to collectors. In addition, the company used coupons as part of full-page magazine advertisements. Shortly after the turn of the century a number of full-page and full-color advertisements in national magazines contributed much to the growth of the business. Advertisements which featured a coupon that could be clipped out and used to obtain a free drink of Coca-Cola were the most successful. In later years, especially after World War I, coupon campaigns were employed successfully to promote bottled Coca-Cola. Numerous examples of these very desirable collectors' items can be found today. The archives of The Coca-Cola Company has a file of sampling coupons dating from 1892.

Soda menus are among the most attractive of the paper goods produced in the early 1900's. Menus have been used throughout the twentieth century, but through the years the advertisements for Coca-Cola have become less conspicuous. As a result many have become less interesting to collectors. Because of this lack of interest as well as the instability of paper products, menus of the 1930's, 1940's, 1950's, and 1960's will soon be a rarity.

The less-durable paper goods used to promote Coca-Cola over the years, although issued in large quantities, were consumed and not generally saved. This means that existing examples can be considered rare and valuable.

1904 blotter (*Archives, The Coca-Cola Company, Atlanta, Georgia*)

1904 blotter (*Archives, The Coca-Cola Company, Atlanta, Georgia*)

1906–1910 blotter (*Archives, The Coca-Cola Company, Atlanta, Georgia*)

1905 blotter (*Archives, The Coca-Cola Company, Atlanta, Georgia*)

1937 blotter

1909 blotter

1938 blotter drawn by Haddon Sundblom

1953 blotter

1956 blotter

1960 blotter

1905 bookmark

1904 card

1894 card. Only one known to exist.

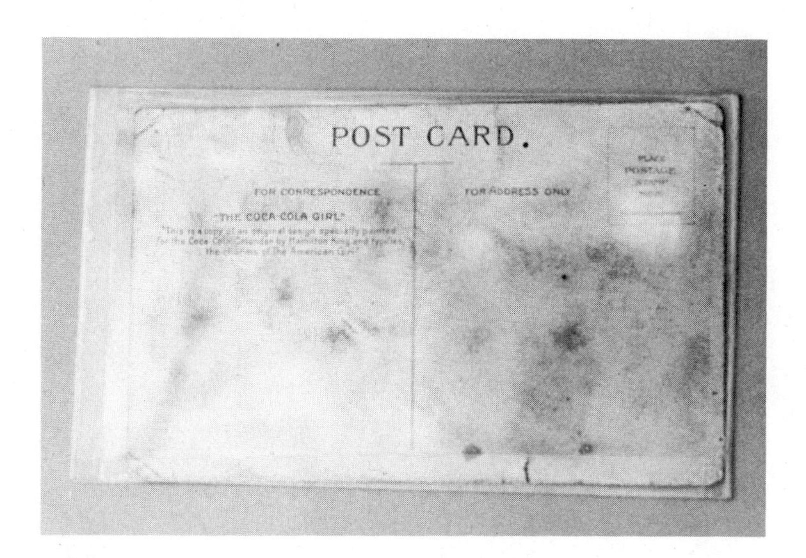

1909 postcard by Hamilton King

This card is worth 5 cents. It pays
for 1 glass Coca-Cola, which cures
your Headache, or wonderfully refreshes
you when exhausted.
ASA G. CANDLER, PROPRIETOR,
ATLANTA, GA.

Earliest known coupon offering a free drink. It was given away in 1890 by Asa G. Candler. (*Archives, The Coca-Cola Company, Atlanta, Georgia*)

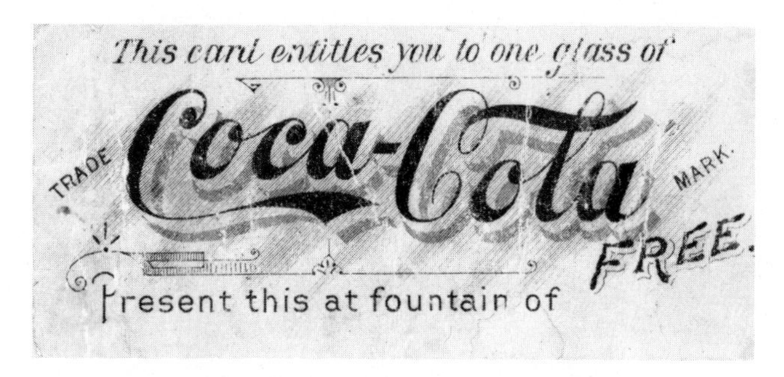

This card entitles you to one glass of
TRADE Coca-Cola MARK.
FREE.
Present this at fountain of
Any Dispenser of COCA-COLA.

Coupons from the 1890's (*Archives, The Coca-Cola Company, Atlanta, Georgia*)

Complimentary Ticket
Enclosed For One Glass
Coca-Cola
TRADE MARK

Coupon, a "Complimentary Ticket," from the 1890's (*Archives, The Coca-Cola Company, Atlanta, Georgia*)

Coupons of 1895–1905 (*Archives, The Coca-Cola Company, Atlanta, Georgia*)

1905 advertisement with Lillian Nordica and a coupon

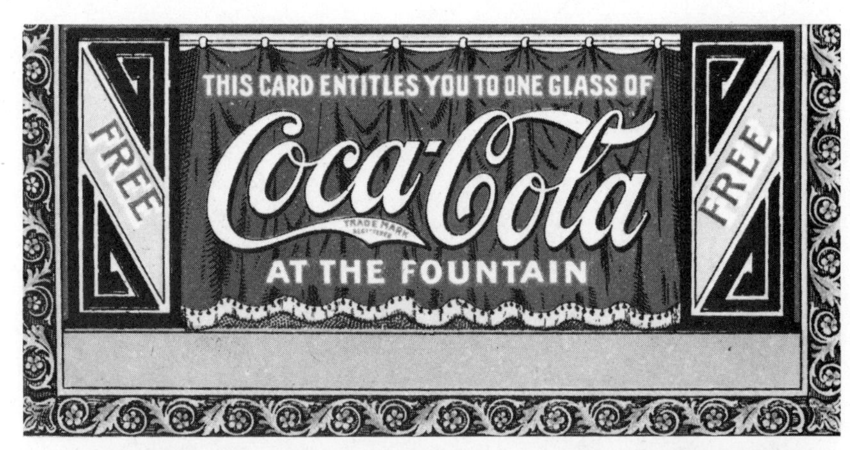

Free-drink coupons

1920 coupon (*Archives, The Coca-Cola Company, Atlanta, Georgia*)

1905 magazine advertisement with coupon

1970 coupon

1904 soda-fountain menu. One of the earliest and most sought menus.

1905 menu

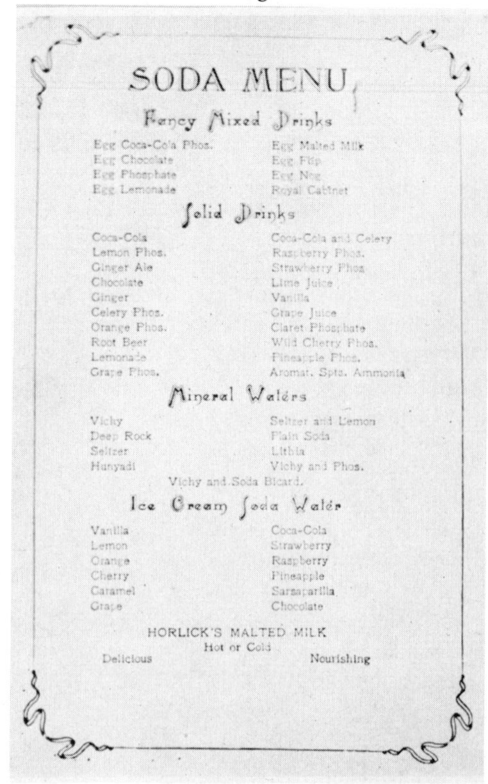

SODA MENU

Fancy Mixed Drinks

Egg Coca-Cola Phos.	Egg Malted Milk
Egg Chocolate	Egg Flip
Egg Phosphate	Egg Nog
Egg Lemonade	Royal Cabinet

Solid Drinks

Coca-Cola	Coca-Cola and Celery
Lemon Phos.	Raspberry Phos.
Ginger Ale	Strawberry Phos.
Chocolate	Lime Juice
Ginger	Vanilla
Celery Phos.	Grape Juice
Orange Phos.	Claret Phosphate
Root Beer	Wild Cherry Phos.
Lemonade	Pineapple Phos.
Grape Phos.	Aromat. Spts. Ammonia

Mineral Waters

Vichy	Seltzer and Lemon
Deep Rock	Plain Soda
Seltzer	Lithia
Hunyadi	Vichy and Phos.

Vichy and Soda Bicard.

Ice Cream Soda Water

Vanilla	Coca-Cola
Lemon	Strawberry
Orange	Raspberry
Cherry	Pineapple
Caramel	Sarsaparilla
Grape	Chocolate

HORLICK'S MALTED MILK
Hot or Cold
Delicious Nourishing

Reverse of the 1904 soda-fountain menu

CHAPTER 28

GAMES AND TOYS

The Coca-Cola Company has long considered children an important market for its products, and consequently it has aimed much of its advertising at young people. Games and toys in great variety have often been a part of advertising campaigns. However, not all games and toys used in the promotion of Coca-Cola were designed to appeal only to children; numerous games and a few toys have been produced for adult amusement. Almost all of these games and toys are liberally marked with the trademark(s) "Coca-Cola" or "Coke," slogans, or statements, but a few are only casually identified. Collectors must be alert to items in the latter group, for they are easily overlooked.

Playing cards and other types of cards are among the most often used by the company. From the early 1900's on, cards bearing advertising for Coca-Cola have been a commonly used advertising item. On the collectors' market, complete decks of playing cards are frequently broken up and sold one card at a time. The older the cards the more collectors are apt to locate examples on a one-card basis. Cards issued in recent decades, on the contrary, are most often located in complete decks. Chances of obtaining original boxes or carrying cases are enhanced as the newer decks are sought.

Among the most unusual of the decks of playing cards produced to advertise Coca-Cola are the ones issued during World War II. These cards are called Airplane Spotter Playing Cards. These cards have the markings of a regular deck of cards, but they are predominantly a series of illustrations and informative hints that could be used to facilitate airplane identification. Such airplane identification materials were popular during the early 1940's, when the nation faced the threat of invasion by air. Groups of volunteers organized and stood watch for foreign aircraft. As part of their training which enabled them to distinguish between foreign and domestic aircraft, the groups liberally used the materials produced by The Coca-Cola Company. At least two sets of small poster-like cards featuring American aircraft of World War II were used in the promotion of Coca-Cola.

Besides playing cards, numerous other games have been used to promote Coca-Cola. The list is incomplete because of a lack of complete records, but some of the most often used include checker games, cribbage boards, sets of dominos, puzzles of several types, dice, and marbles.

Toys for children have been produced for a number of years for The Coca-Cola Company. Such toys include dolls, badges, trucks, whistles, balls, blocks, Yo-Yos, kites, Ping-Pong paddles, and numerous miniature items. Miniature advertising items are especially interesting to collectors. Most of the miniatures produced to advertise Coca-Cola have been replicas of actual items used by the company in its business. Miniature bottles and cases in great variety and delivery trucks are among the most frequently seen small items.

1909 playing cards, produced for The Coca-Cola Company by S.L. Whitten, of Chicago

These "Airplane Spotter Playing Cards" were issued in the early 1940's. They were used both as playing cards and as training aids for civilian volunteers who scanned the skies for hostile aircraft.

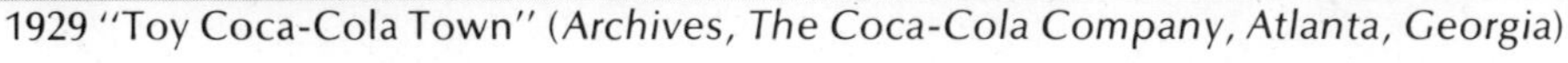
1929 "Toy Coca-Cola Town" (*Archives, The Coca-Cola Company, Atlanta, Georgia*)

1962 playing cards

1960's bridge set in simulated-alligator case

Jigsaw puzzle and can

Dominos from the 1950's. Antiques dealers often sell old domino sets in pieces.

Poker dice set of the late 1960's from Mexico

Rare promotional game of 1922 called "Coca-Cola Anna-Lizas"

1930's metal delivery truck with bottles

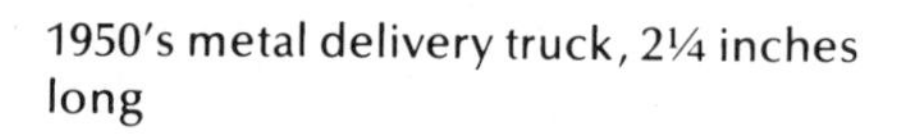

1950's metal delivery truck, 2¼ inches long

These whistles were made in Mexico from modified bottle caps.

Yo-Yos from Mexico

1968 advertisement for free Christmas decorations with six-bottle cartons of Coke, from the December 6 issue of *Life*

CHAPTER 29

OPENERS AND ICE PICKS

Bottle openers and ice picks are among the most common of the advertising items that are practically related to marketing a bottled beverage.

When the crown-cap bottle replaced the popular Hutchinson-stoppered bottle in the very early 1900's, an immediate search for opening devices began. It continues to this day. A large variety of openers carry embossed or debossed advertisements for Coca-Cola. Collectors who occupy themselves with building a representative gathering of Coca-Cola bottle openers quickly find their collections far exceed a hundred. As with other objects of advertising, the oldest examples are the most difficult to find and the most valuable.

Certain types of bottle openers have proved more successful, and as can be expected, are found in greater abundance. Further distinction can be made between stationary and portable openers. Stationary openers are permanently attached to some object such as a cooler, and portable openers are designed to be carried with the user—perhaps in his pocket. Collectors can expect to find fewer of the stationary openers because not as many were made.

During the first fifty years that Coca-Cola was on the market, ice was the chief means of chilling the beverage both at the fountain and in the bottle. To reduce blocks of ice to usable pieces, ice picks were a necessity. Ice picks, then, were a natural item on which to print advertising, and many different kinds were used to promote Coca-Cola. The Coca-Cola Company began to produce ice picks for advertising during the 1890's, and they predate the use of bottle openers by at least ten years. The era of the ice pick is past, and as they become more obsolete as a tool, more examples will become available to collectors.

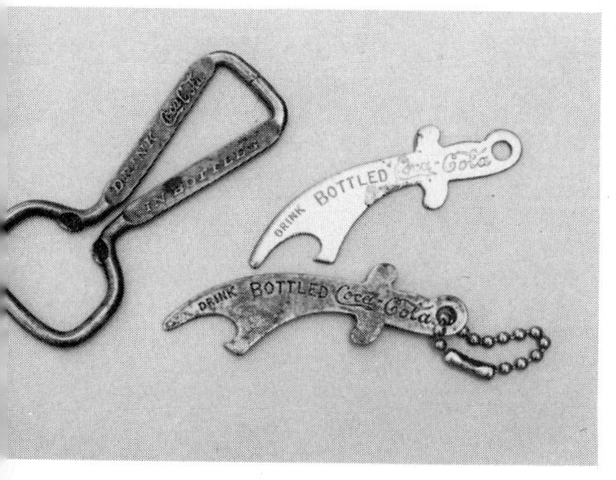

Bottle openers from the 1920's

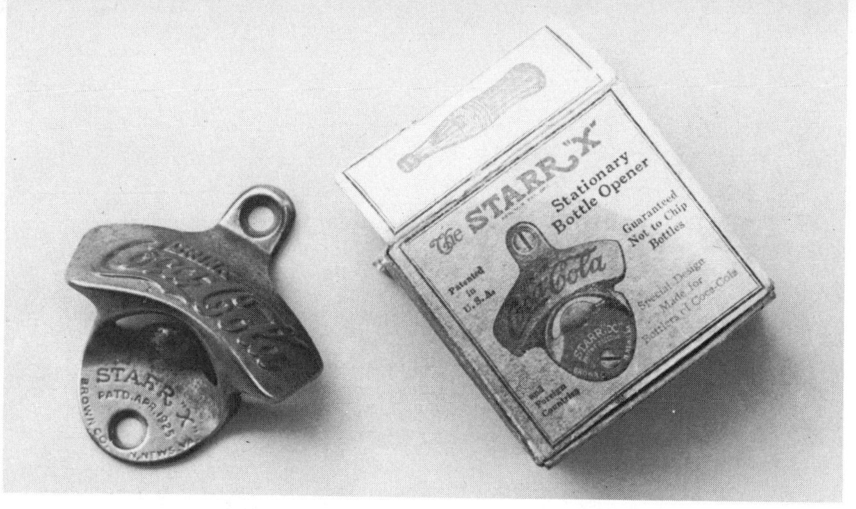

1925 bottle opener. "The Starr 'X' " was made especially for bottlers by the Brown Co., of Newport News, Virginia.

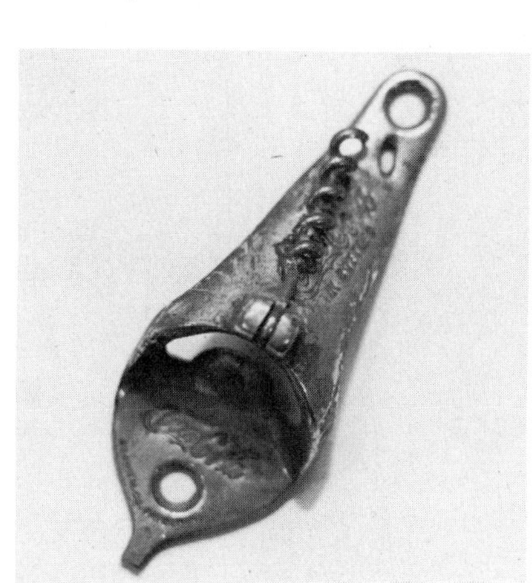

Stationary bottle opener from 1900's

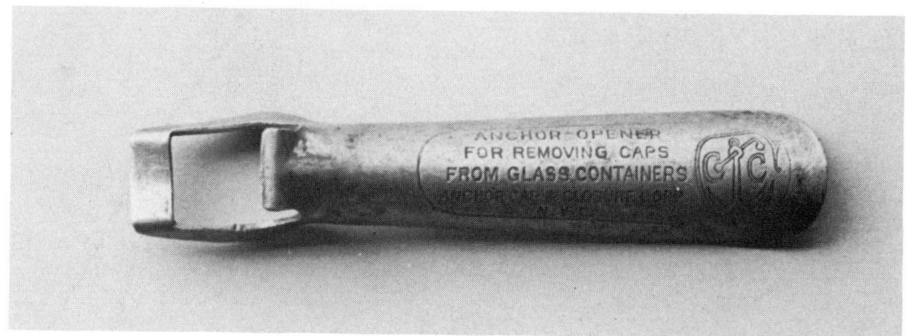

1940's–1950's portable bottle opener

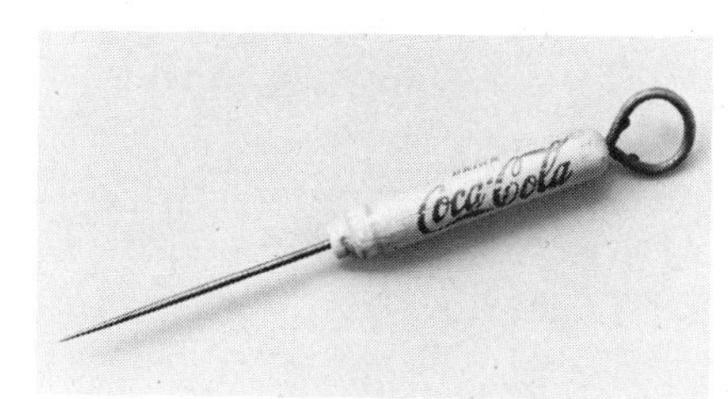

Circa 1940 ice pick/bottle opener

Bottle opener, measuring 3½ inches in length

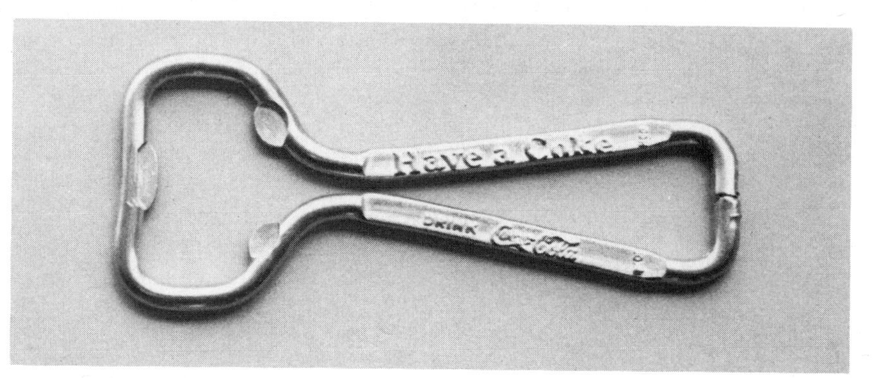

One of the most common bottle openers

CHAPTER 30

THERMOMETERS

The Coca-Cola Company has successfully distributed thousands of outdoor and a few indoor thermometers since the early 1920's. A mark of the success and durability of this type of promotional item is that many of the original thermometers are still in use almost fifty years after they were first placed on the market. As collector interest continues to mount, however, more and more of the earliest specimens are quietly being removed from active use and are finding their way into collections of Coca-Cola memorabilia.

Although a few thermometers advertising Coca-Cola were issued prior to the 1920's, the vast majority came into being after the mid-1920's. Outdoor thermometers were a natural result of the increasing interest in bottled Coca-Cola. As the number of retail outlets for the bottled beverage grew, so did the acceptance of such practical advertising items as thermometers. The end result is that thousands of retailers conspicuously display thermometers—each one a potential collectors' item.

Outdoor thermometer produced in the late 1920's, tin-plated, 16½ by 5 inches

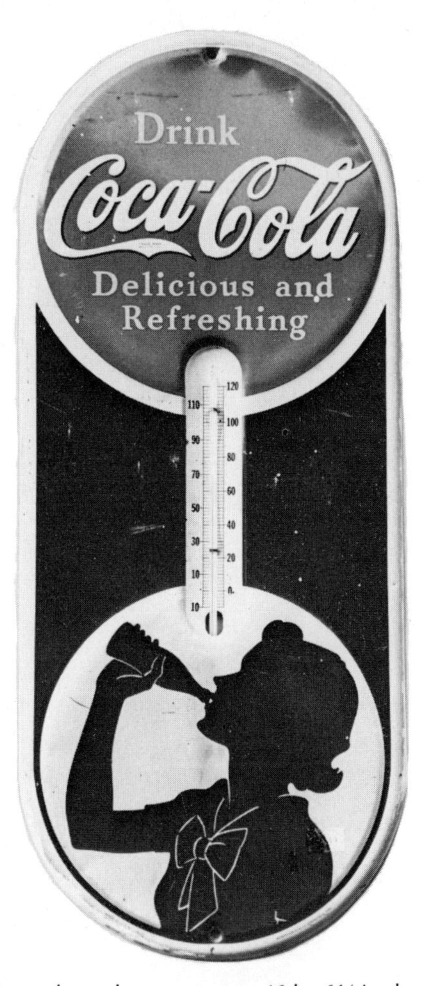

1939 outdoor thermometer, 16 by 6½ inches

1958 outdoor thermometer, tin-plated

Red and white 12½-inch thermometer

CHAPTER 31

POCKET KNIVES, PENS, PENCILS, PENCIL HOLDERS, AND PENCIL SHARPENERS

Pocket knives, pens, pencils, pencil holders, and pencil sharpeners carrying advertisements for Coca-Cola have been distributed since the 1890's. Collectors of any of these items find that they must compete with the numerous general collectors who gather such items. Pocket knives are the most difficult to locate, although many were produced and many collections of Coca-Cola memorabilia have at least several examples. One-, two-, or three-blade knives abound. Knives with blades for unusual purposes have also been produced but are harder to find. Some of the knives advertising Coca-Cola feature mother-of-pearl, wood, bone, metal, or plastic handles.

Ink pens were used for promotion during the first years of The Coca-Cola Company, but no examples advertising Coca-Cola have yet been found. The refillable fountain pen was the first ink-writing tool to be used as a promotional idea for Coca-Cola. Fountain pens remained a favorite advertising object until after World War II, when they were replaced with the more durable and less expensive ballpoint pens.

Frequently pens were paired with mechanical pencils to make a set. Early examples of the pen-and-pencil sets have been separated and are hard to find, but more recent sets occasionally can be located intact and in their original boxes.

Wooden lead pencils, in various conditions, are frequently found. The variety of this type of writing tool is extensive, and a few collectors have gathered a representative selection.

Holders for pencils are not to be found in

great variety or quantity. This is disappointing for collectors, because the few pencil holders produced were very handsome items. The miniature replica of the classical 1890's syrup urn that was produced in the 1960's is possibly the most attractive of the two dozen or so pencil holders used to advertise Coca-Cola.

Pencil sharpeners are other useful items that have frequently been employed to carry advertising for Coca-Cola. The several bottle-shaped examples seem to have attracted the most collector attention, but all sharpeners are considered desirable.

1908 pocket knives

Circa 1930's pocket knife

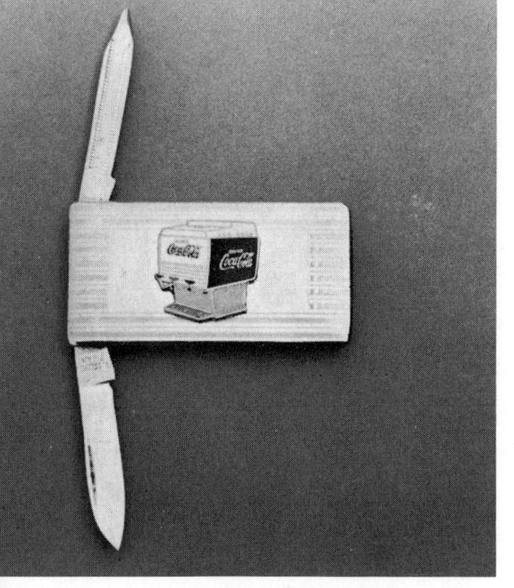

1950's pocket knife/money clip

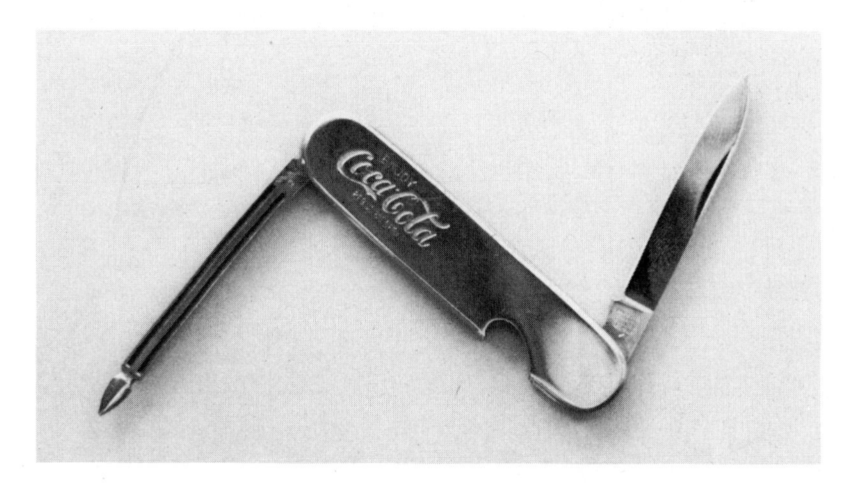

Late 1960's chrome-plated pocket knife, three inches long

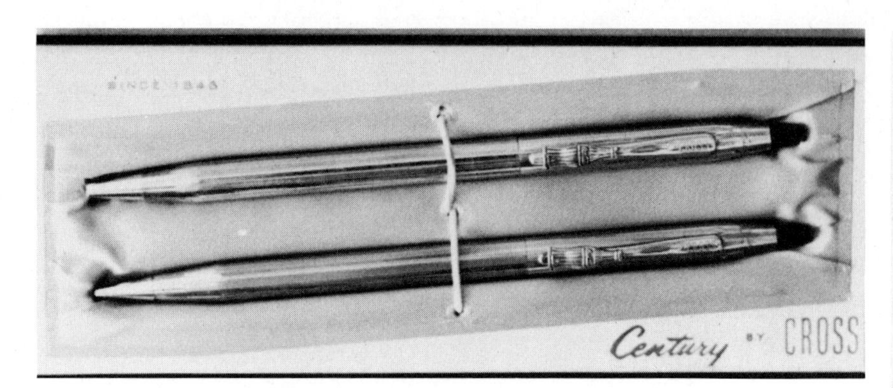

Gold-plated pen and pencil set of the 1960's. Made by the A. T. Cross Company, of Providence, Rhode Island.

1963 tin-plated pencil holder

Mechanical pencils of the 1950's

1933 red metal pencil sharpener

Plastic pencil sharpener made in the 1960's, one inch long

Ceramic pencil holder made in the 1960's

CHAPTER 32

MUSIC BOXES, PAPERWEIGHTS, AND RADIOS

Some items which were produced in limited quantity are the few music boxes, paperweights, and radios used off and on as promotional pieces for Coca-Cola.

Music boxes are few in number and type, but each specimen is a most interesting collectible piece. Music boxes have been occasionally used to promote Coca-Cola since the early 1950's. It is possible that they were used earlier, but it cannot yet be stated with certainty. Music boxes most generally are figural; that is, they are manufactured in the shape of some object. The two most popular items that have been replicated in music boxes are coolers and bottles. Both coolers and bottles are critical to the successful promotion of Coca-Cola because of their standardized shapes, and as a result they are always prime candidates for advertising items.

Paperweights, unlike music boxes, are not generally figural. The basic characteristics of paperweights are their relatively standardized size (about three inches in diameter) and weight (about sixteen ounces). The Coca-Cola Company began to use paperweights for advertising in the early 1900's and has occasionally issued different types since. The earliest and most valuable paperweights have movable objects sealed in the weight, whereas most of the later examples are solid pieces. In 1948 the round glass paperweight with the embedded copy "Coke is Coca-Cola" was introduced. Separate background colors included red, blue, and white.

Radios are relatively new objects in the field of advertising. The Coca-Cola Company first began to use them in the 1930's. The bulkiness of radios before the 1930's made them impractical as advertising items. Like music boxes, radios are replicas of coolers or bottles. One of the latest radios, however, is made in the shape of a Coca-Cola can. With mechanical and electrical devices such as music boxes and radios, value is proportional to condition.

1909 paperweights: hollow glass, tin bottoms

1950's music box

Solid glass paperweights promoting the abbreviation Coke for Coca-Cola. Made in 1948. *Left to right*: blue, red, clear.

Plastic paperweights. Made by Advertising Attractions, Inc., of New York City. *Left:* 1960. *Right:* 1962.

1949 cooler-shaped radio

1971–1972 can radio made by General Electric

Left: 1963 transistor radio

CHAPTER 33

SMOKING PARAPHERNALIA

Like numerous other firms The Coca-Cola Company has over the years promoted its product by advertising on smoking items.

Book matches have been a favorite medium for advertising Coca-Cola since the early 1900's. Since matches were designed to be consumed, few examples of the millions produced still exist. Collectors interested in obtaining examples of the book matches used to advertise Coca-Cola have consistently discovered that groups or individuals who specialize in collecting book matches of all kinds are their best sources.

When it was a custom for smokers to carry wooden matches, small metal boxes called match safes were developed, and they are today among the most popular of advertising items promoting Coca-Cola. During the early 1900's The Coca-Cola Company produced several different types carrying the trademark and a slogan—sometimes two. In at least one instance a picture of one of the many young female models used on calendars and trays was used. These safes were comparatively expensive to manufacture, so relatively few were produced. Most bottlers preferred book matches which could be purchased cheaply and given away by the hundreds. Match safes have therefore become rare and valuable collectors' items. Current research has not turned up any record or specimens of boxed matches used to advertise Coca-Cola. One suspects that match safes were thought to be a better and more lasting advertising item during the early years of this century. In recent years there does not seem to be a logical explanation for the absence of boxed matches advertising Coca-Cola, unless cigarette lighters are considered to be a more durable item.

The Coca-Cola Company has issued a wide variety of cigarette lighters over the years. Because of manufacturing refinements in the 1930's cigarette lighters could be mass-produced inexpensively. Since the 1930's thousands of lighters have been distributed (usually free) by The Coca-Cola Company and its bottlers.

Other smoking paraphernalia used to promote Coca-Cola include cigarette boxes, ashtrays, and cigarette cases. Ashtrays advertising Coca-Cola were made in large varieties and circulated widely. They have been made of tin plate, aluminum, and other metals, glass, ceramic, foil-covered cardboard, and heat-resistant plastic. A collection of ashtrays featuring advertisements for Coca-Cola would not only be fairly easy to assemble but also extensive in number and type.

Perhaps the highlight of any collection of memorabilia focusing on smoking would be a cigar. Unknown to many people who have studied the sketchy history of The Coca-Cola Company, the trademark is known to have been used on cigars (see Chapter 9).

1958 ashtray given away at main office of The Coca-Cola Company of Atlanta

Painted aluminum ashtray made in Mexico

Ashtray. Came with match holder, not shown. Manufactured by the American Pullmatch Corp., of Piqua, Ohio.

1950's aluminum ashtray

1936 frosted-glass cigarette box commemorating the fiftieth anniversary of Coca-Cola (*Dr. Burton Spiller, Rochester, New York; photograph by Richard P. Daley*)

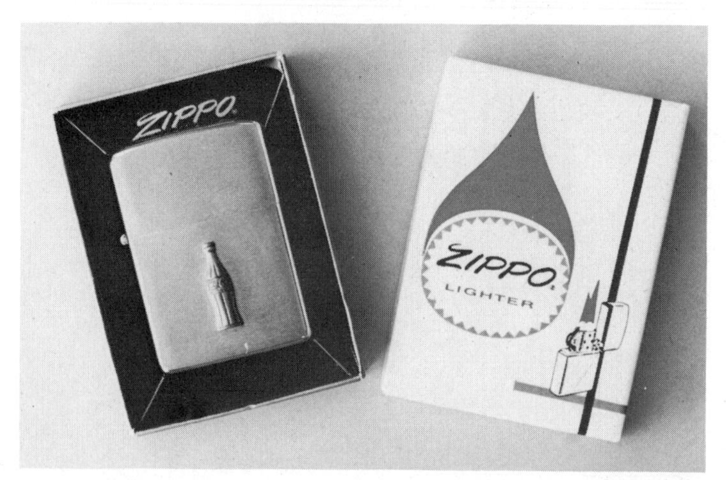

Cigarette lighter, made by the Zippo Manufacturing Company, of Bradford, Pennsylvania, in the 1950's and 1960's

Cigarette lighter and music box. Plays "Dixie" when struck.

1954 plastic cigarette lighter

1963 aluminum lighter, 2½ inches tall, made by Park Lighter in U.S.A.

Book matches

Silver-plated match safe

CHAPTER 34

BILLBOARD POSTERS

The first billboard advertising issued by The Coca-Cola Company, in May, 1925, featured a hotel bellhop nicknamed the Ritz Boy. The Ritz Boy carried a tray with a full bottle of Coca-Cola and an empty glass. The advertising copy was a simple "6,000,000 a day." Four other subjects were used during the following months of June, July, August, and September. The entire five-month campaign was on billboards in 5,270 cities and towns across the country. It was sponsored jointly by the company and 893 bottlers.

In 1926 the first bathing beauty billboard was displayed. In addition to the girl there was the slogan "It had to be good to get where it is. 7,000,000 a day."

In 1927 the five-month campaigns were expanded to six. By 1930 the campaigns were ten months in duration, and by 1934 a full twelve-month campaign was used. In 1948 the twelve-month campaigns were changed to two posters each month. In 1949 the company returned to the use of one poster a month, with an extra billboard poster available during certain months. The same plan is being used today.

It is not only very difficult for a collector to obtain the twenty-four-foot-long billboard posters of the past but nearly impossible to display such items. Nevertheless some collectors collect billboard posters even if they don't have appropriate display facilities. Most collectible billboard posters are specimens that for one reason or another were never used but perhaps were purchased by a bottler and stored. Few if any posters are obtained after they have been pasted to a billboard.

Billboard posters promoting Coca-Cola have long been recognized by the advertising industry as outstanding examples of art. As a matter of fact, since 1931 such posters have won honors at annual competitions staged by the outdoor advertising industry and the art directors' clubs of New York and Chicago. In the first twenty-seven years of competition, eighty-six posters were selected on the average of three each year as being among the "100 Best Posters of the Year." The 1941 "Girl on Beach Robe" and the 1946 "Yes Girl" both won the first award victory medal, and the 1945 "Girl in Garden" poster won the Kerwin Fulton medal.

"Ritz Boy" billboard poster, the first one used, in May, 1925 (*Archives, The Coca-Cola Company, Atlanta, Georgia*)

1929 billboard poster (*Archives, The Coca-Cola Company, Atlanta, Georgia*)

Posters from 1929 to 1935 (*Archives, The Coca-Cola Company, Atlanta, Georgia*)

1929

1932

1932

1935

Late 1930's poster (*Archives, The Coca-Cola Company, Atlanta, Georgia*)

1936 poster celebrating the fiftieth anniversary of Coca-Cola (*Archives, The Coca-Cola Company, Atlanta, Georgia*)

1941 "Girl on Beach Robe" won first place and grand-prize medal in the annual poster contest sponsored by the outdoor advertising industry. (*Archives, The Coca-Cola Company, Atlanta, Georgia*)

1943 poster (*Archives, The Coca-Cola Company, Atlanta, Georgia*)

1944 poster was awarded a first-place medal in an outdoor advertising contest. (*Archives, The Coca-Cola Company, Atlanta, Georgia*)

1945 "Girl in Garden" won the coveted Kerwin Fulton medal for outdoor advertising. (*Archives, The Coca-Cola Company, Atlanta, Georgia*)

July, 1946, "Yes Girl" poster won a first place and grand-prize medal in annual contest sponsored by outdoor advertising industry. (*Archives, The Coca-Cola Company, Atlanta, Georgia*)

Posters from 1948 to 1957

1948

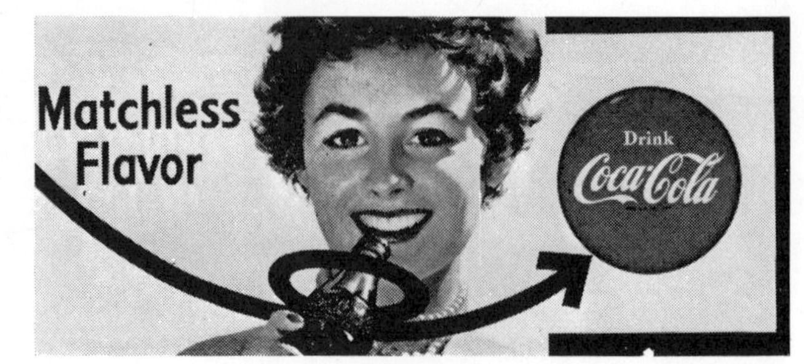

1954

1956

1957

CHAPTER 35

RADIO ADVERTISING

If any single area of the collecting of Coca-Cola memorabilia has been overlooked, it is radio advertising. Under the guidance of Robert W. Woodruff, The Coca-Cola Company first used radio to promote Coca-Cola in 1927. The campaign began on Tuesday, May 10, 1927, at nine P.M. (Eastern Standard Time), and America heard for the first time the voice of the Coca-Cola girl. For fourteen weeks listeners of National Broadcasting Company (NBC) affiliated radio stations in New York, Buffalo, Philadelphia, Washington, Pittsburgh, Detroit, St. Louis, Louisville, Nashville, Atlanta, Memphis, Chicago, and Davenport listened to episodes in a romance between the Coca-Cola girl (called Vivian) and the public, personified as "Jim." This historic series of broadcasts was a prototype of the radio, and later the television, serial.

In 1930 Coca-Cola sponsored a program featuring Grantland Rice, Graham McNamee, and sports figures, with Leonard W. Joy and his thirty-one-piece "string symphony." This also was an NBC-beamed program that was carried from coast to coast. Mr. Joy wrote the theme song for the program, which was broadcast from 1930 to 1932. The theme song does not have a name and was simply called the "Coca-Cola Signature" (a "signature" means "theme song" in radio jargon). Shortly after being hired to do the series of programs for Coca-Cola, Joy was asked to write the theme. He went home and worked all night to produce the resulting thirty-two bars of music. He wrote the theme originally as a tango for an all-brass orchestra. Like the famous John Philip Sousa, who wrote waltzes that almost always turned out to be his best marches, Joy changed the tempo of the "Coca-Cola Signature" to waltz time and substituted strings for the brass when nobody liked his original effort. The results were, of course, the incomplete (it is always faded out before the ending) but ever-popular "Coca-Cola Signature."

Again, during all of 1934 and the first part of 1935, The Coca-Cola Company turned to radio to promote its product. The Coca-Cola Company sponsored a program, "The Pause That Refreshes on the Air," a half-hour of popular music by a sixty-five-piece orchestra and twenty-five-member vocal group directed by Dr. Frank Black, who was the musical director of NBC Radio at the time. The program was unusual and successful because it was among the first not to introduce each musical number individually. The selections for the first fourteen minutes were announced at the beginning of the program after a commercial announcement. The music was then played, followed by one commercial announcement. The next fourteen minutes of music was announced and played, and the program ended with another commercial announcement.

At first thought it might seem that advertising for Coca-Cola on radio is outside the realm of collecting and could only be considered history. A very active hobby in recent years, however, is the collecting of old radio programs. Some of the earliest programs were recorded on transcription disks (records), and later many of the recorded programs were transferred to tape and wire recordings. Today such programs are traded by collectors, rerecorded, and traded to other collectors. Among the numerous programs from the early days of radio that exist as a result of this unusual collecting interest are those sponsored by the makers and distributors of Coca-Cola. No collection of memorabilia would be complete without at least one of the early radio broadcasts. A recent survey shows that pre-1930 radio programs are extremely difficult to obtain, but more recent broadcasts have been saved and are fairly easy to acquire.

Late in 1935 the famous Ray Noble, broadcasting from the Rainbow Room in New York City, presented a musical program advertising Coca-Cola called "Refreshment Time." This broadcast was followed by others, and certainly tapes of the "Refreshment Time" series are not only a collector's dream but a pleasure to listen to.

A very famous radio voice of the 1930's was "Singin' Sam." After preliminary test broadcasts late in 1936 "Singin' Sam" transcribed fifteen-minute programs sponsored by The Coca-Cola Company for the next five years. With a small orchestra led by Victor Arden, he made over a thousand of the transcriptions. The short programs were produced entirely at the expense of The Coca-Cola Company and made available to bottlers with the stipulation that they pay the relatively small cost of four dollars a program to broadcast them five times a week over their local radio stations.

Radio became such an important part of the company's advertising activities that it sponsored more than one radio program at a time. While the "Singin' Sam" transcriptions were being used, another network program was sponsored simultaneously in September of 1937. "The Song Shop," as it was titled, presented a variety of music conducted by Gustav Haenschen.

From 1940 to 1944 André Kostelanetz and his orchestra with Albert Spalding and a number of guest artists entertained a national radio audience every Sunday afternoon at four P.M. This program was aired over the Columbia Network.

In November, 1941, Kay Kayser introduced a series of broadcasts for Coca-Cola called "Spotlight Bands." This show featured a series of different bands selected to please young Americans in the Armed Forces. After the outbreak of World War II, in December, 1941, the broadcasts were increased to six a week in an attempt to entertain service men and women and war plant workers. The programs, with some modifications, were aired from 1941 to 1946. Of all the "Spotlight Bands" programs the classic is one presented on Christmas Day in 1942. This program began at noon with a half-hour introductory show and continued for eleven hours with time out only for dinner. The format of the program was designed so that forty-two different bands from all over the country presented fifteen minutes of entertainment each. The program, impressively titled "The Victory Parade's Christmas Party of Spotlight Bands," was broadcast on 142 Blue Network stations. Collectors who own tapes of this marathon presentation for Coca-Cola have a portion of radio, as well as Coca-Cola, history.

Morton Downey, famous as a singer in the 1940's and later well known as a wealthy bottler of Coca-Cola, did a series of radio broadcasts for Coca-Cola from 1943 to the mid-1950's.

From 1946 to 1959 Percy Faith and his orchestra did radio programs for Coca-Cola. From 1948 to 1950 Spike Jones entertained radio audiences on behalf of the famous beverage. From 1950 to 1952 Edgar Bergen and his dummy, Charley McCarthy, did radio programs for Coca-Cola with the musical assistance of Ray Noble, and these were followed by the famous tenor Mario Lanza. John Sebastian, in the serial "Claudia," and singer Eddie Fisher produced another series of transcriptions that were given to individual bottlers for broadcasting over their local radio stations.

When television began to replace radio in the early 1950's as the nation's primary communication medium, The Coca-Cola Company began to withdraw much of its major radio advertising money and pour it into television. Although it is probably possible for a person to obtain video tapes of television programs sponsored by Coca-Cola, it does not appear to be a realistic or practical collector option.

Radio tapes are still the most practical collectors' item. In fact, during 1970 and 1971 there was a boom in radio advertising by The Coca-Cola Company. An example destined to become one of the classic successes took place in 1971, when a song called "I'd Like to Buy the World a Coke" was written for The Coca-Cola Company for use on radio and television. The company sent representatives to Italy to gather youths of a variety of nationalities who would be willing to assemble on an Italian hillside and mouth the words to the new song, which was actually sung by a British group called the New Seekers. The whole incident was photographed for a television commercial, and the New Seekers' recording was used on radio. The company also sent records of the commercial to radio disk jockeys when the commercial became extremely popular. The disk jockeys would not play the records as part of their regular programs. The Coca-Cola Company revised the song and eliminated any mention of Coke. The New Seekers made a recording, as did a country-western group called the Hillside Singers. Within a few months the two recordings combined had sold over a million copies. The whole project cost The Coca-Cola Company $225,000, but the advertising value was certainly worth many times that. Collectors can add the recorded commercials, the record of the revised commercial ("I'd Like to Teach the World to Sing"), and the published sheet music to their collection of radio advertising memorabilia.

Above left: The "Coca-Cola Signature," composed in 1930 by Leonard W. Joy for a Coca-Cola–sponsored radio program that featured Grantland Rice and Graham McNamee interviewing sports personalities and Joy conducting the thirty-one-piece orchestra. *Left:* Joy as he appeared in 1930. *Above right:* Joy as he appeared in 1954 as an executive for Decca Records, Inc. *(Archives, The Coca-Cola Company, Atlanta, Georgia)*

Necktie "Designed for Morton Downey by Altman & Co., Fifth Avenue, New York, N.Y." Downey was a singer in the 1940's; then he became a Coca-Cola bottler.

Graham McNamee, the pioneer radio sports commentator (*Nostalgia Photos, Inc., Los Angeles, California*)

45-rpm record of three 1971 hit radio and TV commercials for Coke

Sheet music for the hit radio and TV commercial "I'd Like to Buy the World a Coke." This sheet music was given away to the thousands of people who wrote to the company.

In 1971, when disc jockeys were asked to include "I'd Like to Buy the World a Coke" in their regular programming, they refused. The Coca-Cola Company then rewrote the song, eliminating any mention of Coke, and it became "I'd Like to Teach the World to Sing," recorded by the New Seekers. The "Coke" song became a hit record.

CHAPTER 36

THE STEREOTYPING OF SANTA CLAUS

History reveals that there truly was a Santa Claus who lived in the small country of Lycia in Asia Minor around A.D. 300. The real Santa Claus was Saint Nicholas, the Bishop of Myra. Nothing of his life is really known, but many legends paint him as a very generous man with a tremendous interest in children. For those reasons he was elevated to the position of the patron saint of children.

To honor Saint Nicholas, people in many countries set aside a special day each year and in his memory gave gifts to the needy. Over the years the concept changed to gift giving to friends and loved ones. The day of celebration, in America and in some other countries, eventually became Christmas Day.

The colonists from Holland brought the concept of Saint Nicholas to America, where his name was eventually corrupted to Santa Claus. Many of the immigrants to America in the eighteenth and nineteenth centuries embraced the Santa Claus concept and added their own refinements. The idea that Santa Claus rides in a sleigh drawn by reindeer most likely comes from Scandinavia. Other sources added the ideas that he wears fur-trimmed clothes and lives at the North Pole. The pipe he smokes and the idea that he descends through chimneys into houses seem to be Dutch contributions to the legend. One of the most recent additions has been a new lead reindeer, Rudolph, who with his bright-red nose guides Santa Claus on foggy Christmas Eves.

The Coca-Cola Company, through its advertising, has made one of the largest contributions to the legend of Santa Claus. To fully understand how the makers of Coca-Cola could have such an influence on the Santa Claus myth, it should be noted that for about the first two hundred years in America the Saint Nicholas concept prevailed. It was in 1844 that the famous poet and educator Clement Clarke Moore published a volume of his poetry. Within the collection was a narrative poem called " 'Twas the Night before Christmas," which he had written in 1822. Moore's description of Santa Claus deviated from the Saint Nicholas concept:

He had a broad face and a round little belly
That shook when he laughed like a bowlful of jelly.
He was bubbly and plump, a right jolly old *elf* [italics added],
And I laughed when I saw him in spite of myself.

For at least fifty years after Moore's poem was published, artists drew inspiration from the "elf" concept and pictured Santa Claus as a gnomelike character. Shortly before the turn of the century artists began to deviate from Moore's stereotype, and Santa Claus was drawn in a wide range of sizes. Even more confusion abounded regarding the color and type of clothing worn by the legendary gentleman. Some artists insisted on a long coat; others, a short one; still others added more confusion by coloring his clothes green, blue, red, and/or brown. Some of the confusion was caused by the importing of Christmas cards from Europe, where artists were not influenced by Moore's poem. However, the vast majority of the artistic renditions associated Santa Claus with toys, children, a Christmas tree, and portrayed him with a long white beard. Out of the turn-of-the-century confusion came one consistency: Santa Claus lost the image of an elf and became the height of an average human being.

In 1930 The Coca-Cola Company produced a magazine advertisement featuring a realistic version of Santa Claus. The advertisement was well received, and as a result it was decided that Santa Claus would become a regular feature in the company's seasonal advertising.

By mid-1931 artist Haddon Sundblom was hard at work for The Coca-Cola Company developing a Santa Claus that would be both realistic and symbolic. In 1931 the first of the now-famous Sundblom portraits of Santa Claus appeared on posters and in magazines advertising Coca-Cola.

The quality of Haddon Sundblom's work, teamed with the company's extensive advertising, has created what is probably the most common conception of Santa Claus. Almost without exception the legendary patron saint of children is portrayed in a long red coat, with white fur trim, red trousers, high boots, and a large leather belt with an imposing brass buckle. White hair and a flowing beard complete the stereotype.

According to Haddon Sundblom, "The model [for Santa Claus] for years was a retired salesman named Lou Prentice, who embodied all the features and spirit of Santa Claus, including the wrinkles which were so evident when he smiled or laughed. Lou passed away several years ago, and since that time I have been using my own face as a model for Santa Claus."

Every year since 1930 Santa Claus has appeared on posters, cardboard cutouts, blotters, Christmas cards, billboards, and in magazines promoting Coca-Cola. Each of these items is of tremendous collecting interest. The numerous poses over the years with toys, Christmas trees, elfin helpers, a dog, a fawn, reindeer, and children make Santa Claus memorabilia a very interesting collection in themselves, or they can be a part of a more extensive collection of memorabilia.

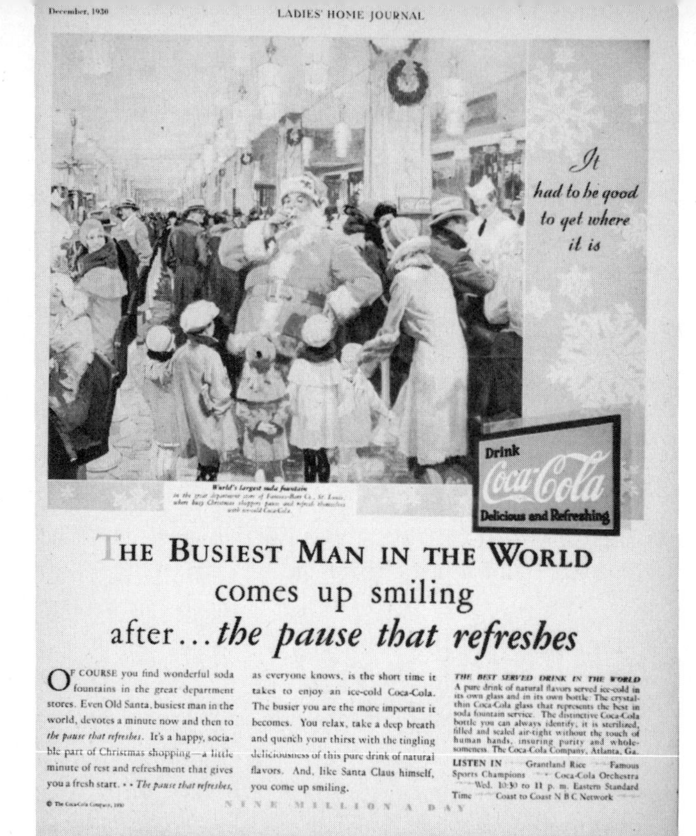

Left: Advertisement from December, 1930, *Ladies' Home Journal*, featuring the first Santa Claus used by The Coca-Cola Company (*Archives, The Coca-Cola Company, Atlanta, Georgia*)

Circa 1900's Christmas card

Left: This is the first Santa Claus created for The Coca-Cola Company by artist Haddon Sundblom (1931).

1932 Santa Claus (*Archives, The Coca-Cola Company, Atlanta, Georgia*)

1933 Santa Claus (*Archives, The Coca-Cola Company, Atlanta, Georgia*)

1934 Santa (*Archives, The Coca-Cola Company, Atlanta, Georgia*)

1935 Santa (*Archives, The Coca-Cola Company, Atlanta, Georgia*)

1936 Santa (*Archives, The Coca-Cola Company, Atlanta, Georgia*)

1937 Santa (*Archives, The Coca-Cola Company, Atlanta, Georgia*)

1938 Santa (*Archives, The Coca-Cola Company, Atlanta, Georgia*)

1939 cardboard cutout Christmas display (*Archives, The Coca-Cola Company, Atlanta, Georgia*)

Below: 1941 Santa (*Archives, The Coca-Cola Company, Atlanta, Georgia*)

1940 Santa (*Archives, The Coca-Cola Company, Atlanta, Georgia*)

1943 Santa (*Archives, The Coca-Cola Company, Atlanta, Georgia*)

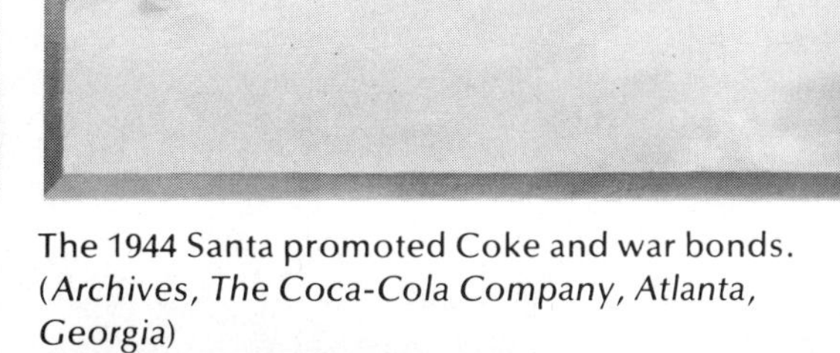

1944 Sprite with Santa (*Archives, The Coca-Cola Company, Atlanta, Georgia*)

The 1944 Santa promoted Coke and war bonds. (*Archives, The Coca-Cola Company, Atlanta, Georgia*)

1945 Santa (*Archives, The Coca-Cola Company, Atlanta, Georgia*)

1946 Santa (*Archives, The Coca-Cola Company, Atlanta, Georgia*)

1946 Santa (*Archives, The Coca-Cola Company, Atlanta, Georgia*)

1947 Santa (*Archives, The Coca-Cola Company, Atlanta, Georgia*)

1948 Santa (*Archives, The Coca-Cola Company, Atlanta, Georgia*)

1947 Santa

1949 Santa

1950 Santa (*Archives, The Coca-Cola Company, Atlanta, Georgia*)

1951 Santa (*Archives, The Coca-Cola Company, Atlanta, Georgia*)

1951 Santa

1952 blotter

By 1953 Sundblom's Santa Claus had become a classic. The two children represented lived next door to Sundblom in Tucson, Arizona.

1954 Santa (*Archives, The Coca-Cola Company, Atlanta, Georgia*)

1955 Santa (*Archives, The Coca-Cola Company, Atlanta, Georgia*)

1956 Santa (*Archives, The Coca-Cola Company, Atlanta, Georgia*)

1959 Santa (*Archives, The Coca-Cola Company, Atlanta, Georgia*)

1960 Santa (*Archives, The Coca-Cola Company, Atlanta, Georgia*)

1954 cardboard cutout display

1958 Santa

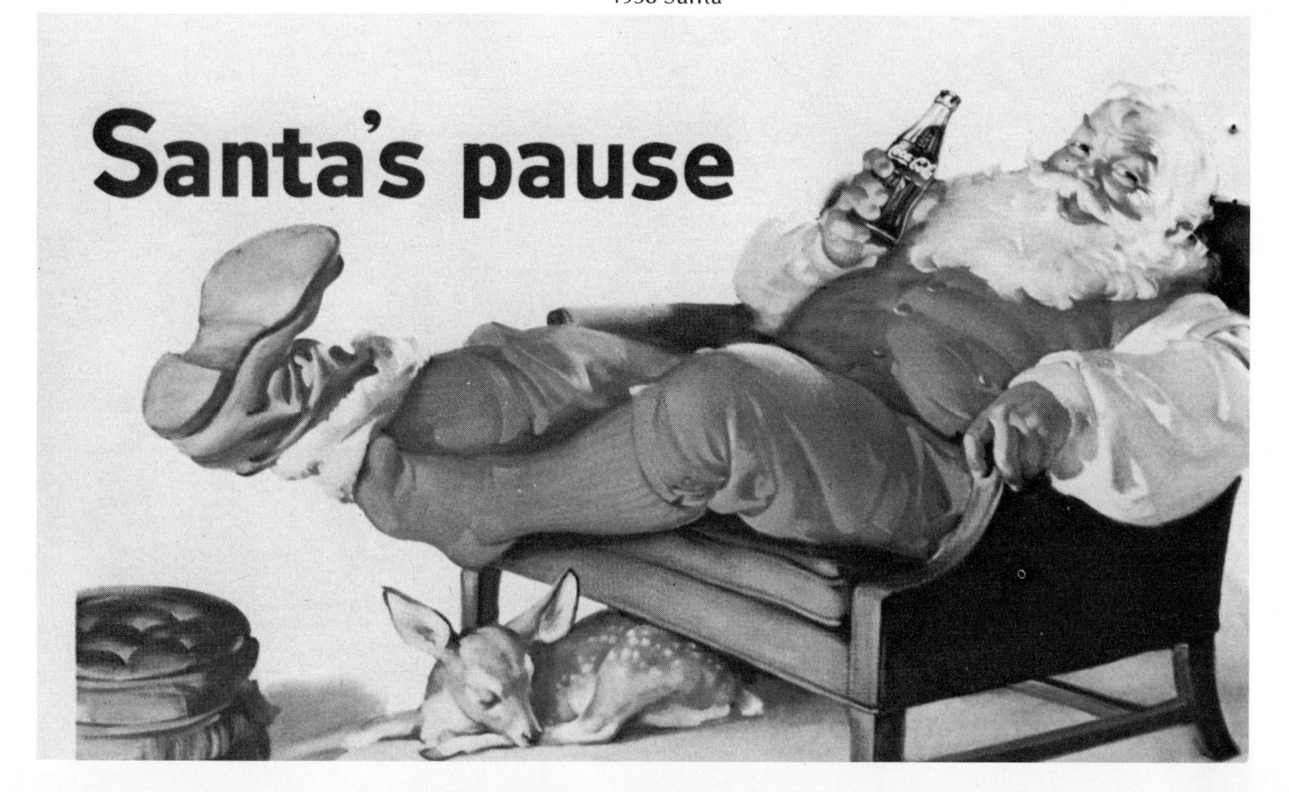

1960 Santa. This advertisement appeared in *Life*, *The Saturday Evening Post*, *Look*, *Time*, *Sports Illustrated*, and *National Geographic*. (*Archives, The Coca-Cola Company, Atlanta, Georgia*)

1961 Santa

1962 Santa (*Archives, The Coca-Cola Company, Atlanta, Georgia*)

1964 Santa (*Archives, The Coca-Cola Company, Atlanta, Georgia*)

1965 Santa (*Archives, The Coca-Cola Company, Atlanta, Georgia*)

1967 Santa (*Archives, The Coca-Cola Company, Atlanta, Georgia*)

1968 Santa (*Archives, The Coca-Cola Company, Atlanta, Georgia*)

1970 Santa Claus

1969 Christmas card. *Left:* front. *Below:* inside.

1971 Christmas card

1970 live Santa Claus (*Archives, The Coca-Cola Company, Atlanta, Georgia*)

CHAPTER 37

JEWELRY

New collectors are generally surprised to learn that jewelry is very much a part of the advertising history of The Coca-Cola Company. From around the turn of the century to the present, jewelry of various types and quality has been regularly produced featuring advertising for Coca-Cola.

Perhaps one of the first pieces of jewelry ever used to promote Coca-Cola was a watch fob. Dangling outside the pocket, fobs were a very effective means of calling attention to the product. During the early years of the century at least several different watch fobs were produced and employed to promote Coca-Cola. Each of these is a valuable collectors' item today.

Cuff links are another type of jewelry used in promotions. Numerous styles have been issued off and on over the years. Frequently tie tacks and/or tie clips are also produced.

Belt buckles are another item which appeared early in the use of promotional jewelry. One handsome brass specimen, 3 by 3¼ inches, with "Coca-Cola" embossed in a circle on the front, has puzzled collectors and historians for years because on the back is stamped "Anson Mills, Pat., Feb. 1, 1881, T. C. Arndorff Sole, Manf. Worcester, Mass., U.S.A." The most logical explanation for the 1881 date, which is five years before Coca-Cola was invented, is that the buckle design was developed and patented in 1881. Another series of three brass buckles was produced between 1909 and 1912. On the reverse of each of the buckles is a design of a bottle crown cap inscribed "Coca-Cola"; above the crown cap "THE COCA-COLA BOTTLER" is inscribed; and beneath the crown cap "J. J. Willard—Phila." is inscribed (Willard was the first editor of *The Coca-Cola Bottler* in 1909). "Tiffany Studio, New York"—the manufacturer—is stamped near the other inscriptions. On the obverse of the three buckles is embossed "The Coca-Cola Company/U.S. Patent Office Trade Mark, January 31, 1886. DELICIOUS AND REFRESHING." (This date is in error; the trademark was actually registered on January 31, 1893.) The difference in the three buckles appears in an insert panel on the obverse: On one panel appears "Seth W. Fowle & Sons, Boston, Mass."; on another "Thomas & Whitehead, Chattanooga, Tenn."; and on the third panel there appears "J. A. Biedenharn, Vicksburg, Miss."

Pins, rings, necklaces, earrings, wrist and pocket watches, stick pins, lapel buttons, compacts, and money clips are only a few of the jewelry items produced. Perhaps it is better to say that almost everything that could be considered a standard piece of jewelry has been used at one time to advertise the drink Coca-Cola. A collection limited to jewelry would be extensive.

A very popular jewelry item is key chains. From about the 1930's, when the automobile ceased being a luxury and became a necessity, car key chains became a more popular type of promotional jewelry.

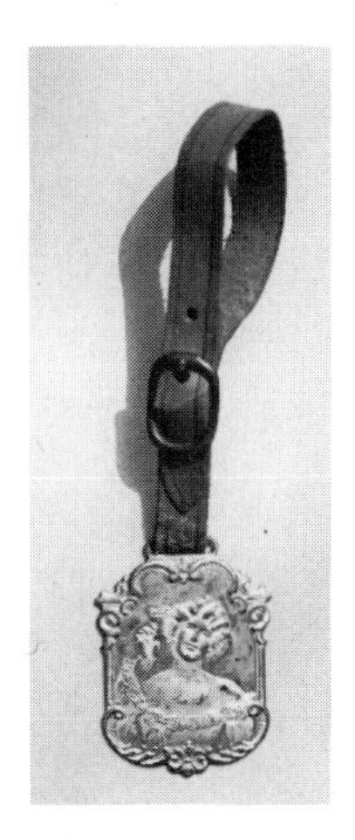

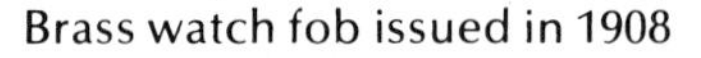

Brass watch fob issued in 1908

Gold-plated watch fob of the early 1900's

1905–1925 watch fobs

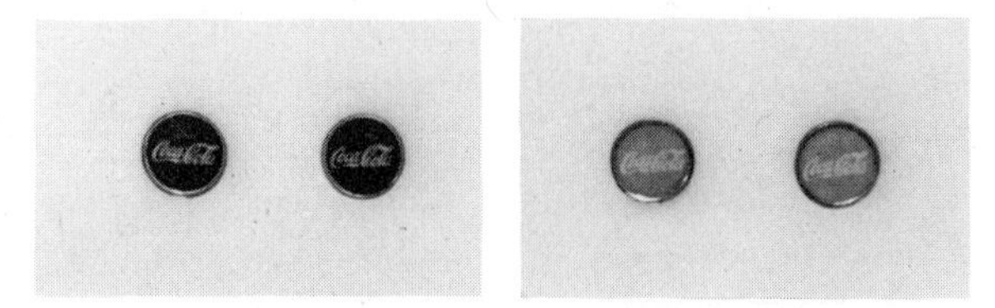

Sterling-silver cuff links made in 1923

Sterling-silver cuff links and tie tack, produced in 1930's for salesmen to wear while working

Solid brass buckle made in the 1900's. This buckle was originally designed to be part of a shipping-case strap but was converted into a belt buckle by an innovative route salesman. It is stamped "Anson Mills, Pat., Feb. 1, 1881, T.C. Arndorff Sole, Manf. Worcester, Mass., U.S.A."

Sterling-silver tie tack

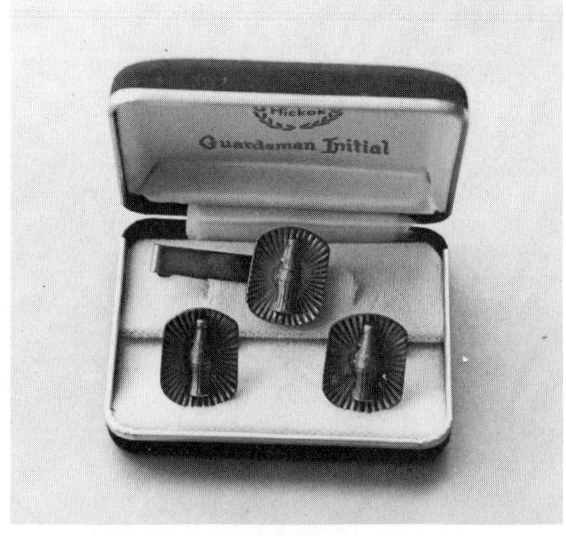

Burnished-gold cuff links and tie clip made in the 1950's by the Hickok Company

1950's cuff links made from bottle caps

Ladies' gold lapel pins produced in the 1950's and 1960's. Such jewelry is frequently given away by bottlers at various celebrations.

Portion of a page from the April, 1959, issue of *The Coca-Cola Bottler* advertising promotional jewelry manufactured by the L.G. Balfour Company, of Attleboro, Massachusetts

Key chains. Left: circa 1936, issued for fiftieth anniversary celebration. Right: circa 1960.

1964 brass key chain with amber replica of bottle

1960 key chains. The obverse of the left key chain is a St. Christopher medal.

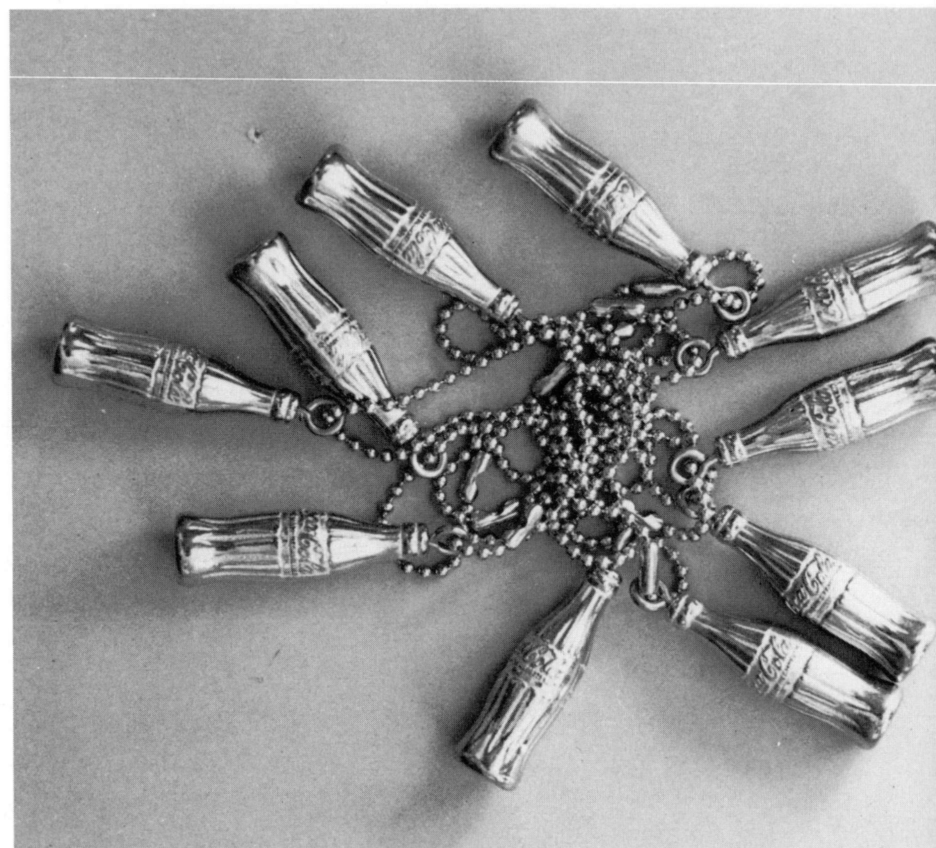

1950 gold-dipped key chains

CHAPTER 38

EDUCATIONAL MATERIALS

Advertising items of an educational nature issued by The Coca-Cola Company date from the early 1900's. The idea that children are not only a current, but potential, market for the beverage and that advertising items designed for them are an effective promotional tool resulted in a large variety of educationally oriented objects produced over the years.

Educational items include dictionaries, nature study cards, famous American portraits, units of study designed specifically for school use, airplane identification pictures, educational charts, note pads with educational information imprinted on them, and illustrated biographical magazines designed for school enrichment. That brief listing is by no means exhaustive; numerous other items designed for educational enrichment have been issued over the years.

A very well received promotional item in the 1920's was Webster's *Little Gem Dictionary.* This small vest-pocket reference book was one of The Coca-Cola Company's first highly successful educationally oriented items. By 1925 the book was in its third edition. In subsequent years the small volumes, debossed "Compliments of The Coca-Cola Bottling Company," became a standard promotional piece.

In the early 1930's a series of "Nature Study Cards" was issued. The cards focused on many aspects of nature and offered both written and illustrative information. Many educators used these cards as part of their science presentations.

In 1932 the makers of Coca-Cola issued two series of portraits, great Americans and famous doctors. The great American portraits featured one great American with his birth and death dates plus a facsimile of his handwritten signature. The famous doctor series was a grouping of some of the most famous medical men in history. Their portraits were presented with their names, birth and death dates, and a brief statement regarding their most significant contribution to medical thought.

In 1940, among several brief supplemental paperbound social studies booklets, the attractive *Our American Neighbors* booklet was given to appropriate grade-school pupils. This series was followed in the mid-1940's by several series of World War II airplane pictures. Each picture was executed in full color, came with a simulated picture frame which was actually part of the piece, and was imprinted with the name of the plane and other statistics. The advertisement for Coca-Cola was in the form of a standard red circular sign with the slogan "Drink Coca-Cola" and a picture of a full bottle of Coke.

Postwar educational materials developed by The Coca-Cola Company began in 1946 with a six-booklet series entitled "Our America." Each of the booklets is fifteen pages long and came with twenty colored pictures related to the subject of the booklet. School children, after studying the printed material, pasted the pictures in the book. Subjects covered were oil, glass, cotton, lumber, transportation, and electricity.

In later years boating charts explaining the rules of the sea, notebooks imprinted with America's famous landmarks, and note pads displaying weights and measures tables were among the most circulated of the educational items advertising Coca-Cola.

Among the most recent and effective of The Coca-Cola Company's educational materials is "The Golden Legacy" series of thirty-two-page magazines featuring beautifully illustrated stories of great Negroes in American history. This series of magazines was so popular that it eventually consisted of well over a dozen pieces —each a collectors' item.

1925 edition of *Webster's Little Gem Dictionary*

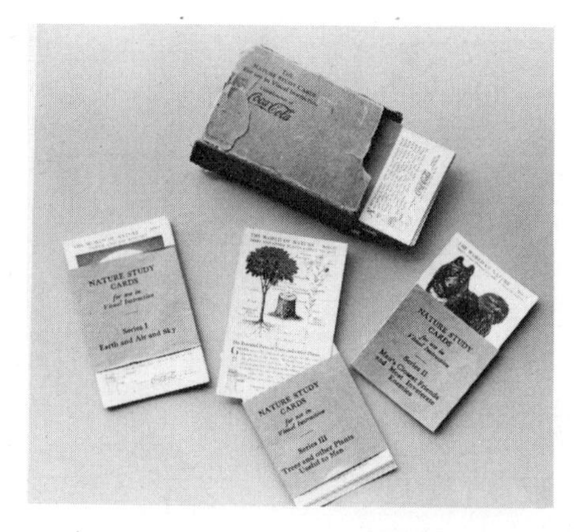

Left and below: From 1928 to 1933 several series of nature study cards were issued bearing advertisements for Coca-Cola.

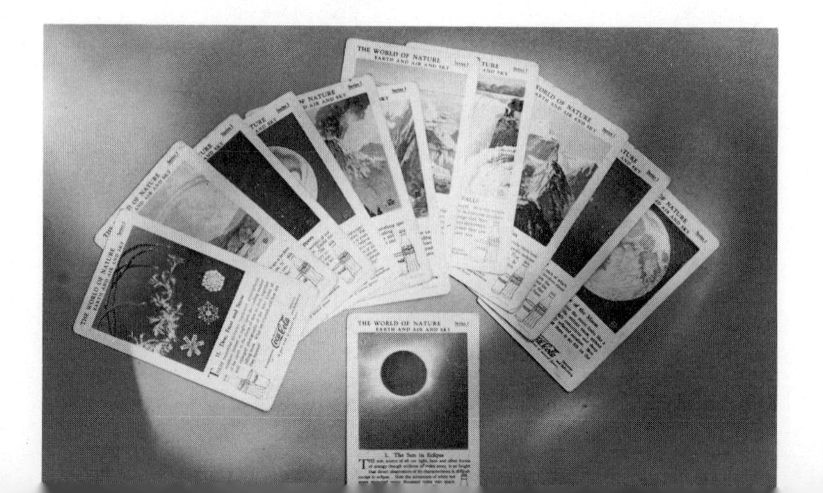

"Great American" portrait of Benjamin Franklin, 1932 (*Archives, The Coca-Cola Company, Atlanta, Georgia*)

"Great American" portrait of George Washington, 1932 (*Archives, The Coca-Cola Company, Atlanta, Georgia*)

"Great American" portrait of Abraham Lincoln, 1932 (*Archives, The Coca-Cola Company, Atlanta, Georgia*)

"Great American" portrait of Robert E. Lee, 1932 (*Archives, The Coca-Cola Company, Atlanta, Georgia*)

Two of the "Famous Doctor" series, 1932 (*Archives, The Coca-Cola Company, Atlanta, Georgia*)

Two of the "Famous Doctor" series, 1932 (*Archives, The Coca-Cola Company, Atlanta, Georgia*)

Two of the "Famous Doctor" series, 1932 (*Archives, The Coca-Cola Company, Atlanta, Georgia*)

1940 social-studies supplementary booklet

DRINK
Coca-Cola
Boeing "Flying Fortress" · U. S. Army Air Force
B-17 Four-engine Heavy Bomber

Consolidated Vultee "Privateer" · U. S. Navy
Four-engine Heavy Bomber
DRINK
Coca-Cola

DRINK
Coca-Cola
Douglas Super Transport · U. S. Army Air Force
DC-7 Carries 108 troops and Crew of 13

DRINK
Coca-Cola
Douglas "Invader" · U. S. Army Air Force
A-26 Twin-engine Fighter Bomber

World War II airplane pictures

Left: 1946 series of educational booklets. The pictures came separately and were then glued into the booklets.

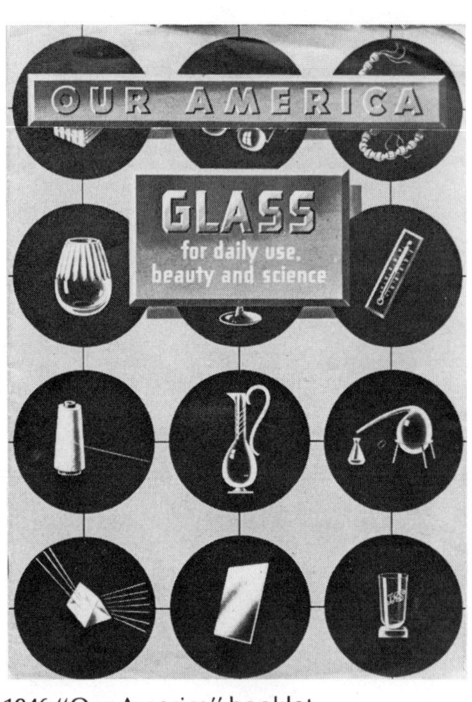

1946 "Our America" booklet

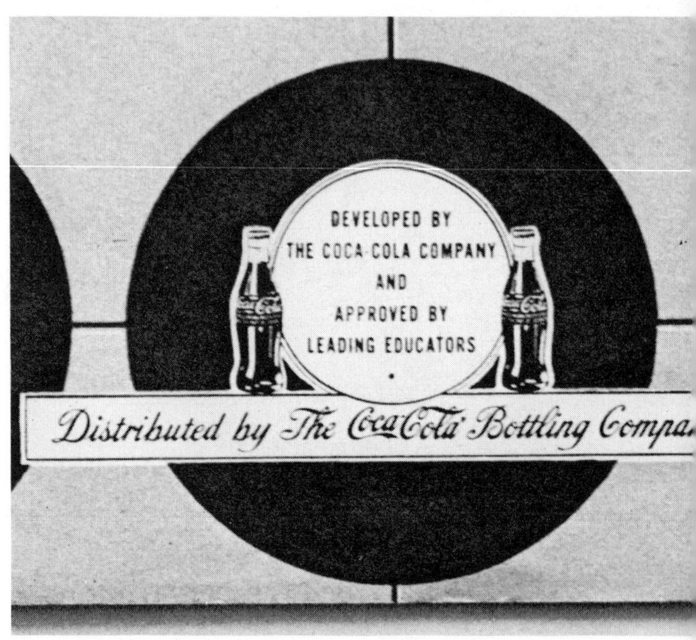

1946 "Our America" booklets were stamped with advertising for Coca-Cola.

1946 "Our America" booklets

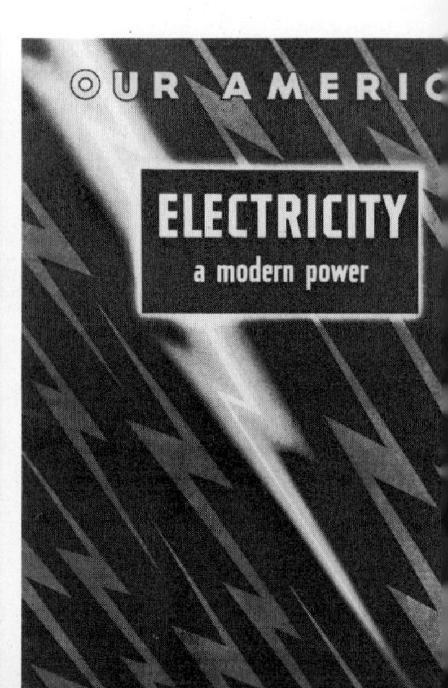

1946 "Our America" booklets

1960 nautical wall chart

1960 notebook with national landmarks

1968 booklet

1960's weights and measures chart

Advertisement that appeared in the February, 1969, issue of *Ebony*. It explains how readers could obtain copies of the 32-page historical magazines featuring stories of great Negroes in American history.

1970 "The Golden Legacy" series

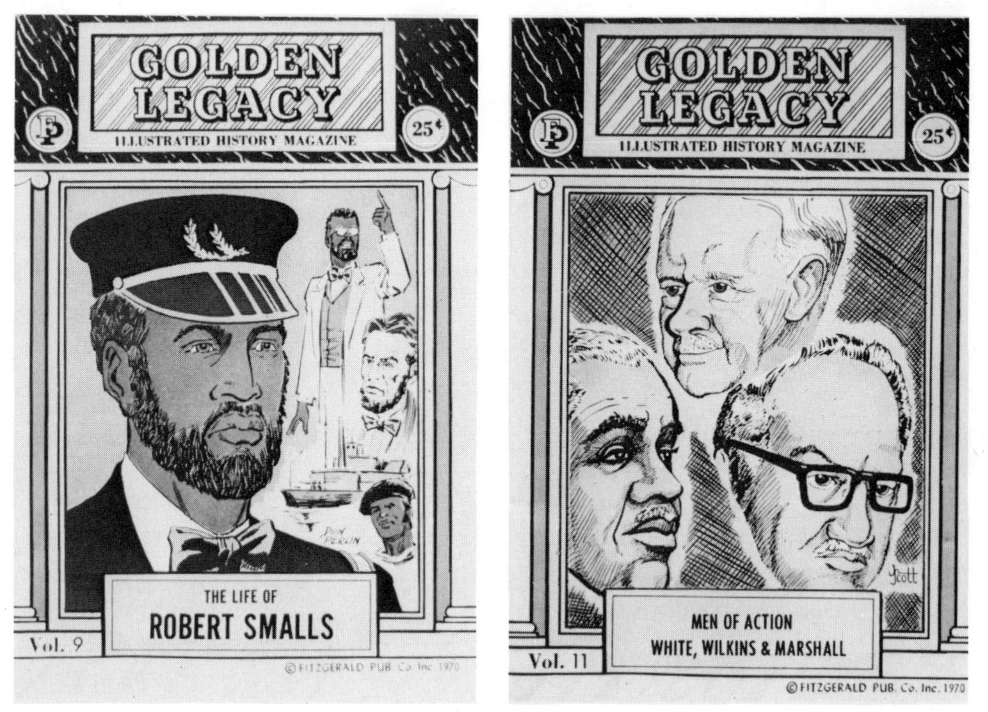

1970 "The Golden Legacy" series

CHAPTER 39

COLLECTIBLE LITERATURE

Over the years much has been published about and by The Coca-Cola Company. The most sophisticated collections almost always feature a selection of literature. The literature often informs the collector about the objects that are available, and he is therefore better able to recognize and obtain collectible items.

Literature produced by The Coca-Cola Company is almost exclusively of a promotional nature. Although such books, booklets, pamphlets, and brochures are issued to advertise and promote Coca-Cola, they frequently are devoted to such subjects as flower arranging, history, economics, and so forth. All of these qualify as "collectible literature" and could be included in a literature portion of a collection.

Magazines and other periodicals feature articles about Coca-Cola. Those magazines carrying such articles (especially if the cover reflects the featured article) make excellent collectibles. While it is certainly true that these articles about Coca-Cola cannot be considered as authentic Coca-Cola items, they are still very popular with collectors. Since there is little chance for deception in dealing with such materials, collectors accept them almost without question as being worthy of inclusion in a collection. Perhaps the most popular in this grouping are the magazines and/or periodicals that are small in circulation and therefore harder to find.

First issue of *The Coca-Cola Bottler,* printed in April, 1909

This booklet describes the history of Coca-Cola from 1886 to 1916. Printed in 1916.

Booklet by Laura Lee Burroughs on flower arranging

1957 booklet given by The Coca-Cola Company to bottlers who had been in business for fifty years. It contains a list of all bottlers who had celebrated their fiftieth anniversary.

"50th Anniversary Issue" of *The Coca-Cola Bottler*, printed in April, 1959

The Refresher Magazine, produced in 1961 by The Coca-Cola Company, commemorating the seventy-fifth anniversary of Coca-Cola

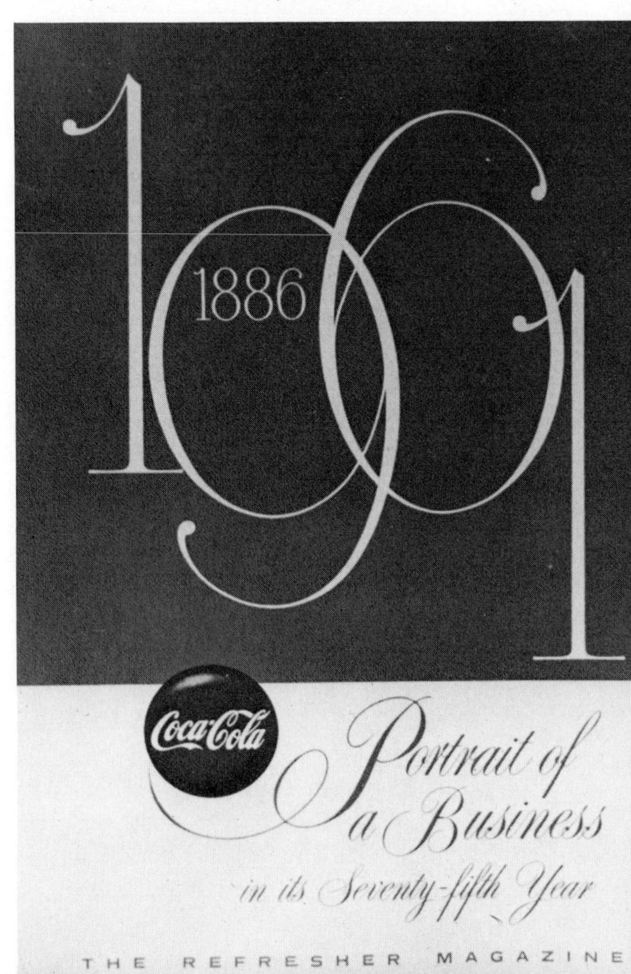

(continued from page 4) the Islands but given a special [illegible] your own ideas of hospitality. Whatever your party plans, [illegible] you want to make sure that your guests are really refreshed. [illegible] have plenty of ice-cold Coca-Cola on hand, the perfect [illegible] ment to good food—in our fifty States and the whole wide [illegible]

holders for flowers and candles are easy to make by sawing a bamboo carpet pole into sections. Cut just below the joint and you'll discover that each container has a built-in bottom. These containers may be used in a variety of different ways.

gladioli and papyrus, here arranged with beeswax candles in a container made of three sections of bamboo which are laced together with rattan. The tops are cut diagonally. Bamboo grille forms base and background for a dramatic grouping.

coconut shells make attractive bowls for serving chicken Hawaiian. An inverted coconut shell forms a base for a second one which holds flowers. Six pandanus leaves, knotted in the Polynesian manner, and a cluster of nasturtiums are in [illegible]

unique lei, made from sprigs of Hawaiian pine which are lightly bound to a string of plastic rose lights and a few pompon chrysanthemums decorate a dessert tray. The dessert is a fruit-stuffed pineapple, topped with whipped cream and strawberries.

1961 bound collection of issues of *Pause for Living,* from Spring, 1959, to Autumn, 1961

Reprint of two articles on collecting Coca-Cola memorabilia written by Cecil Munsey in 1967. The reprint was made especially for The Coca-Cola Company and was distributed by them.

Reprint of an article that appeared in the February 9, 1969, issue of *West* magazine, which is the Sunday supplement of the Los Angeles *Times*

1969 issue of *Momentum*, a magazine produced by The Coca-Cola Company

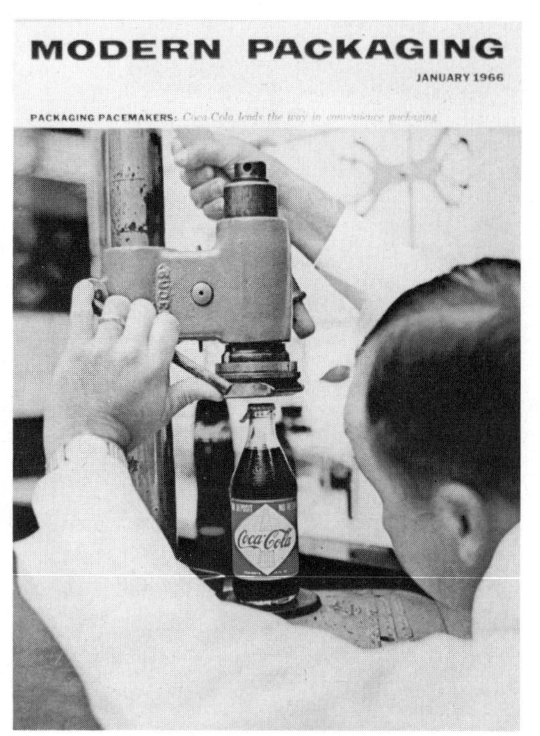

January, 1966, issue of *Modern Packaging*, which features an article on no-deposit bottles

October, 1966, issue of *Dun's Review*, which features an article entitled "Greatest Franchise of All"

January/February, 1971, issue of *The Western Collector*, which features an article by Cecil Munsey on collecting memorabilia of Coca-Cola

CHAPTER 40

UNAUTHORIZED AND AUTHORIZED INDIVIDUAL BOTTLER ADVERTISING ITEMS

The relationship between The Coca-Cola Company and its bottlers has always allowed an individual bottler to create and produce his own advertising items. The original contract Asa Candler made with B. F. Thomas and J. B. Whitehead contained a clause that promised that the company would help bottlers with advertising. The help, or "advertising allowance," was ten cents of advertising money for each gallon of syrup bought from the company by bottlers. A later amendment reduced the sum to five cents, and today advertising is generally split fifty-fifty between the bottler and The Coca-Cola Company.

As mentioned above, individual bottlers were offered financial help with advertising. In certain cases, where bottlers wanted to expend additional funds for advertising in their respective territories, they were encouraged to do so. Soon, however, the company realized that to encourage a bottler to advertise beyond his allowance also encouraged him to create his own materials. The results soon amounted to a fragmentation of advertising, with much poorly written newspaper and magazine copy being produced by bottlers. Although poorly written copy was discouraged by The Coca-Cola Company, bottler-produced items, which were considered in poor taste, worried the company most. The unauthorized items produced over the years have special significance in collecting circles; they were generally produced in limited quantities, and many were in "poor taste" for the times. Some of the most valued collectors' items related to Coca-Cola are the unauthorized items of "questionable" taste produced in the early years of the twentieth century.

In 1910 The Coca-Cola Company realized that it must stop, as much as possible, the practice of individual bottlers producing their own advertising copy and items. Legally the company could not forbid an individual bottler to create his own advertising materials, so the firm began to produce an increasing amount of standardized material for bottler use. In addition, the company produced a steady stream of written material explaining why a bottler should use only company-approved materials. Almost everything offered to bottlers by The Coca-Cola Company was offered on a cost-plus-nothing basis, or in some cases even free, to encourage use of company-approved and standardized material.

Progress in reducing the production and use of individual bottler items for advertising was slow but effective. While bottlers still retain the right to produce their own advertising materials, few do it, because the parent company does almost everything it can to meet the needs of its bottlers by producing a wide variety of materials and sharing costs. Almost without exception, any bottler wishing to produce individualized materials today will seek the guidance of The Coca-Cola Company.

As discussed in the chapters dealing with bottles and bottling pioneers, the original bottling contract gave B. F. Thomas and J. B. Whitehead exclusive bottling rights for almost the entire country. It should also be recalled that after Whitehead split his half of the contract with J. T. Lupton, the country was divided into geographical territories. The largest of the Whitehead-Lupton territories was the Western Coca-Cola Bottling Company, which originally comprised Michigan, Wisconsin, Minnesota, Iowa, Missouri, North and South Dakota, Nebraska, Montana, Idaho, Wyoming, Utah, Colorado, Nevada, Arizona, and practically all of Illinois, Kansas, and New Mexico.

The Western Coca-Cola Bottling Company, under its chief officer, S. L. Whitten, produced a great number of controversial items. The Western Coca-Cola Bottling Company was chartered as an Illinois Corporation on October 2, 1905, and maintained its headquarters in Chicago until it was sold to The Coca-Cola Company on December 12, 1935.

The Western Coca-Cola Bottling Company was a "parent bottler," and as such this firm supplied syrup and advertising materials to the individual bottlers within its territory. Many of the advertising items found are identified with "Western Coca-Cola Bottling Company" and a city within the territory. This means that the identified items originated in the company's headquarters in Chicago but were localized by an individual bottler within Western's territory. Although Western Coca-Cola Bottling Company was large in acreage, in the early years it did not have bottlers in all of its designated territory; for that reason collectors should not expect to find advertising items of this firm widely distributed. Most items are found in and around Chicago.

Throughout the collecting world there has been confusion about the Western Coca-Cola Bottling Company and its controversial advertising materials. The prolific firm is often called "a small Mid-Western bottler," which, as already shown, is not the case. There are many stories about how The Coca-Cola Company punished the rebel in its midst. In fact there was no punishing, and the firm was not really considered a rebel. The Coca-Cola Company did not control Western and other bottlers to any great extent in the early years of the century when the controversial items were used. It can be noted, however, that the Western Coca-Cola Bottling Company very clearly illustrated to The Coca-Cola Company (in Atlanta) the need for standardization in advertising. Once inspired, the Atlanta group worked, and are still working, to achieve that end.

The Western Coca-Cola Bottling Company produced most of its controversial advertising materials between 1905 and 1912; after that it began to heed suggestions of The Coca-Cola Company and bring its advertising more in line with the standardized materials issued from Atlanta. A cursory examination of the controversial items of the Western Coca-Cola Bottling Company will quickly reveal why collectors have long been fascinated with this romantic firm and why collectors pay hundreds of dollars for the firm's old advertising items.

One of the first items to raise the eyebrows of company officials in Atlanta was a poster, used in 1905, jointly advertising Coca-Cola and Goldelle Ginger Ale. It had long been suggested that Coca-Cola be advertised alone. Western was not, however, the only firm that did not abide by the Atlanta suggestion; Goldelle Ginger Ale was a popular brand during the early 1900's, and bottlers in many parts of the country produced it and advertised it along with Coca-Cola. Even today in some small communities Coca-Cola bottlers produce beverages made by competitors.

In 1906 the Western Coca-Cola Bottling Company produced a blotter showing a pretty girl in pigtails carrying a tray of glasses filled with Coca-Cola. The glasses are not of the recommended shape.

Between 1905 and 1912 the Western Coca-Cola Bottling Company had produced and distributed a series of metal Vienna art plates. The plates bear a 1905 patent date but were used by Western until 1912. The metal plates came in very ornate frames and were packed in a wooden, velvet-lined case. The only identification is on the back of the plate: "Western Coca-Cola Bottling Co., Chicago." There are well over a dozen of the ten-inch metal plates, each one with a picture of a different girl. The plates are very colorful and very much sought by antiques collectors. The value of the plates is enhanced if they are acquired with the frame and original wooden case.

Like many of the advertising materials used by the Western Bottling Company, the Vienna art plates were made by an organization specializing in advertising items. Such items are generally unmarked when purchased by the firm wishing to use them. The purchasing firm (in this case the Western Coca-Cola Bottling Company) adds its message and then uses the item(s) to promote its product. Because of this, only Vienna art plates stamped "Western Coca-Cola Bottling Co., Chicago" can be considered true Coca-Cola items.

The most famous of the Vienna art plates used by Western to promote Coca-Cola is one featuring a girl with long hair, sitting, facing to the right of the plate, and bare to the waist. Most of the women featured on the art plates are shown in from-the-shoulder-up poses. The reason the "topless" plate is so well known, however, is not because of the seminude subject but because the illustration was selected by the executives of Western Coca-Cola Bottling Company to be reproduced on a metal serving tray which was widely circulated. The tray, $12^1/_4$ inches in diameter, was issued in 1908 and was an immediate success. Officials of The Coca-Cola Company in Atlanta were upset by the issuance of this tray but limited their reaction to a letter of disapproval. The tray, which was obviously aimed at the bar trade, proclaimed, "Drink Coca-Cola High Balls," "Drink Coca-Cola Gin Rickies," "Drink Coca-Cola," and "Whenever Ginger Ale, Seltzer or Soda is Good, Coca-Cola is Better—Try It."

The "topless" tray was not the Western Coca-Cola Bottling Company's first truly controversial item. In 1907 they had produced a number of eight-by-ten-inch full-color posters titled "Satisfied." The picture was copyrighted in 1906 by S. L. Whitten, and the posters were made for Western by the Whitehead & Hoag Co., of Newark, New Jersey. Pictured on this fascinating poster is a doll-like young woman with the upper portion of her legs exposed, reclining on a sofa with her feet resting on a tiger rug. On a table next to the sofa are two paper-labeled Coca-Cola bottles—one empty and one full—and a slice of lemon. The girl also holds a half-emptied glass. "Satisfied" has recently been copied and reproduced, and the reproduction is discussed and shown in Chapter 41.

Another very interesting piece of advertising used by the Western Coca-Cola Bottling Company is a folded trade card. Trade cards are about the size of a postcard and were popular in advertising from the 1880's until about 1915. Folded, the trade card pictures a young woman in a bathtub. Only the woman's shoulders and knees are exposed. The bathtub folds down and exposes not the nude girl to be expected but a young waitress in a low-cut blouse serving two bald-headed men Coca-Cola. The tops of the bald heads appear to be the girl's knees when the card is closed.

Like the Vienna art plates, the trade card was a standard advertising item modified by Western Coca-Cola Bottling Company to suit their needs. On the closed portion of the card is printed an appropriate sentence: "Appearances are sometimes deceiving but Coca-Cola can always be relied on as nourishing, refreshing, and exhilarating." On the top portion of the card, which is exposed when the card is closed or open, the slogan "Drink Coca-Cola" is imprinted. At the base of the opened card is the sentence "When thirsty, tired or headachey, or after a night out try a Coca-Cola High Ball. It hits the spot." Even the back of the card is covered with a long message about Coca-Cola.

Along with the long line of advertising items produced by the Western Coca-Cola Bottling Company are others produced by individual bottlers throughout the country. Most individual bottler items are not as controversial as were those produced for Western. For the most part, individual bottler items can be considered authorized or at least sanctioned by The Coca-Cola Company. The Chicago-based parent bottler, Western Coca-Cola Bottling Company, is the exception, and many of their advertising items were obviously unauthorized.

1905 poster produced for the Western Coca-Cola Bottling Company. Advertising any other product with Coke was discouraged by The Coca-Cola Company. The bottles were drawn out of proportion. Goldelle Ginger Ale was popular, and numerous bottlers produced it as well as Coca-Cola. (*Archives, The Coca-Cola Company, Atlanta, Georgia*)

1906 blotter used by the Western Coca-Cola Bottling Company. The glasses shown do not conform to the shape authorized for Coca-Cola at the time. (*Archives, The Coca-Cola Company, Atlanta, Georgia*)

Ten-inch metal Vienna art plate used by the Western Coca-Cola Bottling Company from 1905 to 1912. There were a dozen in the series. These plates were issued in ornate frames and velvet-lined boxes. "Western Coca-Cola Bottling Co., Chicago" is stamped on the back. (*Dr. Burton Spiller, Rochester, New York; photograph by Richard P. Daley*)

Vienna art plate (*Archives, The Coca-Cola Company, Atlanta, Georgia*)

Vienna art plates (*Archives, The Coca-Cola Company, Atlanta, Georgia*)

The most famous Vienna art plate (*above*) issued by the Western Coca-Cola Bottling Company. This plate inspired a matching serving tray (*right*) issued in 1908. Both plate and tray are among the most popular of collectibles. (*Archives, The Coca-Cola Company, Atlanta, Georgia*)

Poster entitled "Satisfied" issued by the Western Coca-Cola Bottling Company. Most officials of The Coca-Cola Company in Atlanta felt this to be in bad taste, but they lacked the power to stop its use. (*Jim Cope, Orange, Texas*)

Standard trade card. *Top:* obverse, folded. *Bottom:* obverse, unfolded.

Coupon used by the San Antonio, Texas, Coca-Cola Bottling Company in 1920 (*Archives, The Coca-Cola Company, Atlanta, Georgia*)

Key chains issued by the Coca-Cola Bottling Company of Los Angeles, California. Left: 1955. Right: 1956.

Glass, 5½ inches tall, produced in 1958 to honor John M. Jones, president of the San Diego Bottling Company on his thirty-fifth anniversary as president

1968 gold key chain issued to commemorate the thirtieth anniversary of the Curacao Beverage Bottling Company

Glass made in 1964 to commemorate the opening of a new bottling plant in San Diego. The glass is clear, with gold design and lettering.

CHAPTER 41

QUESTIONABLE ITEMS

In the past few years, as the artifacts of The Coca-Cola Company have become more valuable as collectors' items and as the search for nostalgia has become a popular diversion, more and more items claiming authentic heritage have appeared on the market. By far the vast majority are truly artifacts of The Coca-Cola Company and should be treated as such. There are, however, a number of items that appear to be authentic but are not. Some of these questionable items are merely an attempt by various manufacturers to produce articles for a nostalgia-conscious market. Such items are most often manufactured with the full knowledge and approval of The Coca-Cola Company, which is proud that its product is so much a part of the American scene and that the general public wants to purchase objects bearing the Coca-Cola trademark. Other questionable items seem to be direct, deceitful attempts to feed a fast-growing collector market.

As is true in most situations where a supply is exceeded by a demand, attempts to increase the supply are sometimes made. In collecting, this is a sensitive situation; the vast majority of collectors seek authentic collectibles and shun specialty, faked, and/or reproduced items. There are a few collectors, however, who will consider questionable objects collectible, for one reason or another, and include them in their collections. Faked and/or reproduced objects sometimes become valued collectors' items. If such items are of good quality and the true story of their origin is well known, collectors will consider them, eventually, as collectible pieces. Prices for such items seldom reach the level of their original and authentic counterparts. In some cases where original items are few in number, collectors who feel that they might never be able to own an original piece will settle for a known fake or reproduced item if they can obtain it for a fair price.

It would be presumptuous to make absolute statements regarding the authenticity of any item of a questionable nature because the records of The Coca-Cola Company are incomplete. As a result there will probably never be either a complete or an accurate list of the items used by The Coca-Cola Company over the years. It does not seem presumptuous, however, to label an item as questionable and offer reasons for the labeling; such will be the format for the specific illustrations and their discussions. If the reader should find the reasons offered illogical and/or unfair, it would be wise not to consider the item(s) as questionable. Basically the illustrations that follow are divided into two categories: (1) those items made to appear old and/or authentic and (2) those items of a specialty nature made with The Coca-Cola Company's approval for a nostalgia-oriented market but never actually used *by* the company.

This full-color illustration, 14 by 20 inches, appears to be a reproduction of a small poster, 8 by 10 inches, used in 1907 by the Western Coca-Cola Bottling Company. The small poster did not carry the slogan "Drink Coca-Cola High Balls and Gin Rickeys" in the upper left corner but was titled "Satisfied" at the base on the brown border. This poster is considered questionable because the illustration, according to experts, is an enlarged photograph mounted on cardboard. An original would most likely be lithographed.

A careful inspection of this clock has revealed that under the face advertising Coca-Cola there is another face without advertising. In addition, Coca-Cola is not known to have been advertised on a Regulator clock of this shape.

Clock faces that have been reproduced in recent years. They are exact replicas of originals, reproduced by special permission from The Coca-Cola Company. These clock faces were produced on off-white and yellow-aged card stock.

This gold decal, 9¼ inches square, has been reproduced and sold to people restoring clocks. Such decals were sometimes applied to the glass in the bottom section of wooden wall clocks advertising Coca-Cola.

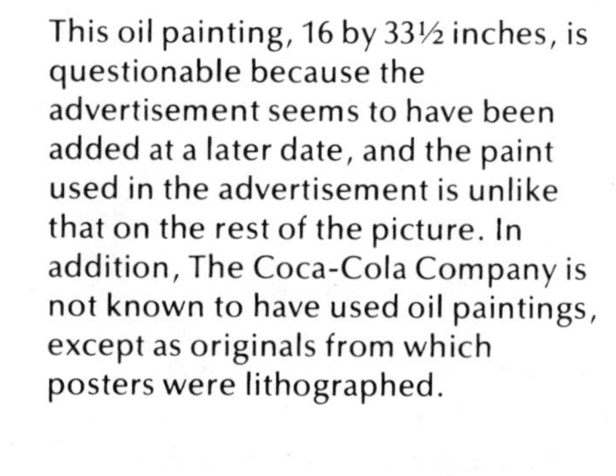

This oil painting, 16 by 33½ inches, is questionable because the advertisement seems to have been added at a later date, and the paint used in the advertisement is unlike that on the rest of the picture. In addition, The Coca-Cola Company is not known to have used oil paintings, except as originals from which posters were lithographed.

This poster (*left*), 14 by 21 inches, is considered questionable because the advertisement for Coca-Cola is not part of the original lithography and appears to have been added at a later date by a silk-screening process. Analysis of the advertisement ink (*below*) suggests that it is of a type used after World War II, whereas the poster itself dates from 1904.

Ceramic mug produced for the pop-art market. It is questionable as a collector's item because it was not produced for The Coca-Cola Company.

Drink coasters produced for the pop-art market

Glass produced for the pop-art market

Ceramic mug

Old-Fashioned Coke® Glasses

☐ They echo other times when every drugstore had a soda fountain where you stopped after school for a cherry Coke! It's delightful nostalgia to have these crystal-clear copies that serve everything from breakfast juices to summer coolers and cocktails. Both the six- and ten-ounce glasses fit in the assorted-color metal holders. All in sets of six.

0802-1—Six-ounce .. **1** set, **$2.50**
0803-1—Ten-ounce .. **1** set, **$3.29**
0804-1—Coke Holders, **1** set, **$3.49**

An advertisement for "Coke Glasses" and "Coke Holders." They were not produced for The Coca-Cola Company.

Advertisement for "Contemporary Waste Cans"

1971 newspaper advertisement promoting "Tiffany Lamps." The lamp is a rather crude reproduction of the original stained-glass lamp of the early 1900's. The firm selling the lamps left out the hyphen in the trademark. The Coca-Cola Company dislikes such misuses of its trademark.

CHAPTER 42

ET CETERA

The Coca-Cola Company has used thousands of advertising items to promote its products. There seems to be no absolute method of categorizing the advertising artifacts involved. The advertising industry is based to a great extent on imagination, and historically The Coca-Cola Company has proceeded with vigor, using almost every idea presented by its advertising consultants. From 1886, when such items as oilcloth signs were used to advertise Coca-Cola, to 1971, when 350,000 red and white hip-hugger pants with the Coca-Cola trademark and the slogan "It's the Real Thing" were used, the company can boast one of the most successful advertising records in history. The challenge for collectors is great, and the assembling of a collection is bound to be thoroughly enjoyable.

Celluloid-covered note pad issued in 1902

1902 celluloid postage-stamp carrier

1905 sheet music for "Ben Bolt." Other songs printed by The Coca-Cola Company were "Juanita," "The Palms," "Old Folks at Home," "Lead Kindly Light," "My Old Kentucky Home," "Nearer, My God, to Thee," and "Rock Me to Sleep, Mother."

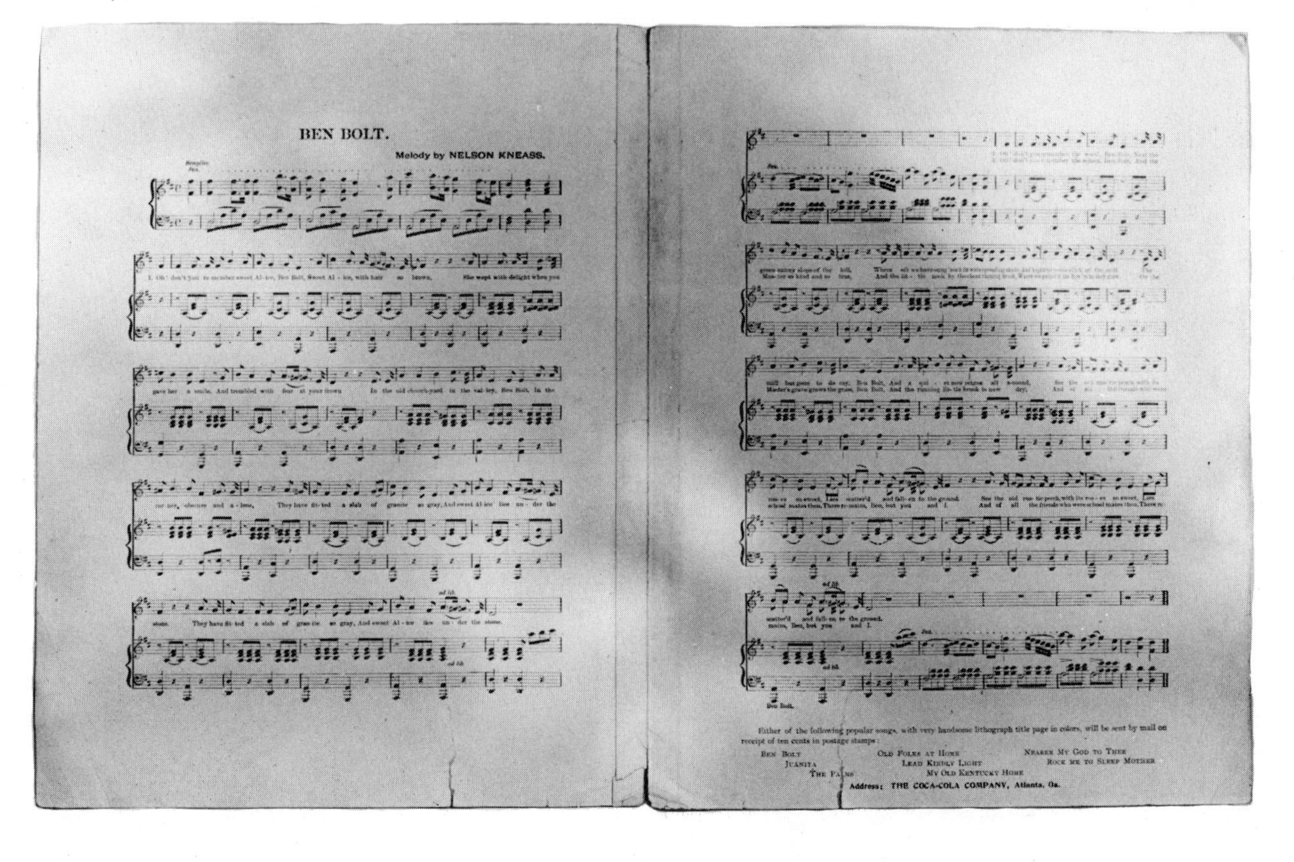

1906 brown leather postage-stamp holder with stamped gold lettering

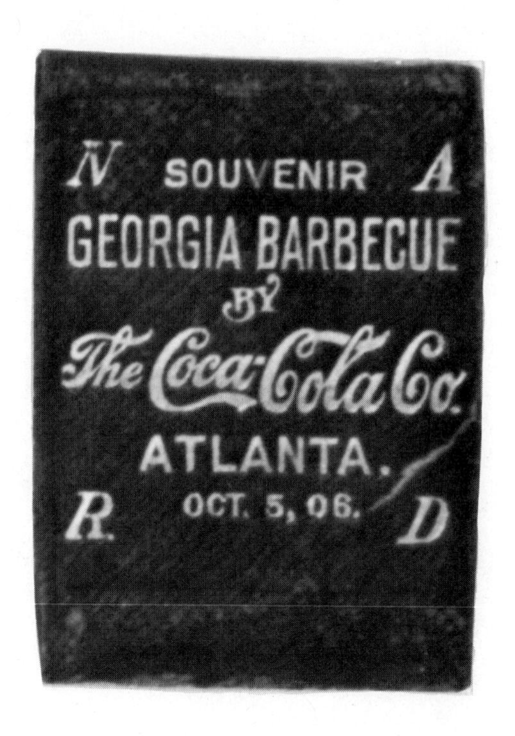

Brown leather coin purse issued in 1910

1911 fan

At annual bottlers' conventions identification badges are given to participants. These are early badges. Left to right: 1912, 1915, 1916, and 1917.

1918 black leather wallet

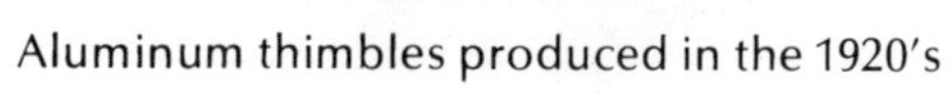
Aluminum thimbles produced in the 1920's

1925 fan

1925 needle case

1932 Olympic record indicator. Information is revealed by rotating the inner piece.

1932 bottle bags designed to fit a Coke bottle and protect the drinker from water dripping from the freshly iced bottle. Electric coolers eliminated the need for bottle bags.

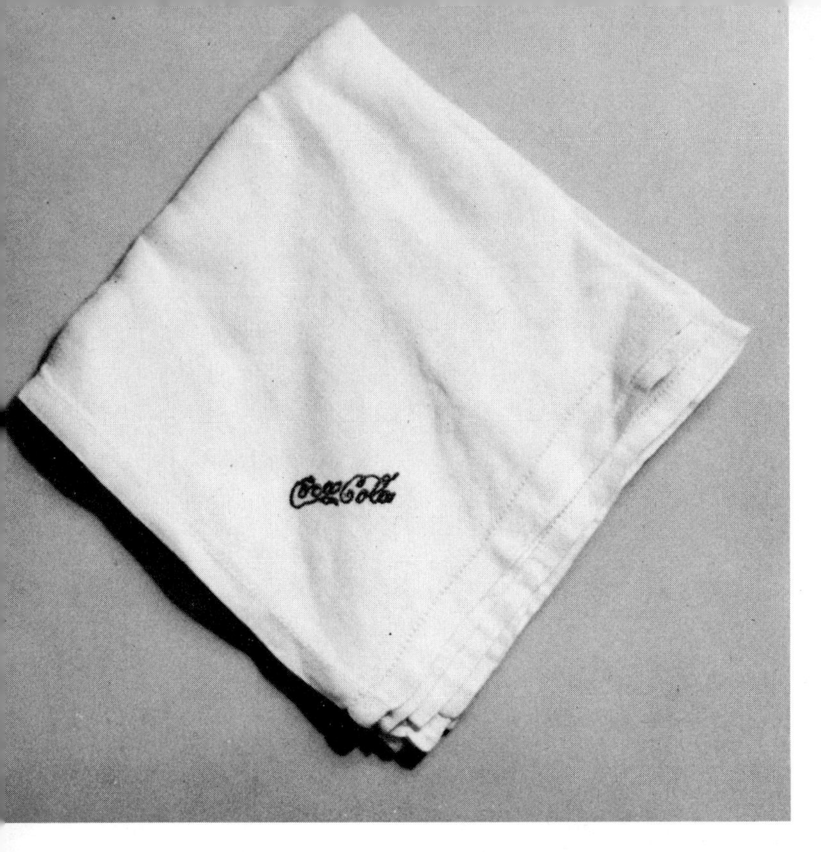

1936 handkerchief

1940 book cover made by the Holden Book Cover Company, of Springfield, Massachusetts

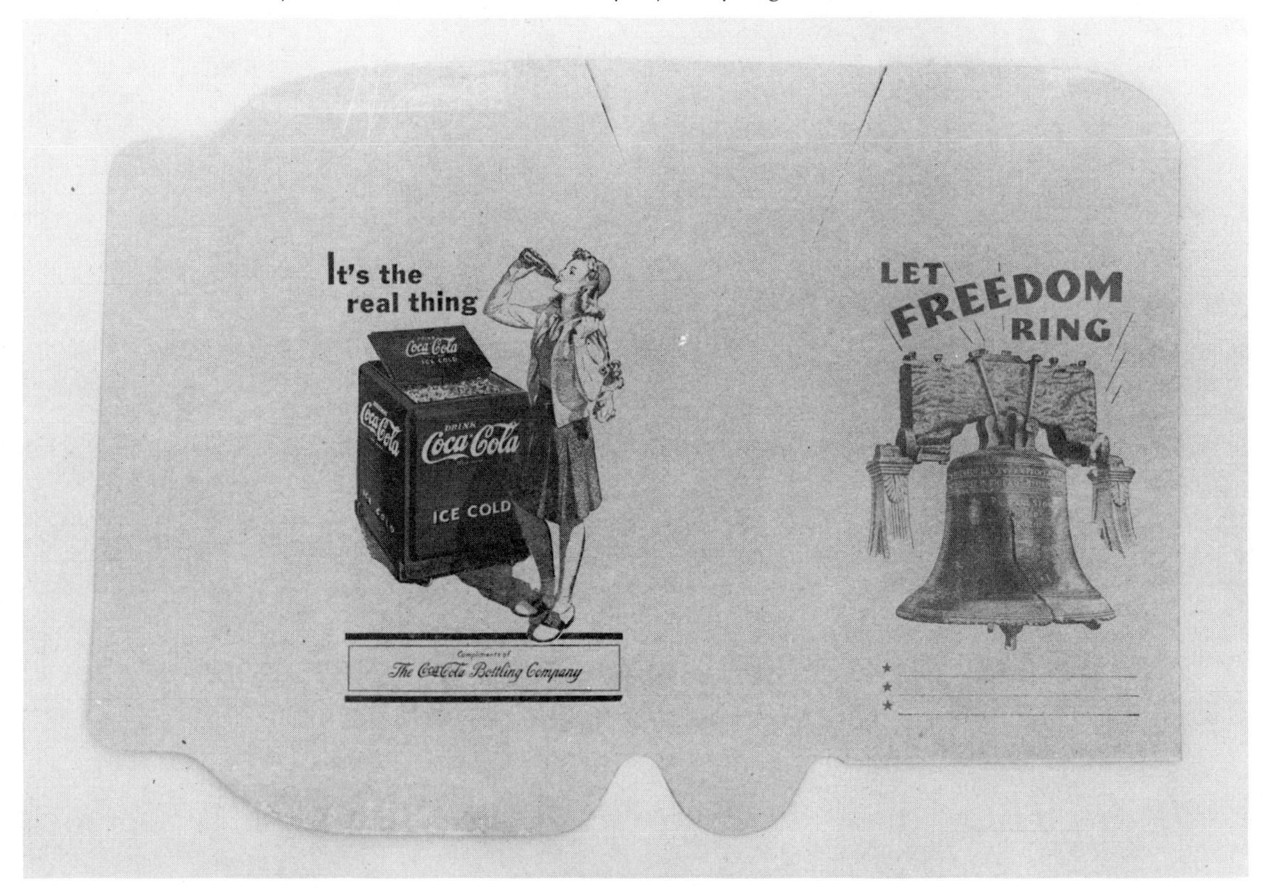

During the 1940's The Coca-Cola Company provided typing awards for high-school youngsters. Sometimes company officials ran the contests. (*Jani Gardner, Cincinnati, Ohio*)

During World War II this brown plastic sewing kit was made for soldiers.

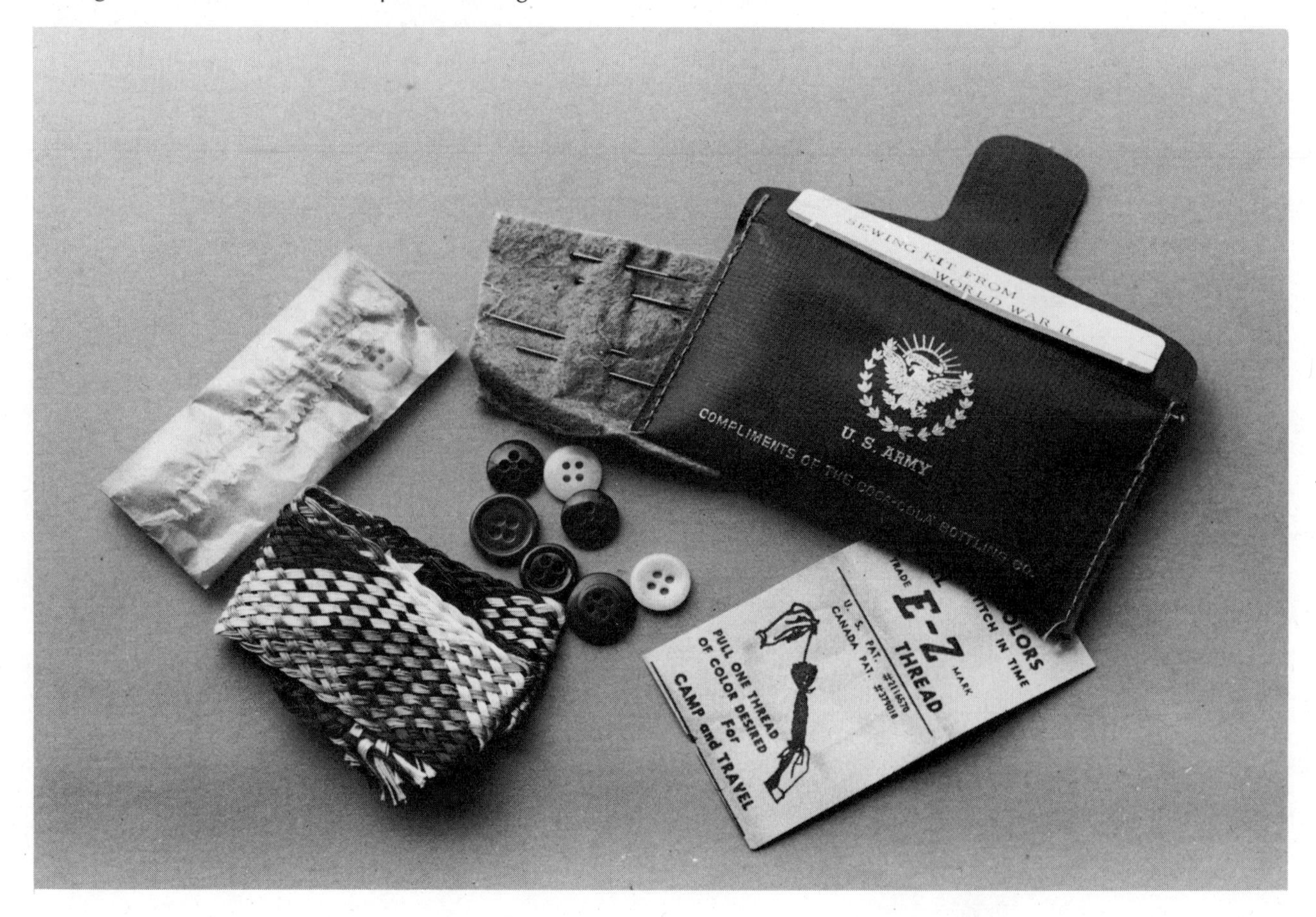

1950's handkerchief advertising Coke and the Kit Carson TV show (*Dr. Burton Spiller, Rochester, New York; photograph by Richard P. Daley*)

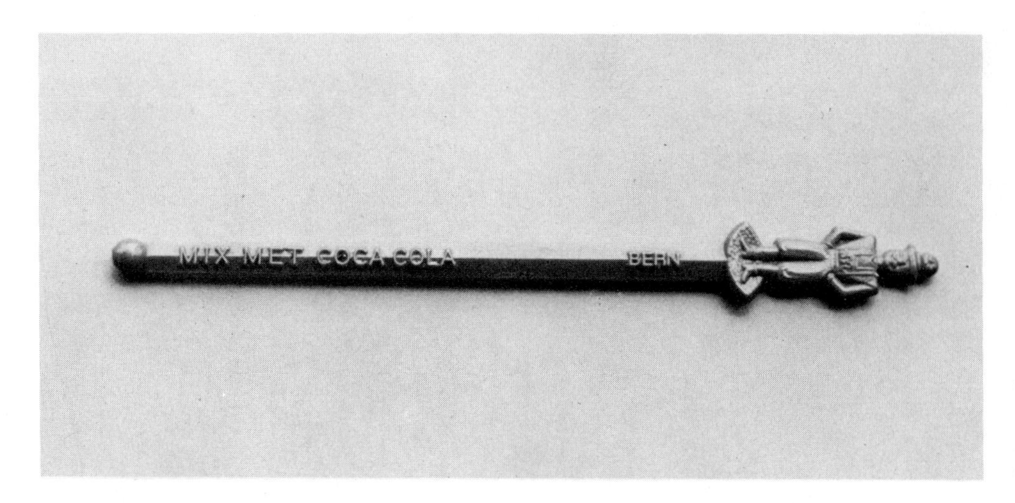

6½-inch long red plastic swizzle stick made to promote Coca-Cola as a drink mixer

Trade tokens made in Mexico. Such tokens were necessary because the first automatic coin-operated vending machines were American-made, accepting only U.S. coins.

In the late 1950's keys became promotional items.

1960's red plastic telephone dialer

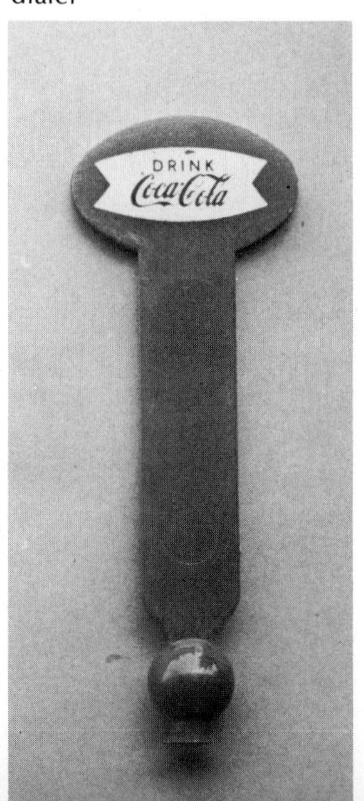

Mid-1960's clothes brush. The brush collapses into the 5½-inch handle for traveling.

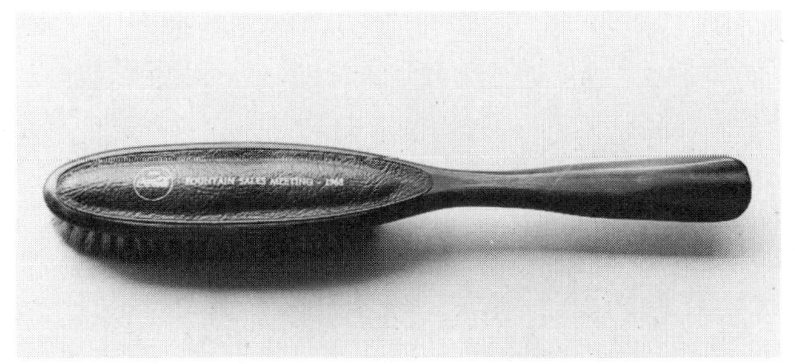

1968 imitation black leather clothes brush with wire bristles, issued to bottlers at fountain sales meeting

1960's black plastic note-pad holder

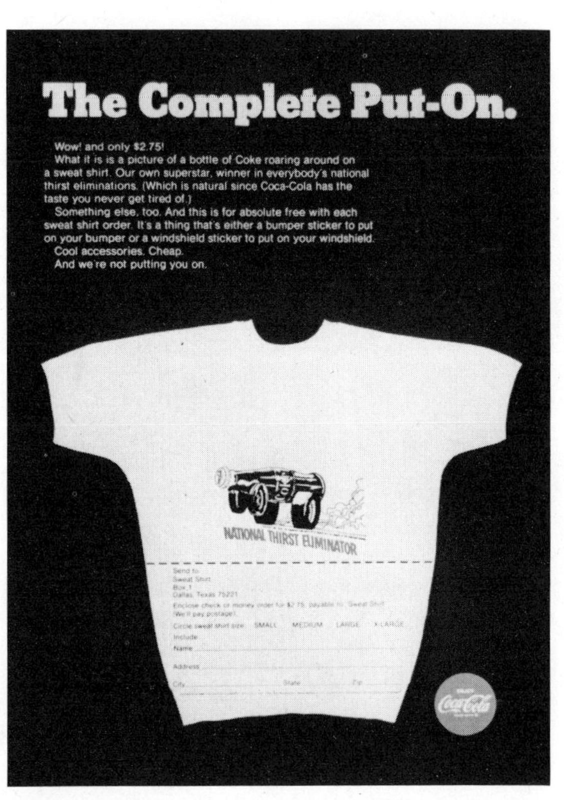

1969 magazine advertisement for sweat shirt and bumper sticker

APPENDIX A

COCA-COLA BOTTLERS AND THE DATES THEY STARTED IN BUSINESS

The following is an alphabetical listing by state and city of most bottlers of Coca-Cola. The list is incomplete because it was taken both from records of those bottlers who were in business long enough to celebrate their fiftieth anniversary and from other sources. The bottlers not listed would be those who did not stay in business very long. In addition to being alphabetized, the list states the year in which each bottler started in business.

Collectors and historians will find this list valuable in placing tentative dates on the memorabilia of The Coca-Cola Company identified by an individual bottler marking. Although the list will provide only the date the firm started in business, such information will narrow dating down to the earliest possible year a specific firm could have used the object in question. Other information that will assist in dating is to be found throughout this book.

ALABAMA

Aliceville 1910
(Aliceville Coca-Cola Bottling Company)
Andalusia 1909
(Andalusia Coca-Cola Bottling Company)
Anniston 1903
(Alabama Coca-Cola Bottling Company)
Birmingham 1902
(The Birmingham Coca-Cola Bottling Company)
Decatur 1909
(Decatur Coca-Cola Bottling Company)
Demopolis 1915
(Demopolis Coca-Cola Bottling Company)
Dothan 1906
(Dothan Coca-Cola Bottling Company)
Fayette 1910
(Fayette Coca-Cola Bottling Company)
Florence 1908
(Florence Coca-Cola Bottling Company)
Frisco City 1908
(Coca-Cola Bottling Company of Frisco City)
Gadsden 1903
(Alabama Coca-Cola Bottling Company)

Gordo 1911
(Coca-Cola Bottling Company of Gordo)
Huntsville 1902
(Huntsville Coca-Cola Bottling Company)
Jasper 1907
(Jasper Coca-Cola Bottling Company)
Mobile 1902
(Coca-Cola Bottling Company, Inc.)
Montgomery 1903
(Montgomery Coca-Cola Bottling Company)
Opelika 1902
(Opelika Coca-Cola Bottling Company, Inc.)
Russellville 1911
(Coca-Cola Bottling Company)
Scottsboro 1915
(Scottsboro Coca-Cola Bottling Company)
Selma 1903
(Coca-Cola Bottling Company of Selma)
Talladega 1904
(Coca-Cola Bottling Company)
Tuscaloosa 1903
(Tuscaloosa Coca-Cola Bottling Company)
West Blockton 1913
(Coca-Cola Bottling Company)

ALASKA

Anchorage 1947
(Anchorage Cold Storage Company, Inc.)
Fairbanks 1947
(Alaska Beverage Company)
Juneau 1947
(Juneau Cold Storage Company, Inc.)
Ketchikan 1947
(Ketchikan Soda Works)
Sitka 1958
(Sitka Bottling Company)

ARIZONA

Ajo 1916
(Ajo Coca-Cola Bottling Company)
Clifton 1903
(Greenlee Coca-Cola Bottling Company)
Douglas 1912
(Coca-Cola Bottling Company of Douglas)
Phoenix 1905
(Phoenix Coca-Cola Bottling Company)
Prescott 1916
(Coca-Cola Bottling Company of Prescott)
Safford 1910
(Safford Coca-Cola Bottling Company)
Tucson 1906
(Coca-Cola Bottling Company of Tucson, Inc.)
Yuma 1910
(Coca-Cola Bottling Company of Yuma)

ARKANSAS

Batesville 1909
(Coca-Cola Bottling Company of Arkansas)
Blytheville 1906
(Coca-Cola Bottling Company of Blytheville)
Camden 1910
(Coca-Cola Bottling Company of Southwest Arkansas)
Fayetteville 1906
(Fayetteville Coca-Cola Bottling Company)
Fort Smith 1903
(The Coca-Cola Bottling Company of Fort Smith)
Harrison 1913
(Coca-Cola Bottling Company of Arkansas)
Hope 1909
(Hope Coca-Cola Bottling Company)
Hot Springs 1908
(Coca-Cola Bottling Company of Hot Springs)
Jonesboro 1903
(Jonesboro Coca-Cola Bottling Company)
Little Rock 1903
(Coca-Cola Bottling Company of Arkansas)
Magnolia 1908
(Magnolia Ice & Coca-Cola Bottling Company, Inc.)
Nashville 1911
(Coca-Cola Bottling Company of Nashville)
Newport 1906
(Coca-Cola Bottling Company of Arkansas)
Pine Bluff 1911
(Coca-Cola Bottling Company of Southeast Arkansas)
Rogers 1912
(Rogers Coca-Cola Bottling Company)

CALIFORNIA

Bakersfield 1910
(Coca-Cola Bottling Corporation of Bakersfield)
Bishop 1917
(Inyo-Mono Coca-Cola Bottling Company)
Blythe 1917
(Coca-Cola Bottling Company of Blythe)
El Centro 1910
(Coca-Cola Bottling Company of El Centro)
Eureka 1911
(The Coca-Cola Bottling Company of California)
Fresno 1905
(Coca-Cola Bottling Company of Fresno)
Los Angeles 1902
(Coca-Cola Bottling Company of Los Angeles)
Modesto 1911
(Coca-Cola Bottling Company of Turlock, Ltd.)
Monterey 1911
(Coca-Cola Bottling Company of Monterey)
Oakland 1908
(The Coca-Cola Bottling Company of California)
Placerville 1911
(Placerville Coca-Cola Bottling Company)

Redding 1910
(Coca-Cola Bottling Company of Redding)
Sacramento 1909
(Coca-Cola Bottling Company of Sacramento)
San Bernardino 1911
(Coca-Cola Bottling Company of San Bernardino & Riverside)
San Diego 1910
(Coca-Cola Bottling Company of San Diego)
San Francisco 1905
(The Coca-Cola Bottling Company of California)
San Jose 1912
(Coca-Cola Bottling Company of San Jose)
Santa Barbara 1910
(Coca-Cola Bottling Company of Santa Barbara)
Santa Maria 1916
(Coca-Cola Bottling Company of Santa Maria)
Santa Rosa 1914
(Coca-Cola Bottling Company of Santa Rosa)
Stockton 1911
(Coca-Cola Bottling Company of Stockton, Ltd.)
Ventura 1911
(Coca-Cola Bottling Company of Ventura)

COLORADO

Alamosa 1911
(Alamosa Coca-Cola Bottling Company)
Colorado Springs 1910
(Coca-Cola Bottling Company)
Delta 1910
(Delta Coca-Cola Bottling Company)
Denver 1902
(Denver Coca-Cola Bottling Company)
Durango 1915
(Durango Coca-Cola Bottling Company)
Glenwood Springs 1917
(Coca-Cola Bottling Company of Glenwood Springs)
Grand Junction 1910
(Grand Junction Coca-Cola Bottling Company)
Greeley 1916
(The Greeley Coca-Cola Bottling Company)
Salida 1910
(The Salida Coca-Cola Bottling Company)
Sterling 1910
(Sterling Coca-Cola Bottling Company)
Trinidad 1910
(Trinidad Coca-Cola Bottling Company)

CONNECTICUT

Bridgeport 1912
(Coca-Cola Bottling Company of New York, Inc.)
East Hartford 1912
(Coca-Cola Bottling Company of Hartford)
Middletown 1912
(Coca-Cola Bottling Company of Middletown, Inc.)
New Haven 1912
(Coca-Cola Bottling Company of New Haven, Inc.)

DELAWARE

Dover 1916
(Dover Coca-Cola Bottling Company)
Wilmington 1905
(Delaware Coca-Cola Bottling Company)

DISTRICT OF COLUMBIA

Washington 1905
(Washington Coca-Cola Bottling Works, Inc.)

FLORIDA

Apalachicola 1907
(Apalachicola Coca-Cola Bottling Company)
Arcadia 1909
(Arcadia Coca-Cola Bottling Company)
Avon Park 1914
(Highlands Coca-Cola Bottling Company)
Bradenton 1908
(Bradenton Coca-Cola Bottling Company)
Cocoa 1913
(Brevard Coca-Cola Bottling Company)
Dade City 1911
(Dade City Coca-Cola Bottling Company)
Daytona Beach 1908
(Daytona Coca-Cola Bottling Company)
DeLand 1912
(DeLand Coca-Cola Bottling Company)
Fort Lauderdale 1914
(Fort Lauderdale Coca-Cola Bottling Company)
Fort Myers 1911
(Fort Myers Coca-Cola Bottling Company)
Fort Pierce 1914
(Fort Pierce Coca-Cola Bottling Company)
Gainesville 1908
(Gainesville Coca-Cola Bottling Company)
Green Cove Springs 1915
(Green Cove Coca-Cola Bottling Company)
Inverness 1907
(Inverness Coca-Cola Bottling Company)
Jacksonville 1902
(Jacksonville Coca-Cola Bottling Company)
Key West 1903
(Key West Coca-Cola Bottling Company)
Kissimmee 1909
(Kissimmee Coca-Cola Bottling Company)
Lake City 1907
(Lake City Coca-Cola Bottling Company)
Lakeland 1908
(Lakeland Coca-Cola Bottling Company)
Leesburg 1908
(Leesburg Coca-Cola Bottling Company)
Live Oak 1907
(Live Oak Coca-Cola Bottling Company)

Madison 1907
(Madison Coca-Cola Bottling Company)
Marianna 1907
(Marianna Coca-Cola Bottling Company)
Miami 1907
(Miami Coca-Cola Bottling Company)
Monticello 1907
(Monticello Coca-Cola Bottling Company)
Ocala 1908
(Ocala Coca-Cola Bottling Company)
Orlando 1910
(Orlando Coca-Cola Bottling Company)
Palatka 1908
(Palatka Coca-Cola Bottling Company)
Panama City 1907
(Panama City Coca-Cola Bottling Company)
Pensacola 1903
(Hygeia Coca-Cola Bottling Company)
Perry 1907
(Perry Coca-Cola Bottling Company)
Plant City 1910
(Plant City Coca-Cola Bottling Company, Inc.)
Punta Gorda 1915
(Punta Gorda Coca-Cola Bottling Company)
Quincy 1907
(Quincy Coca-Cola Bottling Company)
Saint Petersburg 1909
(Saint Petersburg Coca-Cola Bottling Company)
Sanford 1908
(Sanford Coca-Cola Bottling Company)
Tallahassee 1905
(Tallahassee Coca-Cola Bottling Company)
Tampa 1902
(Tampa Coca-Cola Bottling Company)
Tarpon Springs 1913
(Tarpon Springs Coca-Cola Bottling Company)
Wauchula 1910
(Wauchula Coca-Cola Bottling Company, Inc.)
West Palm Beach 1911
(Palm Beach Coca-Cola Bottling Company)
Winter Haven 1909
(Ridge Coca-Cola Bottling Company)

GEORGIA

Albany 1903
(The Albany Coca-Cola Bottling Company)
Americus 1905
(Americus Coca-Cola Bottling Company)
Athens 1903
(The Athens Coca-Cola Bottling Company)
Atlanta 1900
(The Atlanta Coca-Cola Bottling Company)
Augusta 1902
(Augusta Coca-Cola Bottling Company)
Bainbridge 1904
(Bainbridge Coca-Cola Bottling Company)
Brunswick 1903
(Brunswick Coca-Cola Bottling Company)
Carrollton 1906
(Carrollton Coca-Cola Bottling Company)
Cartersville 1906
(Cartersville Coca-Cola Bottling Company)
Claxton 1916
(Claxton Coca-Cola Bottling Company)
Columbus 1902
(Columbus Coca-Cola Bottling Company)
Conyers 1909
(Conyers Coca-Cola Bottling Company)
Cordele 1907
(Cordele Coca-Cola Bottling Company)
Cornelia 1907
(Cornelia Coca-Cola Bottling Company)
Cuthbert 1906
(Cuthbert Coca-Cola Bottling Company)
Dalton 1906
(Dalton Coca-Cola Bottling Company)
Douglas 1912
(The Douglas Coca-Cola Bottling Company)
Dublin 1912
(Dublin Coca-Cola Bottling Company)
Elberton 1913
(Elberton Coca-Cola Bottling Company)
Fitzgerald 1909
(Fitzgerald Coca-Cola Bottling Company)
Fort Valley 1912
(Fort Valley Coca-Cola Bottling Company)
Gainesville 1905
(Gainesville Coca-Cola Bottling Company)
Griffin 1907
(Griffin Coca-Cola Bottling Company)
Hartwell 1905
(Coca-Cola Bottling Company)
Hawkinsville 1903
(Hawkinsville Coca-Cola Bottling Company)
Hinesville 1915
(Hinesville Coca-Cola Bottling Company)
LaFayette 1915
(Coca-Cola Bottling Works of LaFayette)
LaGrange 1903
(LaGrange Coca-Cola Bottling Company)
Macon 1902
(Macon Coca-Cola Bottling Company)
McRae 1905
(McRae Coca-Cola Bottling Company)
Manchester 1905
(Georgia-Alabama Coca-Cola Bottling Company)
Marietta 1910
(Marietta Coca-Cola Bottling Company)
Milledgeville 1912
(Milledgeville Coca-Cola Bottling Company)
Monroe 1907
(Monroe Coca-Cola Bottling Company)

Moultrie 1913
(Moultrie Coca-Cola Bottling Company)
Pelham 1912
(Pelham Coca-Cola Bottling Company)
Richland 1909
(Richland Coca-Cola Bottling Company)
Rome 1901
(Rome Coca-Cola Bottling Company)
Sandersville 1913
(Sandersville Coca-Cola Bottling Company)
Savannah 1902
(The Savannah Coca-Cola Bottling Company)
Statesboro 1906
(Statesboro Coca-Cola Bottling Company)
Swainsboro 1907
(Swainsboro Coca-Cola Bottling Company)
Sylvania 1906
(Sylvania Coca-Cola Bottling Company)
Thomaston 1912
(Coca-Cola Bottling Company of Thomaston)
Thomasville 1910
(Thomasville Coca-Cola Bottling Company)
Thomson 1913
(Thomson Coca-Cola Bottling Company)
Tifton 1903
(Tifton Coca-Cola Bottling Company)
Valdosta 1897
(Valdosta Coca-Cola Bottling Works, Inc.)
Vidalia 1909
(Vidalia Coca-Cola Bottling Company, Inc.)
Washington 1906
(Washington Coca-Cola Bottling Company)
Waycross 1905
(The Waycross Coca-Cola Bottling Company)
Waynesboro 1912
(Waynesboro Coca-Cola Bottling Company)
West Point 1904
(Coca-Cola Bottling Company of West Point)
Wrens 1905
(Wrens Coca-Cola Bottling Company)

HAWAII

Honolulu 1907
(Coca-Cola Bottling Company of Honolulu, Ltd.)

IDAHO

Boise 1915
(Inland Coca-Cola Bottling Company)
Coeur d'Alene 1911
(Empire Coca-Cola Bottling Company)
Idaho Falls 1916
(Coca-Cola Bottling Company of Idaho Falls)
Pocatello 1912
(Pocatello Coca-Cola Bottling Company, Inc.)
Twin Falls 1912
(Twin Falls Coca-Cola Bottling Company)

ILLINOIS

Beardstown 1917
(Coca-Cola Bottling Company of Beardstown)
Bloomington 1916
(Coca-Cola Bottling Company of Bloomington)
Cairo 1906
(Cairo Coca-Cola Bottling Company, Inc.)
Champaign 1910
(Champaign Coca-Cola Bottling Company, Inc.)
Chicago 1901
(Coca-Cola Bottling Company of Chicago, Inc.)
Danville 1904
(Danville Coca-Cola Bottling Company)
Decatur 1903
(The Coca-Cola Bottling Company of Decatur)
Duquoin 1913
(Duquoin Coca-Cola Bottling Company)
Freeport 1911
(Freeport Coca-Cola Bottling Company, Inc.)
Galesburg 1905
(Galesburg Coca-Cola Bottling Company)
Harrisburg 1908
(Coca-Cola Bottling Company of Harrisburg)
Herrin 1906
(Herrin Coca-Cola Bottling Company)
Jacksonville 1910
(Jacksonville Coca-Cola Bottling Company)
Kankakee 1911
(Kankakee Coca-Cola Bottling Company)
Kewanee 1905
(Kewanee Coca-Cola Bottling Company)
Lincoln 1910
(Lincoln Coca-Cola Bottling Company)
Litchfield 1905
(Coca-Cola Bottling Company of Litchfield)
Macomb 1907
(Coca-Cola Bottling Company of Macomb)
Marion 1904
(Coal Belt Bottling Company)
Mattoon 1911
(Mattoon Coca-Cola Bottling Company, Inc.)
Mount Carmel 1905
(Coca-Cola Bottling Company of Mount Carmel)
Olney 1905
(Olney Coca-Cola Bottling Company)
Paris 1905
(Paris Coca-Cola Bottling Company, Inc.)
Peoria 1905
(Peoria Coca-Cola Bottling Company)
Petersburg 1904
(Petersburg Coca-Cola Bottling Company)
Quincy 1905
(Coca-Cola Bottling Company of Quincy)
Rockford 1905
(Rockford Coca-Cola Bottling Company)

Rock Island 1905
(Quad Cities Coca-Cola Bottling Company)
Springfield 1910
(Springfield Coca-Cola Bottling Company)
Streator 1905
(Coca-Cola Bottling Company of Streator)

INDIANA

Anderson 1916
(Coca-Cola Bottling Company of Anderson, Inc.)
Bloomington 1915
(Coca-Cola Bottling Company of Bloomington, Inc.)
Columbus 1916
(Coca-Cola Bottling Company of Columbus, Inc.)
Elwood 1915
(Coca-Cola Bottling Company of Elwood, Inc.)
Evansville 1904
(Coca-Cola Bottling Works of Evansville, Inc.)
Fort Wayne 1913
(Coca-Cola Bottling Company of Fort Wayne)
Frankfort 1915
(Coca-Cola Bottling Company of Frankfort, Inc.)
Gary 1919
(Coca-Cola Bottling Company of Gary, Inc.)
Greencastle 1916
(Coca-Cola Bottling Company of Greencastle, Inc.)
Indianapolis 1903
(Coca-Cola Bottling Company of Indianapolis, Inc.)
Jasper 1911
(Coca-Cola Bottling Company of Jasper, Inc.)
Logansport 1907
(Coca-Cola Bottling Company of Logansport, Inc.)
Marion 1916
(Coca-Cola Bottling Company of Marion, Inc.)
Muncie 1915
(Coca-Cola Bottling Company of Muncie, Inc.)
New Castle 1918
(Coca-Cola Bottling Company of New Castle, Inc.)
Plymouth 1919
(Coca-Cola Bottling Company of Plymouth, Inc.)
Portland 1916
(Coca-Cola Bottling Company of Portland, Inc.)
Richmond 1917
(The Richmond Coca-Cola Bottling Company)
Rushville 1916
(Coca-Cola Bottling Company of Rushville, Inc.)
Shelbyville 1917
(Coca-Cola Bottling Company of Shelbyville, Inc.)
South Bend 1905
(Coca-Cola Bottling Company of South Bend)
Terre Haute 1904
(Terre Haute Coca-Cola Bottling Company, Inc.)
Union City 1917
(Union City Coca-Cola Bottling Company, Inc.)
Washington 1904
(Coca-Cola Bottling Company Number Three of Washington)

IOWA

Cedar Rapids 1905
(Cedar Rapids Coca-Cola Bottling Company)
Clarinda 1910
(Clarinda-Shenandoah Bottling Company)
Clinton 1905
(Coca-Cola Bottling Company of Clinton)
Des Moines 1905
(Des Moines Coca-Cola Bottling Company)
Dubuque 1905
(Coca-Cola Bottling Company)
Keokuk 1907
(Coca-Cola Bottling Company)
Marshalltown 1916
(Marshalltown Coca-Cola Bottling Company)
Mason City 1908
(Coca-Cola Bottling Company of Mason City)
Ottumwa 1911
(Coca-Cola Bottling Company of Ottumwa)
Sioux City 1904
(Coca-Cola Bottling Company of Sioux City)
Spirit Lake 1915
(Coca-Cola Bottling Company of Spirit Lake)
Waterloo 1915
(Coca-Cola Bottling Company of Waterloo)

KANSAS

Atchison 1906
(Atchison Coca-Cola Bottling Company, Inc.)
Dodge City 1907
(Coca-Cola Bottling Company of Dodge City, Inc.)
Emporia 1914
(Emporia Coca-Cola Bottling Company)
Fort Scott 1905
(Fort Scott Coca-Cola Bottling Company)
Garden City 1912
(Garden City Coca-Cola Bottling Company, Inc.)
Great Bend 1905
(The Great Bend Coca-Cola Bottling Company)
Hays 1917
(Hays Coca-Cola Bottling Company, Inc.)
Hutchinson 1913
(The Hutchinson Coca-Cola Bottling Company)
Independence 1913
(Independence Coca-Cola Bottling Company, Inc.)
Iola 1909
(The Iola Coca-Cola Bottling Company, Inc.)
Junction City 1915
(The Junction City Bottling Company, Inc.)
Liberal 1912
(The Liberal Coca-Cola Bottling Company)
Manhattan 1912
(Coca-Cola Bottling Company of Manhattan)
Marysville 1915
(The Marysville Bottling Company, Inc.)
Norton 1906
(Norton Coca-Cola Bottling Company, Inc.)

Ottawa 1912
(The Ottawa Coca-Cola Bottling Company)
Parsons 1911
(Parsons Coca-Cola Bottling Company, Inc.)
Salina 1911
(The Salina Coca-Cola Bottling Corporation)
Topeka 1905
(The Topeka Coca-Cola Bottling Company)
Wichita 1904
(The Wichita Coca-Cola Bottling Company)
Winfield 1910
(The Coca-Cola Bottling Company of Winfield)

KENTUCKY

Bowling Green 1905
(Bowling Green Coca-Cola Bottling Works)
Campbellsville 1905
(Coca-Cola Bottling Company of Campbellsville)
Carrollton 1916
(Coca-Cola Bottling Company of Carrollton)
Elizabethtown 1920
(Coca-Cola Bottling Company of Elizabethtown)
Fulton 1913
(Fulton Coca-Cola Bottling Company, Inc.)
Hazard 1914
(Hazard Coca-Cola Bottling Works, Inc.)
Hopkinsville 1916
(Coca-Cola Bottling Company of Hopkinsville, Inc.)
Lexington 1904
(Coca-Cola Bottling Works)
Louisa 1905
(Louisa Coca-Cola Bottling Company)
Louisville 1901
(Coca-Cola Bottling Company of Louisville)
Middlesboro 1904
(Middlesboro Coca-Cola Bottling Works)
Owensboro 1906
(Owensboro Coca-Cola Bottling Company, Inc.)
Paducah 1903
(Paducah Coca-Cola Bottling Company)
Pikeville 1912
(Coca-Cola Bottling Company of Pikeville)
Shelbyville 1920
(Coca-Cola Bottling Company of Shelbyville)
Somerset 1920
(Coca-Cola Bottling Company of Somerset)
Whitesburg 1911
(Coca-Cola Bottling Works of Whitesburg)

LOUISIANA

Alexandria 1906
(Alexandria Coca-Cola Bottling Company, Ltd.)
Baton Rouge 1906
(Baton Rouge Coca-Cola Bottling Company, Ltd.)
Bogalusa 1910
(Bogalusa Coca-Cola Bottling Company, Inc.)
Bunkie 1912
(Bunkie Coca-Cola Bottling Company, Inc.)
DeRidder 1911
(DeRidder Coca-Cola Bottling Company)
Hammond 1910
(Hammond Coca-Cola Bottling Company, Ltd.)
Homer 1914
(Homer Coca-Cola Bottling Company, Inc.)
Jeanerette 1913
(Evangeline Coca-Cola Bottling Company, Inc.)
LaFayette 1919
(LaFayette Coca-Cola Bottling Company)
Lake Charles 1907
(Coca-Cola Bottling Company of Lake Charles, Inc.)
Minden 1905
(Coca-Cola Bottling Company, Inc.)
Monroe 1904
(Ouachita Coca-Cola Bottling Company)
Natchitoches 1909
(Coca-Cola Bottling Company, Inc.)
New Orleans 1902
(The Louisiana Coca-Cola Bottling Company, Ltd.)
Opelousas 1912
(Opelousas Coca-Cola Bottling Company, Inc.)
Ruston 1905
(Ruston Coca-Cola Bottling Company, Inc.)
Shreveport 1904
(Coca-Cola Bottling Company of Shreveport, Inc.)

MAINE

Bangor 1920
(The Coca-Cola Bottling Plants, Inc.)

MARYLAND

Baltimore 1905
(Coca-Cola Bottling Company of Baltimore)
Cambridge 1919
(Coca-Cola Bottling Company of Cambridge, Inc.)
Cumberland 1903
(Cumberland Coca-Cola Bottling Works, Inc.)
Frederick 1911
(Frederick Coca-Cola Bottling Company, Inc.)
Hagerstown 1915
(Hagerstown Coca-Cola Bottling Works, Inc.)
Havre de Grace 1919
(The Coca-Cola Bottling Works, Inc., of Havre de Grace)
Salisbury 1911
(Salisbury Coca-Cola Bottling Company)
Westminster 1920
(Westminster Coca-Cola Bottling Company, Inc.)

MASSACHUSETTS

Boston 1912
(Coca-Cola Bottling Company of Boston)
Fall River 1912
(Coca-Cola Bottling Company of Fall River)

Lowell 1912
(Coca-Cola Bottling Company of Lowell, Inc.)
Lynn 1917
(Coca-Cola Bottling Company of Boston)
Newburyport 1916
(Coca-Cola Bottling Company of Newburyport)
Northampton 1912
(Coca-Cola Bottling Company of Northampton)
Pittsfield 1916
(Berkshire Coca-Cola Bottling Company)
Springfield 1912
(Coca-Cola Bottling Company of Springfield)
Worcester 1912
(Coca-Cola Bottling Company of Worcester)

MICHIGAN

Alpena 1918
(Coca-Cola Bottling Company of Alpena, Inc.)
Battle Creek 1904
(Coca-Cola Bottling Company of Battle Creek)
Bay City 1919
(Coca-Cola Bottling Company of Michigan)
Detroit 1902
(Detroit Coca-Cola Bottling Company)
Escanaba 1913
(Coca-Cola Bottling Company of Delta County)
Flint 1909
(LaSalle Coca-Cola Bottling Company)
Grand Rapids 1911
(LaSalle Coca-Cola Bottling Company)
Jackson 1911
(Midwest Coca-Cola Bottling Company)
Kalamazoo 1905
(Coca-Cola Bottling Company of Kalamazoo)
Lansing 1905
(LaSalle Coca-Cola Bottling Company)
Marquette 1918
(H. W. Elson Bottling Company)
Monroe 1916
(Monroe Coca-Cola Bottling Company)
Muskegon 1912
(Coca-Cola Bottling Company of Muskegon)
Port Huron 1906
(Coca-Cola Bottling Company of Port Huron)
St. Joseph 1910
(Twin City Coca-Cola Bottling Company, Inc.)
Traverse City 1911
(LaSalle Coca-Cola Bottling Company)

MINNESOTA

Austin 1905
(Austin Coca-Cola Bottling Company)
Bemidji 1914
(Coca-Cola Bottling Company of Bemidji, Inc.)
Crookston 1906
(Crookston Coca-Cola Bottling Company)
Duluth 1911
(Coca-Cola Bottling Company of Minnesota, Inc.)
Minneapolis 1919
(Coca-Cola Bottling Midwest, Inc.)
Moorhead 1915
(The Coca-Cola Bottling Company of Fargo, Inc.)
Red Wing 1912
(Coca-Cola Bottling Company of Red Wing, Inc.)
Saint Paul 1919
(Coca-Cola Bottling Midwest, Inc.)
Virginia 1911
(Coca-Cola Bottling Company of Virginia)
Winona 1905
(Coca-Cola Bottling Company of Winona)

MISSISSIPPI

Aberdeen 1908
(Aberdeen Coca-Cola Bottling Company)
Belzoni 1908
(Belzoni Coca-Cola Bottling Company)
Brookhaven 1920
(Brookhaven Coca-Cola Bottling Company)
Clarksdale 1916
(The Coca-Cola Bottling Company of Clarksdale)
Cleveland 1920
(The Coca-Cola Bottling Company of Cleveland)
Columbia 1913
(Columbia Coca-Cola Bottling Company)
Columbus 1904
(Kaye Coca-Cola Bottling Company)
Corinth 1907
(Coca-Cola Bottling Works)
Greenville 1909
(The Coca-Cola Bottling Company of Greenville)
Greenwood 1904
(Coca-Cola Bottling Works of Greenwood)
Grenada 1920
(Grenada Coca-Cola Bottling Company)
Gulfport 1906
(Coast Coca-Cola Bottling Company, Inc.)
Hattiesburg 1906
(Hattiesburg Coca-Cola Bottling Company)
Holly Springs 1916
(The Coca-Cola Bottling Company of Holly Springs)
Houston 1908
(Houston Coca-Cola Bottling Company)
Jackson 1903
(Jackson Coca-Cola Bottling Company)
Laurel 1904
(Laurel Coca-Cola Bottling Company)
Lexington 1908
(Lexington Coca-Cola Bottling Company)
Louisville 1908
(Louisville Coca-Cola Bottling Company)
McComb 1907
(The McComb Coca-Cola Bottling Company)

Meridian 1902
(Meridian Coca-Cola Bottling Company)
Natchez 1906
(Natchez Coca-Cola Bottling Company)
New Albany 1906
(New Albany Coca-Cola Bottling Company)
Newton 1912
(Newton Coca-Cola Bottling Company)
Picayune 1919
(Picayune Coca-Cola Bottling Company)
Sardis 1916
(The Coca-Cola Bottling Company of Sardis)
Starkville 1919
(Starkville Coca-Cola Bottling Company)
Tupelo 1916
(Coca-Cola Bottling Works)
Vicksburg 1894
(Coca-Cola Bottling Company, Inc., of Vicksburg)
West Point 1906
(West Point Coca-Cola Bottling Company)
Yazoo City 1903
(Yazoo Coca-Cola Bottling Company)

MISSOURI

Butler 1919
(Coca-Cola Bottling Company of Butler, Inc.)
Cape Girardeau 1917
(Coca-Cola Bottling Company of Cape Girardeau, Inc.)
Chillicothe 1919
(Coca-Cola Bottling Company of Chillicothe)
Columbia 1910
(Coca-Cola Bottling Company of Missouri)
Flat River 1912
(Coca-Cola Bottling Company of Flat River, Inc.)
Hannibal 1911
(Coca-Cola Bottling Company of Hannibal)
Jefferson City 1905
(Jefferson City Coca-Cola Bottling Company)
Joplin 1903
(The Joplin Coca-Cola Bottling Company)
Kansas City 1902
(Kansas City Coca-Cola Bottling Company)
Kennett 1918
(Coca-Cola Bottling Company of Kennett)
Macon 1905
(Macon Coca-Cola Bottling Company)
Mexico 1910
(Mexico Coca-Cola Bottling Company)
Poplar Bluff 1904
(Coca-Cola Bottling Company of Poplar Bluff)
Saint Joseph 1905
(Hund and Eger Bottling Company)
Saint Louis 1902
(Coca-Cola Bottling Company of Saint Louis)
Salem 1913
(Salem Coca-Cola Bottling Company)
Sedalia 1905
(Coca-Cola Bottling Company of Sedalia, Inc.)
Springfield 1905
(Springfield Coca-Cola Bottling Company)
Trenton 1904
(Trenton Coca-Cola Bottling Company)
West Plains 1910
(West Plains Coca-Cola Bottling Company)

MONTANA

Billings 1916
(Coca-Cola Bottling Company of Billings)
Bozeman 1914
(Bozeman Coca-Cola Bottling Company)
Butte 1912
(Butte Coca-Cola Bottling Company)
Kalispell 1920
(Coca-Cola Bottling Company of Kalispell)
Lewistown 1917
(Lewistown Coca-Cola Bottling Company)
Missoula 1916
(Coca-Cola Bottling Company of Missoula)

NEBRASKA

Beatrice 1911
(Coca-Cola Bottling Company of Beatrice)
Columbus 1917
(Coca-Cola Bottling Company of Columbus)
Falls City 1910
(Coca-Cola Bottling Company of Falls City)
Grand Island 1916
(Grand Island Bottling Company)
Holdredge 1911
(Coca-Cola Bottling Company)
Kearney 1910
(Midway Coca-Cola Bottling Company)
Lincoln 1904
(Coca-Cola Bottling Company of Lincoln)
Long Pine 1914
(Coca-Cola Bottling Company of Long Pine)
Nebraska City 1911
(Nebraska City Coca-Cola Bottling Company)
Norfolk 1919
(Norfolk Coca-Cola Bottling Company)
North Platte 1911
(Coca-Cola Bottling Company of North Platte)
Omaha 1905
(Omaha Coca-Cola Bottling Company)

Superior 1905
(Superior Coca-Cola Bottling Company)

NEVADA

Ely 1912
(Coca-Cola Bottling Company of Ely)
Las Vegas 1919
(Desert Coca-Cola Bottling Company)
Reno 1918
(Shoshone Coca-Cola Bottling Company)

NEW HAMPSHIRE

Keene 1913
(Coca-Cola Bottling Company of Keene, Inc.)
Salem 1919
(Salem Coca-Cola Bottling Company, Inc.)
Somersworth 1916
(Coca-Cola Bottling Company of Somersworth)

NEW JERSEY

Atlantic City 1920
(Coca-Cola Bottling Company of South Jersey)
Newark 1904
(The Coca-Cola Bottling Company of New York, Inc.)
Trenton 1909
(The Coca-Cola Bottling Company of New York, Inc.)

NEW MEXICO

Albuquerque 1904
(The Coca-Cola Bottling Company)
Carlsbad 1917
(Carlsbad Coca-Cola Bottling Company)
Deming 1916
(Deming Coca-Cola Bottling Company)
Gallup 1917
(Coca-Cola Bottling Company of Gallup)
Las Cruces 1917
(Las Cruces Coca-Cola Bottling Company)
Las Vegas 1912
(Las Vegas Coca-Cola Bottling Company)
Raton 1918
(Raton Coca-Cola Bottling Company)
Roswell 1912
(Pecos Valley Coca-Cola Bottling Company, Inc.)
Santa Fe 1919
(Coca-Cola Bottling Company of Santa Fe, Inc.)
Tucumcari 1914
(Coca-Cola Bottling Company of Tucumcari)

NEW YORK

Binghamton 1920
(Binghamton Coca-Cola Bottling Company)
Brooklyn 1920
(The Coca-Cola Bottling Company of New York, Inc.)
Buffalo 1902
(The Coca-Cola Bottling Company of New York, Inc.)
Elmira 1918
(Elmira Coca-Cola Bottling Works, Inc.)
Massena 1919
(Coca-Cola Bottling Company of Massena, Inc.)
New York 1904
(The Coca-Cola Bottling Company of New York, Inc.)
Plattsburgh 1919
(Plattsburgh Coca-Cola Bottling Corporation)
Rochester 1906
(Rochester Coca-Cola Bottling Corporation)
Syracuse 1917
(Syracuse Coca-Cola Bottling Company)

NORTH CAROLINA

Albemarle 1909
(Albemarle Coca-Cola Bottling Company)
Aberdeen 1913
(Aberdeen Coca-Cola Bottling Company, Inc.)
Asheville 1904
(Coca-Cola Bottling Company of Asheville)
Biscoe 1909
(Biscoe Coca-Cola Bottling Company, Inc.)
Burlington 1904
(Burlington Coca-Cola Bottling Company)
Charlotte 1902
(The Charlotte Coca-Cola Bottling Company)
Concord 1908
(Coca-Cola Bottling Company of Concord)
Durham 1905
(Durham Coca-Cola Bottling Company)
Elizabeth City 1908
(Elizabeth City Coca-Cola Bottling Works, Inc.)
Fayetteville 1904
(Fayetteville Coca-Cola Bottling Company)
Forest City 1908
(Coca-Cola Bottling Company)
Gastonia 1907
(The Gastonia Coca-Cola Bottling Company)
Goldsboro 1909
(Goldsboro Coca-Cola Bottling Company, Inc.)
Greensboro 1902
(Greensboro Coca-Cola Bottling Company)
Greenville 1905
(Coca-Cola Bottling Company)
Hamlet 1902
(Hamlet Coca-Cola Bottling Company)

Henderson 1912
(Coca-Cola Bottling Company of Henderson, Inc.)
Hickory 1905
(Hickory Coca-Cola Bottling Company)
Kelford 1914
(Kelford Coca-Cola Bottling Company, Inc.)
Kinston 1909
(Coca-Cola Bottling Company)
Leaksville 1913
(Coca-Cola Bottling Company)
Lexington 1908
(Coca-Cola Bottling Company of Lexington)
Lincolnton 1913
(Lincolnton Coca-Cola Bottling Company)
Lumberton 1912
(Lumberton Coca-Cola Bottling Company)
Marion 1916
(Coca-Cola Bottling Company of Marion)
Mayodan 1915
(Mayodan Coca-Cola Bottling Company)
Monroe 1913
(Monroe Coca-Cola Bottling Company)
Mount Airy 1907
(Mount Airy Coca-Cola Bottling Company, Inc.)
New Bern 1904
(New Bern Coca-Cola Bottling Works, Inc.)
North Wilkesboro 1906
(The North Wilkesboro Coca-Cola Bottling Company, Inc.)
Raleigh 1903
(The Capitol Coca-Cola Bottling Company, Inc.)
Reidsville 1905
(Reidsville Coca-Cola Bottling Company)
Rocky Mount 1910
(Coca-Cola Bottling Company of Rocky Mount, Inc.)
Roxboro 1908
(Roxboro Coca-Cola Bottling Company)
Salisbury 1904
(Coca-Cola Bottling Company of Salisbury)
Sanford 1908
(Sanford Coca-Cola Bottling Company)
Shelby 1908
(Coca-Cola Bottling Company of Shelby)
Statesville 1909
(Statesville Coca-Cola Bottling Company)
Tarboro 1912
(Tarboro Coca-Cola Bottling Company)
Washington 1911
(Coca-Cola Bottling Company of Washington, Inc.)
Weldon 1910
(Weldon Coca-Cola Bottling Works, Inc.)
Wilmington 1902
(Wilmington Coca-Cola Bottling Works, Inc.)
Wilson 1909
(The Barnes-Harrell Company)
Winston-Salem 1906
(Winston Coca-Cola Bottling Company)

NORTH DAKOTA

Bismarck 1910
(Coca-Cola Bottling Company of Bismarck)
Grand Forks 1907
(Coca-Cola Bottling Company of Grand Forks)
Minot 1911
(Coca-Cola Bottling Company of Minot)

OHIO

Akron 1909
(The Akron Coca-Cola Bottling Company)
Alliance 1916
(The Coca-Cola Bottling Company of Alliance)
Ashtabula 1909
(The Painesville Coca-Cola Bottling Company)
Canton 1906
(The Coca-Cola Bottling Company of Canton)
Cincinnati 1901
(The Coca-Cola Bottling Works Company)
Circleville 1919
(Scioto Coca-Cola Bottling Company)
Cleveland 1905
(The Cleveland Coca-Cola Bottling Company)
Columbus 1905
(Coca-Cola Bottling Company of Ohio)
Dayton 1905
(The Dayton Coca-Cola Bottling Company)
Dennison 1918
(Dennison Coca-Cola Bottling Company)
Elyria 1914
(The Elyria Coca-Cola Bottling Company)
Findlay 1916
(The Findlay Coca-Cola Bottling Company)
Lima 1914
(The Lima Coca-Cola Bottling Works, Inc.)
Mansfield 1916
(The Mansfield Coca-Cola Bottling Company)
Marion 1916
(The Marion Coca-Cola Bottling Company)
Mount Vernon 1916
(Coca-Cola Bottling Company of Mount Vernon, Inc.)
Newark 1919
(Newark Coca-Cola Bottling Works, Inc.)
Piqua 1917
(The Piqua Coca-Cola Bottling Company)
Portsmouth 1914
(Portsmouth Coca-Cola Bottling Company, Inc.)
Springfield 1914
(The Springfield Coca-Cola Bottling Company)
Steubenville 1919
(Steubenville Coca-Cola Bottling Company, Inc.)
Tiffin 1919
(The Tiffin Coca-Cola Bottling Company)

Toledo 1905
(LaSalle Coca-Cola Bottling Company)
Warren 1919
(Warren Coca-Cola Bottling Company)
Youngstown 1906
(Coca-Cola Bottling Company of Youngstown)
Zanesville 1909
(The Zanesville Coca-Cola Bottling Company)

OKLAHOMA

Ada 1905
(Ada Coca-Cola Bottling Company)
Altus 1905
(Altus Coca-Cola Bottling Company)
Alva 1917
(Alva Coca-Cola Bottling Company, Inc.)
Ardmore 1904
(Ardmore Coca-Cola Bottling Company)
Bartlesville 1905
(Bartlesville Coca-Cola Bottling Company)
Clinton 1908
(Coca-Cola Bottling Company of Clinton)
Cushing 1909
(Cushing Coca-Cola Bottling Company)
Durant 1919
(Durant Coca-Cola Bottling Company)
Enid 1905
(Coca-Cola Bottling Company of Enid)
Guthrie 1915
(The Coca-Cola Bottling Company of Guthrie)
Idabel 1909
(Idabel Coca-Cola Bottling Company, Inc.)
Lawton 1910
(Lawton Coca-Cola Bottling Company)
McAlester 1906
(McAlester Coca-Cola Bottling Company)
Miami 1913
(Miami Coca-Cola Bottling Company)
Muskogee 1904
(Coca-Cola Bottling Company of Muskogee)
Oklahoma City 1903
(Oklahoma Coca-Cola Bottling Company)
Okmulgee 1910
(Coca-Cola Bottling Company of Okmulgee)
Sapulpa 1909
(The Coca-Cola Bottling Company of Sapulpa)
Shawnee 1902
(The Coca-Cola Bottling Company of Shawnee)
Tulsa 1905
(Coca-Cola Bottling Company of Tulsa)
Vinita 1910
(Coca-Cola Bottling Company)
Woodward 1912
(Woodward Coca-Cola Bottling Company)

OREGON

Canyon City 1911
(Coca-Cola Bottling Company of Canyon City)
Eugene 1910
(Coca-Cola Bottling Company of Eugene)
Hood River 1915
(Mid-Columbia Coca-Cola Bottling Company)
Klamath Falls 1916
(Coca-Cola Bottling Company of Klamath Falls)
Medford 1911
(Medford Coca-Cola Bottling Company)
Portland 1907
(Coca-Cola Bottling Company of Oregon)
Roseburg 1910
(Roseburg Coca-Cola Bottling Company)

PENNSYLVANIA

Altoona 1916
(Coca-Cola Bottling Company of Altoona, Inc.)
Beaver 1919
(Beaver Coca-Cola Bottling Company)
Berlin 1919
(Coca-Cola Bottling Works, Inc., of Berlin)
Bethlehem 1917
(Quaker State Coca-Cola Bottling Company)
Butler 1919
(Quaker State Coca-Cola Bottling Company)
Chambersburg 1919
(Chambersburg Coca-Cola Bottling Works, Inc.)
Charleroi 1919
(Coca-Cola Bottling Company of Charleroi)
Clearfield 1919
(Clearfield Coca-Cola Bottling Company, Inc.)
Coatesville 1918
(Coatesville Coca-Cola Bottling Works, Inc.)
Erie 1911
(Erie Coca-Cola Bottling Company)
Greensburg 1919
(Greensburg Coca-Cola Bottling Company, Inc.)
Harrisburg 1902
(Harrisburg Coca-Cola Bottling Works, Inc.)
Indiana 1915
(Coca-Cola Bottling Company of Indiana)
Johnstown 1919
(Coca-Cola Bottling Company of Johnstown, Inc.)
Lancaster 1919
(Lancaster Coca-Cola Bottling Company, Inc.)
Lewistown 1919
(Lewistown Coca-Cola Bottling Works, Inc.)
Philadelphia 1902
(The Philadelphia Coca-Cola Bottling Company)
Pittsburgh 1902
(Quaker State Coca-Cola Bottling Company)

Pottsville 1919
(Coca-Cola Bottling Company of Pottsville)
Reading 1919
(Reading Coca-Cola Bottling Works, Inc.)
Scranton 1907
(Coca-Cola Bottling Company)
Sharon 1919
(Coca-Cola Bottling Company, Inc.)
Sunbury 1919
(Sunbury Coca-Cola Bottling Company, Inc.)
Uniontown 1919
(Coca-Cola Bottling Company of Uniontown)
Washington 1919
(Coca-Cola Bottling Company of Washington, Inc.)
Wilkes-Barre 1916
(Keystone Coca-Cola Bottling Company)
Williamsport 1912
(Williamsport Coca-Cola Bottling Works, Inc.)
York 1914
(York Coca-Cola Bottling Works, Inc.)

RHODE ISLAND

Providence 1912
(Coca-Cola Bottling Company of Rhode Island)

SOUTH CAROLINA

Abbeville 1907
(Abbeville Coca-Cola Bottling Company)
Aiken 1919
(Aiken Coca-Cola Bottling Company)
Allendale 1911
(Allendale Coca-Cola Bottling Company)
Anderson 1904
(Coca-Cola Bottling Company of Anderson)
Beaufort 1907
(Beaufort Coca-Cola Bottling Company)
Charleston 1902
(Charleston Coca-Cola Bottling Company)
Chester 1904
(Carolina Coca-Cola Bottling Company)
Columbia 1902
(Columbia Coca-Cola Bottling Company)
Darlington 1907
(Darlington-Hartsville Coca-Cola Bottling Company, Inc.)
Denmark 1912
(The Denmark Coca-Cola Bottling Company)
Dillon 1907
(Dillon Coca-Cola Bottling Company)
Estill 1919
(Estill Coca-Cola Bottling Company)
Florence 1907
(Florence Coca-Cola Bottling Company, Inc.)
Gaffney 1905
(Coca-Cola Bottling Company of Gaffney)
Georgetown 1907
(Georgetown Coca-Cola Bottling Company)
Greenville 1902
(Coca-Cola Bottling Company of Greenville)
Greenwood 1904
(Greenwood Coca-Cola Bottling Company)
Hampton 1908
(Hampton Bottling Works)
Lane 1915
(Lane Coca-Cola Bottling Company)
Laurens 1906
(The Laurens Coca-Cola Bottling Company)
Marion 1906
(Marion Coca-Cola Bottling Company)
Newberry 1907
(Newberry Coca-Cola Bottling Company)
Orangeburg 1904
(Orangeburg Coca-Cola Bottling Company)
Pageland 1913
(Pageland Coca-Cola Bottling Works)
Ridgeland 1909
(Ridgeland Coca-Cola Bottling Company)
Rock Hill 1906
(Rock Hill Coca-Cola Bottling Company)
Spartanburg 1903
(Spartanburg Coca-Cola Bottling Company)
Summerville 1915
(Dorchester Coca-Cola Bottling Company)
Sumter 1903
(Carolina Coca-Cola Bottling Company)
Union 1905
(Union Coca-Cola Bottling Company)
Walterboro 1913
(Walterboro Coca-Cola Bottling Company)

SOUTH DAKOTA

Aberdeen 1916
(Coca-Cola Bottling Company of Aberdeen, Inc.)
Huron 1911
(Coca-Cola Bottling Company of Huron)
Mitchell 1911
(Coca-Cola Bottling Company of Mitchell)
Pierre 1911
(Coca-Cola Bottling Company of Pierre)
Rapid City 1917
(Coca-Cola Bottling Company of the Black Hills)
Sioux Falls 1908
(Coca-Cola Bottling Company of Sioux Falls)
Watertown 1918
(Coca-Cola Bottling Company, Inc., of Watertown)

TENNESSEE

Chattanooga 1899
(Chattanooga Coca-Cola Bottling Company, Inc.)

Clarksville 1905
(Clarksville Coca-Cola Bottling Company)
Cleveland 1907
(Cleveland Coca-Cola Bottling Company)
Columbia 1913
(Coca-Cola Bottling Works)
Cookeville 1915
(Coca-Cola Bottling Company)
Covington 1909
(The Coca-Cola Bottling Company of Covington)
Dayton 1914
(The Coca-Cola Bottling Company of Dayton)
Dickson 1914
(Dickson Coca-Cola Bottling Company)
Dyersburg 1911
(Coca-Cola Bottling Company of Dyersburg, Inc.)
Etowah 1908
(Etowah Coca-Cola Bottling Company)
Fayetteville 1908
(The Coca-Cola Bottling Works of Fayetteville)
Jackson 1905
(Coca-Cola Bottling Works)
Johnson City 1906
(The Coca-Cola Bottling Works of Johnson City)
Knoxville 1902
(Roddy Manufacturing Company)
Lebanon 1919
(Coca-Cola Bottling Works)
Lewisburg 1914
(Coca-Cola Bottling Works, Inc., of Lewisburg)
Lexington 1912
(Coca-Cola Bottling Works)
McMinnville 1916
(Coca-Cola Bottling Company)
Memphis 1902
(Coca-Cola Bottling Company of Memphis)
Murfreesboro 1909
(Coca-Cola Bottling Works of Murfreesboro)
Nashville 1902
(Coca-Cola Bottling Works)
Paris 1916
(The Paris Coca-Cola Bottling Company, Inc.)
Pulaski 1910
(Coca-Cola Bottling Works of Pulaski, Inc.)
Rockwood 1903
(Coca-Cola Bottling Works)
Shelbyville 1914
(Coca-Cola Bottling Works)
South Pittsburg 1914
(Coca-Cola Bottling Works of South Pittsburg)
Tullahoma 1906
(Coca-Cola Bottling Works of Tullahoma, Inc.)
Union City 1909
(Union City Coca-Cola Bottling Company)

TEXAS

Abilene 1904
(Texas Coca-Cola Bottling Company)
Amarillo 1906
(Amarillo Coca-Cola Bottling Company, Inc.)
Austin 1904
(Austin Coca-Cola Bottling Company)
Bastrop 1916
(Bastrop Coca-Cola Bottling Company)
Beaumont 1907
(Beaumont Coca-Cola Bottling Company)
Beeville 1920
(Beeville Coca-Cola Bottling Company)
Big Spring 1910
(Texas Coca-Cola Bottling Company)
Brenham 1911
(Brenham Coca-Cola Bottling Company)
Brownsville 1905
(Brownsville Coca-Cola Bottling Company)
Brownwood 1904
(Brownwood Coca-Cola Bottling Company)
Bryan 1907
(Bryan Coca-Cola Bottling Company)
Cameron 1904
(Coca-Cola Bottling Company)
Clarksville 1904
(Clarksville Coca-Cola Bottling Company)
Cleburne 1909
(Coca-Cola Bottling Company of Cleburne)
Coleman 1915
(Coleman Coca-Cola Bottling Company)
Corpus Christi 1908
(American Bottling Company)
Corsicana 1904
(Corsicana Coca-Cola Bottling Company)
Crockett 1906
(Coca-Cola Bottling Company of Crockett)
Cuero 1910
(Coca-Cola Bottling Company)
Dallas 1902
(The Coca-Cola Bottling Works)
Del Rio 1916
(The Coca-Cola Bottling Company of Del Rio)
El Campo 1917
(El Campo Coca-Cola Bottling Company)
El Paso 1911
(Magnolia Coca-Cola Bottling Company)
Fort Worth 1906
(Coca-Cola Bottling Company of Fort Worth)
Fredericksburg 1911
(Fredericksburg Coca-Cola Bottling Company)
Gainesville 1909
(Gainesville Coca-Cola Bottling Company)
Galveston 1905
(Galveston Coca-Cola Bottling Company)

Glen Rose 1916
(Glen Rose Coca-Cola Bottling Company)
Gonzales 1916
(Gonzales Coca-Cola Bottling Company, Inc.)
Greenville 1908
(Reeves Manufacturing Company)
Henderson 1917
(Henderson Coca-Cola Bottling Company)
Houston 1902
(Houston Coca-Cola Bottling Company)
Jacksonville 1904
(Crown Coca-Cola Bottling Company)
Kenedy 1911
(Kenedy Coca-Cola Bottling Company)
Kerrville 1905
(Kerrville Coca-Cola Bottling Company, Inc.)
Laredo 1910
(The Laredo Coca-Cola Bottling Company, Inc.)
Lockhart 1909
(Lockhart Coca-Cola Bottling Company)
Longview 1912
(Longview Coca-Cola Bottling Company)
Lubbock 1905
(Coca-Cola Bottling Company)
Lufkin 1905
(Lufkin Coca-Cola Bottling Company)
McAllen 1920
(McAllen Coca-Cola Bottling Company)
McKinney 1909
(McKinney Coca-Cola Bottling Company)
Marshall 1908
(Marshall Coca-Cola Bottling Company)
Mexia 1904
(Mexia Coca-Cola Bottling Company)
Nacogdoches 1904
(Nacogdoches Coca-Cola Bottling Company)
New Braunfels 1916
(New Braunfels Coca-Cola Bottling Company, Inc.)
Paducah 1908
(Paducah Coca-Cola Bottling & Ice Company)
Palestine 1905
(Palestine Coca-Cola Bottling Company, Inc.)
Paris 1906
(Paris Coca-Cola Bottling Company)
Pittsburg 1909
(Pittsburg Coca-Cola Bottling Works)
Plainview 1907
(Plainview Coca-Cola Bottling Company)
Port Arthur 1907
(Port Arthur Coca-Cola Bottling Company)
San Angelo 1904
(Coca-Cola Bottling Company)
San Antonio 1903
(San Antonio Coca-Cola Bottling Company, Inc.)
San Marcos 1909
(San Marcos Coca-Cola Bottling Company)
Seguin 1910
(Seguin Coca-Cola Bottling Company)
Sherman 1907
(Sherman Coca-Cola Bottling Company)
Sulphur Springs 1909
(Sulphur Springs Coca-Cola Bottling Company)
Temple 1905
(Temple Coca-Cola Bottling Company)
Texarkana 1905
(Texarkana Coca-Cola Bottling Company)
Tyler 1909
(The Coca-Cola Bottling Works, Inc.)
Vernon 1915
(Vernon Coca-Cola Bottling Company)
Waco 1905
(Waco Coca-Cola Bottling Company)
Waxahachie 1909
(The Coca-Cola Bottling Works, Inc.)
Weatherford 1911
(Coca-Cola Bottling Company of Cleburne)
Wichita Falls 1907
(Wichita Coca-Cola Bottling Company)

UTAH

Logan 1911
(Coca-Cola Bottling Company of Logan)
Ogden 1912
(Coca-Cola Bottling Company of Ogden)
Provo 1916
(Coca-Cola Bottling Company of Provo)
Salt Lake City 1905
(Coca-Cola Bottling Company of Salt Lake)
Vernal 1912
(Coca-Cola Bottling Company of Vernal)

VERMONT

Barre 1917
(Coca-Cola Bottling Company of Barre, Inc.)
Burlington 1917
(Coca-Cola Bottling Company of Burlington)
Rutland 1920
(Coca-Cola Bottling Company of Rutland, Inc.)

VIRGINIA

Alexandria 1913
(Washington Coca-Cola Bottling Company, Inc.)
Bristol 1904
(Dixie Coca-Cola Bottling Company, Inc.)
Charlottesville 1920
(Charlottesville Coca-Cola Bottling Works, Inc.)
Clifton Forge 1902
(Coca-Cola Bottling Company of Clifton Forge, Inc.)
Covington 1910
(Coca-Cola Bottling Works)
Danville 1904
(Danville Coca-Cola Bottling Company, Inc.)

Emporia 1911
(Emporia Coca-Cola Bottling Company, Inc.)
Fredericksburg 1918
(Richmond Coca-Cola Bottling Company, Inc.)
Lynchburg 1906
(Lynchburg Coca-Cola Bottling Works, Inc.)
Martinsville 1919
(Martinsville Coca-Cola Bottling Company, Inc.)
Newport News 1908
(The Newport News Coca-Cola Bottling Company, Inc.)
Norfolk 1901
(Norfolk Coca-Cola Bottling Works, Inc.)
Petersburg 1907
(Petersburg Coca-Cola Bottling Works, Inc.)
Richmond 1903
(Richmond Coca-Cola Bottling Works, Inc.)
Roanoke 1902
(Roanoke Coca-Cola Bottling Works, Inc.)
Saint Paul 1910
(Saint Paul Coca-Cola Bottling Company, Inc.)
Staunton 1908
(Staunton Coca-Cola Bottling Works, Inc.)
Suffolk 1908
(Suffolk Coca-Cola Bottling Works)
Winchester 1916
(Winchester Coca-Cola Bottling Works, Inc.)

WASHINGTON

Bellingham 1905
(The Coca-Cola Bottling Company of Bellingham)
Mount Vernon 1911
(Coca-Cola Bottling Company of Mount Vernon)
Seattle 1906
(Coca-Cola Bottling, Inc.)
Spokane 1910
(Pacific Coca-Cola Bottling Company)
Tacoma 1910
(Pacific Coca-Cola Bottling Company)
Walla Walla 1910
(Coca-Cola Bottling Company of Walla Walla)
Yakima 1911
(Cascade Coca-Cola Bottling Company, Inc.)

WEST VIRGINIA

Beckley 1902
(Raleigh Coca-Cola Bottling Works)
Bluefield 1907
(Bluefield Coca-Cola Bottling Company)
Charleston 1903
(Coca-Cola Bottling Works of Charleston)
Clarksburg 1904
(Clarksburg Coca-Cola Bottling Works, Inc.)
Elkins 1916
(Elkins Coca-Cola Bottling Company)
Fairmont 1915
(Fairmont Coca-Cola Bottling Works, Inc.)
Huntington 1903
(Huntington Coca-Cola Bottling Company)
Logan 1913
(Logan Coca-Cola Bottling Company)
Marlinton 1917
(Coca-Cola Bottling Company of Marlinton)
Morgantown 1908
(Coca-Cola Bottling Company)
Parkersburg 1902
(The Parkersburg Coca-Cola Bottling Company)
Welch 1907
(Northfork Coca-Cola Bottling Company)
Wheeling 1902
(Coca-Cola Bottling Company, Inc., of Wheeling)
Williamson 1907
(Williamson Coca-Cola Bottling Company)

WISCONSIN

Ashland 1910
(Coca-Cola Bottling Company of Pine City, Inc.)
Eau Claire 1911
(Coca-Cola Bottling Company of Eau Claire, Inc.)
Green Bay 1920
(Coca-Cola Bottling Company of Wisconsin)
La Crosse 1911
(La Salle Coca-Cola Bottling Company)
Madison 1911
(Coca-Cola Bottling Company of Madison)
Milwaukee 1911
(La Salle Coca-Cola Bottling Company)
Oshkosh 1911
(La Salle Coca-Cola Bottling Company)
Rhinelander 1905
(Coca-Cola Bottling Company, Inc.)
Rice Lake 1919
(Coca-Cola Bottling Company of Rice Lake, Inc.)
Superior 1910
(Coca-Cola Bottling Company of Superior)
Wisconsin Dells 1914
(Dells Coca-Cola Bottling Company)

WYOMING

Casper 1917
(Coca-Cola Bottling Company of Casper)
Cheyenne 1912
(Coca-Cola Bottling Company of Cheyenne)
Laramie 1912
(Coca-Cola Bottling, Inc., of Laramie)
Sheridan 1910
(Sheridan Coca-Cola Bottling Company)

APPENDIX B

ADVERTISING SLOGANS AND STATEMENTS

The following is an extensive but not exhaustive listing of advertising slogans and statements used by The Coca-Cola Company over the years. The list is alphabetized and features the year in which the slogan or statement was first noted. This list provides perhaps the best dating tool for collectors and historians because the vast majority of Coca-Cola advertising features a slogan and/or a statement. By knowing the earliest date a slogan or statement was used, an interested collector or historian can fairly accurately assign a date to an object in question. One caution, however: Sometimes certain slogans and statements were used for a number of years. In such cases the material offered throughout this book should be examined for further verification of a tentative date assigned an object on the basis of a slogan and/or statement. Throughout the listings, slogans and statements used by individual bottlers have been included, with the responsible bottler named in parentheses.

Adds a refreshing relish to every form of exercise. 1906
After the day's journey drink a glass of delicious, refreshing, Coca-Cola. It satisfies the thirst and pleases the palate. It relieves fatigue and imparts new vigor and new energy. Cooling. Refreshing. Delicious. 1909
All-American choice for "time-out." 1937
All roads lead by Coca-Cola signs. 1925
All trails lead to ice-cold Coca-Cola. 1935
Almost everyone appreciates the best. 1955
Along the highway to anywhere. 1949
Always a delightful surprise. 1924
Always a fresh delight. 1954
Always delightful. 1923
America, give me your tired, your hot, your thirsty, your weary, your parched, your worn-out, etc. 1969
America's family fun drink. 1956
America's favorite moment. 1937
America's preferred taste. 1955
America's year-round answer to thirst. 1940
And the same to you. 1940
The answer to thirst. 1922
Any time is the right time to pause and refresh. 1938
Appearances are sometimes deceiving but Coca-Cola can always be relied on as nourishing, refreshing and ex-

hilarating (Western Coca-Cola Bottling Company, Chicago). 1908
Around the corner from anywhere. 1927
As American as Independence Day. 1946
Ask for it by its full name—then you will get the genuine. 1913
Ask for it either way. 1959
At the little red sign. 1927
At the red cooler. 1938
The ballplayers' one best beverage. 1914
Be really refreshed. 1959
The best beverage under the sun. 1913
The best drink anyone can buy. 1913
The best friend thirst ever had. 1938
The best is always the better buy. 1942
Best-loved sparkling drink in all the world. 1957
The best-served drink in the world. 1929
Big bold taste that's always just right. 1963
A big, bold, unmistakable taste. 1965
Biggest catch—Ice Cold Coca-Cola. 1968
The bold taste of Coke lifts your spirits, boosts your energy. 1965
Bottle that launched 100 summers. 1969
Bounce back to normal. 1933
Bright and bracing as sunshine. 1955
Bright, right taste. 1955
Brighten every bite with Coke. 1959
Bring home the Coke *today*. 1956
Bring in your thirst and go away without it. 1940
The busiest man in the world [Santa Claus]. 1930
By the way—refresh yourself. 1928
Carry a smile back to work. 1934
A casual symbol of pleasant things. 1943
Cheerful lift of Coke. 1958
Cheerful lift that's bright and lively. 1959
A chore's best friend. 1963
Christmas time without Coca-Cola—Bah, humbug! 1966
Coca-Cola . . . along the highway to anywhere. 1949
Coca-Cola . . . a pure drink of natural flavors. 1928
Coca-Cola belongs. 1941
Coca-Cola . . . continuous quality. 1947
Coca-Cola gives a touch of hospitality to sociable moments. 1946
Coca-Cola gives that special zing . . . refreshes best. 1964
Coca-Cola goes along. 1939
Coca-Cola . . . good things from 9 climes poured into a single glass. 1920
Coca-Cola has that extra something. 1942
Coca-Cola has the taste thirst goes for. 1939
Coca-Cola has the taste you never get tired of. 1966
Coca-Cola helps show the world the friendliness of American ways. 1945
Coca-Cola invites you to lunch. 1937
Coca-Cola is a delightful, palatable, healthful beverage. 1904
Coca-Cola is a perfect answer to thirst that no imitation can satisfy. 1919
Coca-Cola is an all-year-round must. 1943
Coca-Cola is full of vim, vigor and go—is a snappy drink. 1907
Coca-Cola is good. 1943
Coca-Cola is the shortest distance between thirst and refreshment. 1926
Coca-Cola makes flow of thought more easy and reasoning power more vigorous. 1899
Coca-Cola . . . makes good things taste better. 1956
Coca-Cola puts *you* at your sparkling best. 1956
Coca-Cola refreshes you best. 1962
Coca-Cola revives and sustains. 1905
Coca-Cola . . . satisfies. 1904
The Coca-Cola Sprite. 1942
Coca-Cola . . . the great temperance beverage—it has none of the ill effects or "let down" qualities of alcoholic stimulants. 1907
Coca-Cola . . . the pause that brings friends together. 1935
Coke. 1941
Coke . . . after Coke . . . after Coke. 1966
Coke and food—refreshing new feeling. 1961
Coke follows thirst everywhere. 1952
Coke has the taste you never get tired of. 1967
Coke is just right. 1957
Coke means Coca-Cola. 1945
Coke on-the-job keeps workers refreshed. 1959
Coke refreshes you best. 1960
Coke Time. 1954
Cold, crisp, refreshing. 1958
Cold, crisp taste of Coke. 1958
Cold, crisp taste that deeply satisfies. 1959
Come up smiling for a fresh start. 1931
Completely refreshing. 1941
Continuous quality is quality you trust. 1947
Cool off with Coke. 1960
Cooling . . . refreshing . . . delicious. 1907
Delicious and refreshing. 1904
Delicious Coca-Cola, sustains, refreshes, invigorates. 1907
Delicious! Refreshing! Exhilarating! Invigorating! 1886
Delicious, sparkling, always refreshing. 1953
Delicious, wholesome, refreshing. 1909
Delicious, wholesome, thirst-quenching. 1909
Deliciously refreshing. 1900
Delightful beverage. 1893
Delightful? Healthful? Refreshing? 1907
Delightful summer and winter beverage. 1895
Delightful summer and winter drink. 1891
Demand the genuine by full name. 1914
Demand the genuine—refuse substitutes. 1912
Dependable as sunrise. 1953
Don't wear a tired, thirsty face. 1933
Drink a bottle of carbonated Coca-Cola. 1905
Drink bottled Coca-Cola—so easily served. 1910

Drink carbonated Coca-Cola in bottles—5¢. 1904
Drink Coca-Cola. 1886
Drink Coca-Cola all the year 'round. 1924
Drink Coca-Cola, anywhere, anytime. 1933
Drink Coca-Cola at soda fountains. 1905
Drink Coca-Cola—High Balls—Gin Rickies (Western Coca-Cola Bottling Company, Chicago). 1906
Drink Coca-Cola in bottles. 1910
Drink Coca-Cola with soda. 1920
Drink delicious Coca-Cola. 1909
The drink everybody knows. 1939
The drink everybody remembers. 1943
A drink of all the year. 1917
The drink of quality. 1906
The drink that adds life and sparkle to living. 1945
The drink that awakens energy. 1934
The drink that cheers but does not inebriate. 1908
The drink that has outgrown the seasons. 1928
The drink that keeps you feeling fit. 1934
The drink that makes the pause refreshing. 1932
Drive safely—drive refreshed. 1953
Enjoy a glass of liquid laughter. 1911
Enjoy Coca-Cola. 1965
Enjoy frozen Coca-Cola. 1969
Enjoy refreshment and be refreshed for enjoyment. 1929
Enjoy that refreshing new feeling. 1962
Enjoy the lively life of Coke. 1962
Enjoy the sociable drink. 1925
Enjoy thirst. 1923
Enjoy thirst through all four seasons. 1923
Even the bubbles taste better. 1956
Every day is election day for Coca-Cola. 1936
Every delicious sip has the flavor of refreshment. 1941
Every glass holds the answer to thirst. 1922
Everybody drinks Coca-Cola—it answers every beverage requirement—vim, vigor, refreshment, wholesomeness. 1913
Everybody likes it. 1925
Everybody likes to work refreshed. 1948
Everybody welcomes Coca-Cola—it's the real thing. 1942
Everybody's club. 1947
Everything your thirst could ask for. 1941
Everywhere the pause that refreshes has become the symbol of good will. 1945
Exhilarating, Invigorating. 1886
Exhilarating, Refreshing. 1914
Experience proves that nothing takes the place of quality. 1941
Extra-bright. 1955
Face the day refreshed. 1939
Face the sun refreshed. 1941
Face Uncle Sam with a Coke in your hand. 1969
Favored above all others for refreshment. 1953
The favorite drink for ladies when thirsty, weary and despondent. 1905
Feel fit for what's ahead. 1934
Feel the difference. 1956
Flows from every fountain. 1905
For extra fun—take more than one! Take an extra carton of Coke! 1965
For headache and exhaustion, drink Coca-Cola. 1893
For headache or tired feeling. 1891
For headache or tired feeling summer or winter. 1890
For home and hospitality. 1951
For people on the go. 1954
For that tired, discouraged feeling—drink Coca-Cola. 1927
Foul-weather friend. 1969
The friendliest club in the world. 1946
The friendliest drink on earth. 1956
Friendliness and Coca-Cola go together, like bread and butter. 1946
A friendly hand no matter where you are. 1920
Friends for life. 1935
From a bottle through a straw. 1909
Fun gets better when you have a Coke. 1957
Fun to be thirsty. 1916
Get that look-alive, be-alive sparkle. 1962
Get the feel of wholesome refreshment. 1936
Get the genuine. 1906
Get the zest that refreshes best. 1960
Get-together club. 1947
Get together with refreshment. 1941
Get what you ask for and see that you get it. 1910
The gift for thirst. 1952
Gives a bright little lift. 1956
Gives so much and asks so little. 1937
A glass of Coke, a pair of straws and thou. 1969
The glass of fashion. 1926
The glass that answers the call of millions. 1919
The global high sign. 1944
Go better refreshed. 1963
Go with Coke. 1969
Good all the way down. 1905
Good food and Coca-Cola just naturally go together. 1951
Good taste is in fashion. 1957
Good things from nine climes poured into a single glass. 1920
Good to the last drop. 1908
Good with snacks. 1959
Good with so many good things. 1951
A gracious place in daily living. 1957
Graduate to Coke. 1963
The great national drink. 1907
The great temperance beverage—a liquid food for brain, body and nerves. 1906
Great to have on ice at home. 1922
Guaranteed under the Pure Food and Drug Act, June 30th, 1906, Serial #3324. 1906
A happy answer to thirst. 1932
Happy Days. 1910

Happy hour . . . have a Coke. 1947
Happy moment of hospitality. 1946
Happy pause for the youth of all ages. 1958
Happy sparkle of Coke. 1955
The happy symbol of a friendly way of life. 1945
Have a Coke and be happy. 1954
"Have a Coke" means . . . 1943
Have fun! Have a Coke! 1957
Heart's desire. 1916
Heed the little thirst—the big one surely takes care of itself. 1926
Help yourself to refreshment. 1950
Here's a Coke for you. 1961
Here's what you want—Coca-Cola. 1913
High sign of friendship. 1944
The high-sign of refreshment. 1929
The hit that saves the day. 1920
Hospitality at its best. 1953
Hospitality is in your hands. 1947
Host of the Highways. 1950
Hot foods call for ice-cold Coke! 1962
Ice-cold Coca-Cola has the taste that charms, and never cloys. 1940
Ice-cold Coca-Cola is everywhere else—it ought to be in your family refrigerator. 1934
Ice-cold every day in the year. 1939
Ice-cold sunshine. 1932
The ideal beverage for discriminating people. 1906
The ideal brain tonic. 1893
I love its flavor. 1902
The inspiring alliance—Coca-Cola, delicious, refreshing, and thirst quenching. 1918
An international passport to refreshment. 1945
In the distinctive bottle. 1924
Invitation to be happy. 1954
Invitation to pause . . . refresh! 1939
Is a delightful, palatable and healthful beverage. 1905
It answers every beverage requirement—vim, vigor, refreshment, wholesomeness. 1913
It had to be good to get where it is. 1925
It has the charm of purity. 1925
It invites a pause. 1933
It is a charming—healthful drink. 1906
It is always nourishing, refreshing, invigorating. More than 250 million bottles (glasses) used last year. For sale everywhere. (Western Coca-Cola Bottling Company, Chicago). 1908
It is the ideal beverage. 1906
It means so much—costs so little. 1932
It never fails to please. 1942
It satisfies. 1910
It satisfies thirst. 1919
It sustains because it is a true food. It refreshes because it has a slightly tonic effect on the system. It invigorates because it supplies the elements for physical and mental exertion. 1907
It will satisfy you. 1913
It's a lucky thirst that meets an ice-cold Coca-Cola. 1939
It's a refreshing little minute that's long enough for a big rest. 1940
It's always summer to your thirst. 1938
It's clean and pure, That's Sure! 1909
It's easy to relax with the pause that refreshes. 1947
It's fun to be thirsty when you can get a Coca-Cola. 1916
It's great to be thirsty when you know the answer. 1922
Its life and sparkle fit any occasion. 1939
It's part of the game to take "time out." 1938
Its taste holds the answer. 1939
It's the real thing (used with "Everybody welcomes Coca-Cola"). 1942
It's the refreshing thing to do. 1936
It's time to drink Coca-Cola. 1911
It's twice time. 1968
I've been thirsty, and I've been refreshed, and believe me refreshed is better. 1969
Just a drink . . . but what a drink! 1928
Just one glass will tell you. 1916
Life, liberty, and the pursuit of thirst. 1926
Lift that livens. 1962
A liquid food for brain, body and nerves. 1907
A little minute—a big rest. 1952
The little red sign at a cool and cheerful place. 1927
Make it a real meal. 1959
Make lunch-time refreshment time. 1939
Make mine a Coke. 1941
Make refreshment complete. 1956
Makes a little moment long enough for a big rest. 1929
Makes good things taste better. 1956
Makes travel more pleasant. 1939
March goes better with Coke. 1969
Matchless flavor. 1954
Matchless—that's Coke—matchless. 1954
Meet me at the soda fountain. 1930
Midsummer magic. 1953
A moment on the sunnyside. 1944
More than just a drink. 1933
The most asked-for soft drink in the world. 1954
The most delicious and refreshing of all summer drinks. Eminent scientists in every section of the country declare it to be no more harmful than tea or coffee. 1910
The most refreshing drink in the world. 1904
The national beverage—and yours. 1914
The national family drink. 1927
National thirst eliminator. 1969
A natural drink of natural flavors. 1926
A natural drink that answers natural thirst. 1919
A natural partner of good things to eat. 1932
Nature's purest and most wholesome drink. 1926
Nicknames encourage substitutions. 1914
No. 1 in the sun. 1969
No wonder Coke refreshes you best. 1960
Nothing like that great taste of Coke! 1956
Nothing refreshes like a Coke. 1943

Nothing soft about the taste of Coca-Cola. 1965
Old Santa says: "Me too." 1930
One little minute that's long enough for a big rest. 1927
One of the simple things that make living pleasant. 1941
Only Coca-Cola refreshes you best. 1962
Only Coke gives you that refreshing new feeling. 1962
The only thing like Coca-Cola is Coca-Cola itself. 1942
The package that gets a welcome at home. 1940
Palate pleasing. 1908
Park your thirst at the familiar red cooler. 1941
Part of the game. 1936
Passport to refreshment. 1945
Pass-words to a delightful experience. 1942
Pause and refresh yourself. 1924
Pause—Go Refreshed. 1944
Pause often, and always drink Coke. 1959
The pause that brings friends together. 1935
The pause that keeps you going. 1934
The pause that refreshes. 1929
People go better refreshed. 1964
People on the go . . . go for Coke. 1954
A perfect blend of many flavors—has a flavor all its own. 1929
A perfect blend of pure products from nature. 1923
A perfect drink—both nourishing and refreshing. 1907
The perfect gift for thirst. 1954
The perfect way to climax a happy occasion . . . to make any occasion happy. 1946
Physically sustaining, good to the taste, and an aid to the digestion. 1907
Pleasure all the way. 1952
Pre-eminently the drink of quality. 1906
Proves big help for tired housewives. 1909
Pure and healthful. 1904
Pure and wholesome. 1914
Pure and wholesome as it is tempting. 1912
Pure as sunlight. 1938
A pure drink of natural flavors. 1928
Quality carries on. 1942
Quality is the reason millions have made it theirs. 1919
The quality of Coca-Cola is a friendly quality you can always trust. 1947
Quality tells the difference. 1919
Quality you can trust. 1942
Quenches the thirst as nothing else can. 1910
Quenching thirst everywhere. 1922
Real satisfaction in every glass. 1911
Refresh—and add zest to the hour. 1950
Refresh yourself. 1923
Refreshes the weary, brightens the intellect, clears the brain. 1905
Refreshing as a morning breeze. 1935
Refreshing as a morning dip. 1935
Refreshing as a summer breeze—Invigorating as a dip in the sea. 1907
The refreshing custom. 1939
The refreshment of friends. 1953
Refreshment that can't be duplicated. 1942
Refreshment the whole world prefers. 1958
Refreshment through the years. 1951
Refreshment time. 1925
Refreshment with the lively-going taste. 1962
Relax refreshed. 1959
Relax with Coke. 1960
Relax with the pause that refreshes. 1947
Relieves fatigue. 1906
Relieves fatigue and calms overwrought nerves without undue stimulation. 1907
Relieves fatigue and is indispensable for business and professional men, students, wheelmen and athletes. 1905
Relieves fatigue of brain, body and nerves. 1909
Relieves mental and physical exhaustion. 1891
Relieves spring fever. 1969
Restful and bracing. 1906
Restores energy. 1906
Revive with Coke. 1960
Right off the ice—Coca-Cola. 1910
Right through the year the best beverage. 1911
The satisfactory beverage. 1908
Satisfied (Western Coca-Cola Bottling Company, Chicago). 1906
Satisfies the thirst and pleases the palate. 1907
Satisfies the thirsty and helps the weary. 1905
The Satisfying Beverage. 1912
See you at the beach. 1969
Serve Ice Cold with sandwiches, cookies, cheese and crackers, and with your meals. 1931
Serving Coca-Cola says you do things right. 1956
Serving Coca-Cola serves hospitality. 1947
Shoppers and Business Men—tired people and thirsty people—nerve worn and brain weary people—people who just like to tickle the palate occasionally with a delicious beverage—all classes, ages and sexes—Drink Coca-Cola. 1909
Sign of good taste. 1957
Simply Delicious. 1909
Sip and see: Coke refreshes you best! 1962
Sip and zip! 1962
Six keys to the popularity of Coca-Cola: Taste, Purity, Refreshing, Sociability, The Nickel, Thirst. 1927
So easily served. 1910
So easy to serve . . . and so inexpensive. 1937
So easy to take home—the six-bottle carton. 1938
So good in taste, in such good taste. 1957
So right, so bright. 1962
The sociability of thirst. 1925
The sociable drink. 1925
Sold everywhere—5¢. 1907
Sold in bottles. 1905
Solutions go better refreshed. 1964
Something more than a *soft* drink. 1965

Something more than mere thirst-slaking. 1906
Sparkling—harmless as water, and crisp as frost. 1908
Specific for Headache. 1893
The spirit of hospitality is in the life and sparkle of ice-cold Coca-Cola. 1948
The standard beverage. 1915
A star drink, Morning, Evening, Night. At home or Abroad, Travelling or Resting. Working or Recreating. 1904
Stay merry—refresh with Coke. 1964
Step into the nearest place and ask for a Coca-Cola. 1907
Stop at the red sign. 1926
Stop at the red sign and refresh yourself. 1925
Stop for a pause . . . go refreshed. 1937
A stop that belongs on your daily time-table. 1941
Strengthens the nerves. 1906
Summer goes better with Coke. 1969
Summertime goodness for winter thirst. 1925
Sure way to get a big smile—get Coke in the picture. 1964
Talk about refreshing. 1943
A taste all its own. 1943
Taste is the lure in ice-cold Coca-Cola. 1935
The taste is the test. 1919
The taste is the test of the Coca-Cola quality. 1917
Taste the difference. 1956
A taste thrill. 1932
Tells your taste to go fly a kite. 1968
That extra something. 1943
That extra something—you can spot it every time. 1943
That taste-good feeling. 1939
That's for me. 1945
There never was a thirst that Coca-Cola couldn't satisfy. 1912
There's a delicious freshness to the flavor of Coca-Cola. 1917
There's a refreshing little minute on the sunny side of things. 1942
There's money in it (Coca-Cola Bottling Company, San Antonio). 1909
There's no drink so easy to get. 1930
There's nothing like it when you're thirsty. 1923
There's nothing like that great taste of Coke! 1956
There's this about Coke. 1954
Things go better with Coke. 1963
Things would have gone better with Coke. 1969
Think of lunchtime as refreshment time. 1948
Thirst and taste for Coca-Cola are the same thing. 1926
Thirst asks nothing more. 1938
Thirst can't be denied. 1922
Thirst come—thirst served. 1932
Thirst is a touch of nature which makes the whole world kin. 1924
Thirst is discriminating. 1925
Thirst knows no season. 1922
Thirst quencher. 1950
Thirst-quenching—delicious and refreshing. 1906
Thirst reminds you—drink Coca-Cola. 1922
Thirst stops here. 1939
Thirst tells you when. 1938
Thirst—the natural call for refreshment. 1925
Thirst, too, seeks quality. 1950
The thirsty one's best beverage. 1914
This is the time for real refreshment. 1965
This is when you want something more than a soft drink. Nothing soft about the taste of Coca-Cola . . . lifts your spirits . . . boosts your energy. 1965
365 shopping days. 1926
Three million a day. 1917
Through all the years since 1886. 1936
Time for a pause—have a Coca-Cola. 1947
A toast to health and happiness. 1906
Travel where you may, they [Coca-Colas] are never more than a thirst apart. 1925
Treat yourself right. 1931
Try it just once and you will know why. 1940
Universal symbol of the American way of life. 1943
Universally popular, always reliable, tested by time and proved good. 1914
Unmistakably Coke. 1956
Unvarying quality. 1954
The upper hand on thirst. 1952
Water when boiled and filtered will do to bathe in or even drink if it costs nothing, but if you have to buy it, get a drink which has something to it more than mere dampness. Get Coca-Cola (Western Coca-Cola Bottling Company, Chicago). 1906
Wave after wave—drink after drink. 1968
A welcome addition to any party—any time—anyplace. 1913
Welcome as springtime. 1959
What a refreshing new feeling you get from Coke. 1960
What refreshment ought to be. 1936
What you want is a Coke. 1952
When it's hard to get started, start with a Coca-Cola. 1934
When thirst comes home to you. 1922
When thirsty, tired or head-achey, or after a night out try a Coca-Cola High Ball. It hits the spot (Western Coca-Cola Bottling Company, Chicago). 1906
When tired Coca-Cola will refresh you: Head-achey, help you; Nervous, relieve you; Thirsty, fill you (Western Coca-Cola Bottling Company, Chicago). 1906
When you feel all hot and sticky and tired and "head-achy," when the life and energy seems to be oozing out of your pores with each drop of perspiration and it just seems you can't go a step further or do a lick more of work, step into any place and Drink a Bottle of COCA-COLA. You'll wonder first thing who turned on the cool wave—your headache will disappear—that nervous, exhausted feeling will be replaced by a gen-

eral all 'round "brace up," the rough spots will be smoothed out of your temper and you'll feel refreshed and exhilarated. The great temperance, tonic beverage for men, women and children—now try a bottle today. 1910

When you get a good thirst—treat it right. 1923

When you need something more than a *soft* drink . . . Coca-Cola. 1965

Whenever you hear "Have a Coke," you hear the voice of America. 1945

Whenever you see an arrow think of Coca-Cola. 1909

Where there's Coca-Cola there's hospitality. 1948

Wherever Ginger Ale, Seltzer or Soda is Good—Coca-Cola is Better—Try it (Western Coca-Cola Bottling Company, Chicago). 1908

Wherever you go, north, east, south or west, you will find Coca-Cola. 1911

Wherever you go you'll find Coca-Cola. 1905

Which?—Coca-Cola or Goldelle Ginger Ale (Western Coca-Cola Bottling Company, Chicago). 1903

Whoever you are, whatever you do, wherever you may be, when you think of refreshment think of ice-cold Coca-Cola. 1939

Wholesome bit of energy. 1955

Why Grow Thirsty. 1945

With a drink so good . . . 'tis folly to be thirsty. 1925

With a taste all its own—It's the Real Thing. 1942

Within easy reach of your thirst. 1940

The wonderful nerve and brain tonic and remarkable therapeutic agent. 1890

Work refreshed. 1948

The world's friendliest club. 1946

Yes. 1946

You can't think of "delicious" or "refreshing" without thinking of Coca-Cola. 1919

You come up smiling for a fresh start. 1931

You taste its quality. 1951

You taste the quality. 1941

You'll enjoy it too. 1923

You'll go better refreshed. 1964

Young America loves it. 1954

Your thirst takes wings when you treat it to an ice-cold Coca-Cola. 1940

Zing! Refreshing New Feeling. 1962

APPENDIX C

ARTISTS WHOSE WORKS APPEAR IN THE ADVERTISING FOR COCA-COLA

The following is a partial listing of artists who have produced advertising art for The Coca-Cola Company between the years 1920 and 1950. The artists listed may provide collectors and historians with some dating information for signed art.

Harry Anderson
McClelland Barclay
Joseph Binder
Al Buell
Pruett Carter
Dean Cornwell
Bradshaw Crandall
Stevan Dohanos
Albert Dorne
Harvey Dunn
Gillett Elvgrin
James Montgomery Flagg
Frank Godwin
Hananiah Harari
Hayden Hayden (Howard Renwick)
Charles Heizerling
Everett Henry
Andrew Loomis
Lougheed
Athos Menaboni
Fred Mizen
Norman Price
Redoute
Norman Rockwell
Georges Schreiber
Lyman Simpson
Robert Skemp
Ben Stahl
Frederic Stanley
Haddon Sundblom
Thorton Utz
Mortimer Wilson
Jack Witrup
N. C. Wyeth

The original art for much of Coca-Cola's advertising has either been retained by The Coca-Cola Company itself or given to bottlers. Collectors cannot expect to obtain much original art, but some pieces have found their way into private collections. This is the original Haddon Sundblom oil "Yachting Girl." This canvas was given to the Coca-Cola Bottling Company of San Diego, California, during the 1969 bottlers' convention and hangs in their private museum of memorabilia.

APPENDIX D

COMPANIES THAT SPECIALIZED IN CHROMO-LITHOGRAPHIC PRINTING ON METAL ADVERTISING ITEMS

The following is a *partial* listing of some of the largest firms involved in the chromo-lithographic printing on metal trays, signs, and the like. Some Coca-Cola artifacts made of metal bear the name of the firm that did the printing; the information provided can be used as an aid in dating any metal advertising item so identified.

1887–1901:	The Tuscarora Advertising Company (Coshocton, Ohio)
1888–1901:	The Standard Advertising Company (Coshocton, Ohio)
1901–1905:	The Meek and Beach Company (Coshocton, Ohio). This firm, in 1901, purchased both the Tuscarora Advertising Company and the Standard Advertising Company.
1901–1909:	The Meek Company (Coshocton, Ohio)
1901–present:	The H. D. Beach Company (Coshocton, Ohio)
1909–1950:	American Art Works (Coshocton, Ohio). This firm was formerly called the Meek Company.
1890–1935:	Charles W. Shonk Manufacturing and Lithograph Company (Chicago, Illinois)
1890–1970:	Kaufmann & Strauss (New York City)
1901–present:	American Can Company
1930–1950:	American Colortype Company (Newark, New Jersey). Advertising printed by this firm is marked "A.C.Co."

SELECTED BIBLIOGRAPHY

BOOKS

Chronological History of the Coca-Cola Company, 1886–1971. Atlanta, Georgia: Public Relations Department, The Coca-Cola Company.

Clymer, Floyd. *Scrapbook of Early Advertising Art.* New York: Bonanza Books, 1955.

Cope, Jim. *Collectible Old Advertising.* Orange, Texas: Privately printed, 1971.

———. *Soda Water Advertising.* Orange, Texas: Privately printed, 1971.

Garrett, Franklin. *Coca-Cola, A Chronological History: 1886–1965.* Atlanta, Georgia: Public Relations Department, The Coca-Cola Company.

Gentry, J. Roy. *A Layman's Comments on Dental Caries.* Atlanta, Georgia: The Coca-Cola Company, 1957.

Griffenhagen, George B. *Private Die Proprietary Medicine Stamps.* Milwaukee, Wisconsin: American Topical Association, 1969.

Kahn, E. J., Jr. *The Big Drink.* New York: Random House, 1960.

Kurtz, Wilbur G., Jr. *A Catalog of Metal Service Trays and Art Plates Since 1898.* Atlanta, Georgia: Archives, The Coca-Cola Company, 1970.

Martin, Milward W. *Twelve Full Ounces.* New York: Holt, Rinehart and Winston, 1962.

Matthews, J. B., and Shalleross, R. E. *Partners in Plunder.* New York: Grosset & Dunlap, 1935.

Munsey, Cecil. *The Illustrated Guide to Collecting Bottles.* New York: Hawthorn Books, 1970.

———. *Would You Believe?* San Diego, California: I.P.S., 1968.

Muzio, Jack. *Collectible Tin Advertising Trays.* Santa Rosa, California: Privately printed, 1972.

Romance of Coca-Cola, The. Atlanta, Georgia: The Coca-Cola Company, 1916.

Rowsome, Frank, Jr. *They Laughed When I Sat Down.* New York: Bonanza Books, 1959.

This Is Your Company. Atlanta, Georgia: The Coca-Cola Company, 1966.

Turner, E. S. *The Shocking History of Advertising.* London: Michael Joseph, 1952.

MAGAZINES

Adams, Charles W. "Letting the Genie Out of the Bottle," *Nation's Business*, LVIII (January, 1970), 64–65.

"Ads for Coca-Cola Bottlers Win Award," *Editor and Publisher*, XCI (September 13, 1958), 44.

"Ads in France Post Coca-Cola as Different Drink," *Advertising Age*, XXIX (November 24, 1958), 22.

"Ad Opportunities for Pepsi and Coke (Test Marketing of Alcoa Aluminum Containers That Hold $2^1/_2$ Gallons)," *Editor and Publisher*, XCVIII (July 17, 1965), 19.

Bell, Lawrence. "Man of Achievement: Robert W. Woodruff," *Forbes*, August 15, 1947, pp. 16–17.

Boroson, Warren. "A Was for Aspirin," *Pageant*, March, 1963.

"Bottle Cap Contest Most Successful, Coke Reports," *Advertising Age*, XXXIII (July 9, 1962), 34.

"Can Orange Juice Fit Pause That Refreshes? (Coke Wants to Sell Orange Juice Like Soft Drink)," *Business Week*, July 25, 1964, p. 100.

"Cap Corks Cover Coke Contest Clues in Cleveland Caper," *Advertising Age*, XXX (February 9, 1959), 26.

"Change That Refreshes, The," *Forbes*, XCII (September 1, 1963), 25–26.

"Coca-Cola—Always a Bargain?", *Financial World*, CXXX (August 14, 1968), 14.

"Coca-Cola: Beware of Maginot Lines," *Forbes*, CIV (January 1, 1970), 35.

Coca-Cola Bottler, The (50th Anniversary Issue), Vol. LI, No. 1 (April, 1959).

"Coca-Cola Calls Double-TV Formation Against Soft Drink Rivals," *Broadcasting*, LXIII (October 15, 1962), 34.

"Coca-Cola Company, The," *Forbes*, C (August 1, 1967), 26–34.

"Coca-Cola Fills Out Its Shape," *Investor's Reader* (Merrill Lynch, Pierce, Fenner & Smith, Inc.), XLIV, No. 10 (May 19, 1965), 19–23.

"Coca-Cola Industry, The," *Fortune*, XVIII, No. 6 (December, 1938), 64–67.

"Coca-Cola Gets Tie-in Push with Ice Cream Group," *Advertising Age*, XXXIII (June 11, 1962), 64.

"Coca-Cola Goes Big for Food," *Printers' Ink*, CCLXXXVI (February 7, 1964), 10.

"Coca-Cola Hikes Sweeps Budget to $2,500,000," *Advertising Age*, XXXIV (April 8, 1963), 3.

"Coca-Cola Life Advertisement Affirms Ownership of Coke Trademark," *Advertising Age*, XXXIII (August 27, 1962), 10.

"Coca-Cola Moves to Franchise Israel's Bottler After Dispute," *Advertising Age*, XXXVII (April 25, 1966), 177.

"Coca-Cola Packaging Pacemakers," *Modern Packaging*, XXXIX (January, 1966), 102–105.

"Coca-Cola Plans Spring Drive for [World's] Fair Promotion," *Advertising Age*, XXXV (March 16, 1964), 117.

"Coca-Cola Plans $3,000,000 7-week Multiple-sale Push," *Advertising Age*, XXXVI (March 15, 1965), 143.

"Coca-Cola Plans Two-Pronged Advertising Drive for Tab," *Advertising Age*, XXXV (March 2, 1964), 118.

"Coca-Cola Promotion; More Gains for Grocers," *Printers' Ink*, CCLXII (January 31, 1958), 22.

"Coca-Cola Schedules Heaviest Advertising Barrage," *Advertising Age*, XXX (February 23, 1959), 3.

"Coca-Cola Sells Business Paper Advertisements for New Dispenser," *Advertising Age*, XXIX (December 1, 1958), 38.

"Coca-Cola Spans Seasons in Massive Preprint Campaign," *Advertising Age*, XXXV (September 21, 1964), 1.

"Coca-Cola's Story—Things Go Better with Broadcast," *Sponsor*, XX (April 18, 1966), 56–57.

"Coca-Cola to Use Winter Picnic Push," *Advertising Age*, XXXVI (December 27, 1965), 59.

"Coca-Cola Wreaks Postal Havoc via Bottle Cap Deal; Automatic Cancelers Upset," *Advertising Age*, XXXIII (June 25, 1962), 10.

"Coke Adds to Teen Appeal Jingle Singers," *Advertising Age*, XXXVI (October 11, 1965), 19.

"Coke Advertising Effort at All Time High," *Advertising Age*, XXXIII (May 14, 1962), 30.

"Coke Again Puts $3,000,000 Behind Warm Weather Push," *Advertising Age*, XXXVII (April 11, 1966), 142.

"Coke and Pepsi Gird for the Non-cola Bottle," *Sales Management*, LXXXV (December 2, 1960), 85.

"Coke's Boast; Tops in Low-calorie, Too," *Printers' Ink*, CCLXXXVI (March 6, 1964), 11.

"Coke Bottlers Tie In with Arnold Palmer Ranges in Contest," *Advertising Age*, XXXVI (June 28, 1965), 64.

"Coke's Fanta Unit Is Testing Fresca in Two Areas; New Green-bottle Drink Pushed as Low Calorie Mixer," *Advertising Age*, XXXVI (July 26, 1965), 4.

"Coke's Formula: Keep the Image Fresh," *Business Week*, April 25, 1970, pp. 66–67.

"Coke in One-way Glass," *Modern Packaging*, XXXV (July, 1962), 114.

"Coke Launches Drive on Spritz Sound of Sprite," *Advertising Age*, XXXVII (January 10, 1966), 1.

"Coke Lifts Its Sights," *Financial World*, CXXI (February 19, 1964), 10–11.

"Coke Makes Switch to a New Staff Set-up," *Business Week*, November 20, 1965, p. 128.

"Coke, Pepsi Rush to Introduce New Aluminum Kegs," *Advertising Age*, XXXVI (July 5, 1965), 2.

"Coke Plans Preprint Xmas Promotion," *Editor and Publisher*, XCV (June 30, 1962), 17.

"Coke Refreshes Ads to Regain Profit Norm as Sociable Pepsi Hosts a Mounting Market," *Printers' Ink*, CCLXVI (February 13, 1959), 44–45.

"Coke, Royal Crown Testing Multi Packs (Plastic Carriers)," *Printers' Ink*, CCXCI (November 26, 1965), 60–61.

"Coke Seeks to Boost Efficiency of Its Export Ads," *Advertising Age*, XXXIII (June 25, 1962), 10.

"Coke Sets Sports Specials on TV in 1966 Media Mix," *Advertising Age*, XXXVII (February 7, 1966), 107.

"Coke's Test of Flip-off Cap," *Modern Packaging*, XXXVIII (March, 1965), 154–155.

"Coke: The Most Exciting Radio Buy of the Year (Teenagers Go for Hi Fi Clubs)," *Sponsor*, XIII (May 30, 1959), 29–31.

"Coke to Offer Ideas for Decorations in Holiday Promotion," *Advertising Age*, XXXVI (September 20, 1965), 52.

"Coke Tries New Ways to Refresh," *Business Week*, August 24, 1963, pp. 100–114.
"Cola in Plastic: The Race to Be First," *Packaging Design*, March/April, 1970, pp. 28–29.
Day, C. "With Coke, Things Go Better and Better," *Sales Management*, XCIV (April 16, 1965), 28–31.
"Devastating Hold of 'Cola' on American Life, The," *Better Nutrition*, March, 1970, pp. 12–13.
Dietz, Lawrence. "Soda Pop Art," *West* (Supplement to the *Los Angeles Times*), February 9, 1969, pp. 9–14.
"Fanta Under Coke Roof," *Advertising Age*, XXXVI (August 9, 1965), 1.
"Farley Denies Coke Backs Arab Boycott of Land of Israel," *Advertising Age*, XXXVII (April 18, 1966), 54.
Fox, J. M. "How Will the FF Industry Be Affected by Coca-Cola–Minute Maid Merger?," *Quick Frozen Foods*, XXIII (October, 1960), 325–326.
Garrett, Franklin M. "Those Coca-Cola Collectibles," *The Antiques Journal*, XXIII, No. 7 (July, 1968), 16–18.
"Has Coke Changed Image?," *Advertising Age*, XXX (October 12, 1959), 98.
"Have a Coke, World," *Newsweek*, January 3, 1972, p. 47.
"How Coca-Cola Sways Youth Music," *Editor and Publisher*, XCII (December 5, 1959), 30.
Hunt, P. R. "Warm Coca-Cola Is Appreciated in Britain," *Advertising Age*, XXXIII (May 14, 1962), 30.
"Its Bottle Becomes Coca-Cola's Trademark," *Modern Packaging*, July, 1960.
Jackson, W. S. "Coca-Cola Company; Common Stock Analysis," *Junior Bankers' Monthly*, LXXIX (December, 1962), 40.
Leigh, K. "Coca-Cola Still the Leader with Pepsi-Cola the Challenger," *Magazine of Wall Street*, CV (February 13, 1960), 576–578.
Lunsford, Julius R., Jr. "Good-Will in Trade Marks: Coca-Cola and Coke," *The Coca-Cola Bottler*, March, 1955.
McGill, Ralph. "Bob Woodruff: Symbol of the 'American Way,'" *Refresher*, December, 1953.
———. "The Multimillionaire Nobody Knows," *Saturday Evening Post*, CCXXIII, No. 45, 26–28.
———. "Robert W. Woodruff," *The Atlanta Journal and Constitution Magazine*, August 19, 1956.
Mackey, W. C., Jr. "Coke Meets Its Goal," *Broadcasting*, LXVI (June 29, 1964), 46.
"Marketing Realignment at Coca-Cola," *Editor and Publisher*, XCVIII (August 21, 1965), 18.
Momentum, The Magazine of The Coca-Cola Company, Worldwide, Vols. I, II, and III (1969), Vol. I (1970).
Morrison, Joseph L. "The Soda Fountain," *American Heritage*, XIII, No. 5 (August, 1962), 10–19.
Munsey, Cecil. "Coca-Cola," *Western Collector*, IX, Nos. 1 & 2 (January/February, 1971), 26–35.
———. "Coca-Cola, Part I: A Refreshing Taste of Americana," *Western Collector*, V, No. 8 (August, 1957), 12–17.
———. "Coca-Cola, Part II: The World's Most Famous Bottle," *Western Collector*, V, No. 9 (September, 1967), 41–46.
———. "Discovery of Coins and [Private Die Proprietary Revenue] Stamps," *Western Collector*, VI, No. 5 (May, 1968), 39–43.
———. "Gold Coca-Cola Bottles," *Western Collector*, VI, No. 7 (July, 1968), 50.
———. "It's Time We Mentioned Clocks," *Western Collector*, VIII, No. 11 (November, 1970), 42.
Muzio, Gloria and Jack. "It's Fun to Collect Old Advertising Trays," *The Antique Trader*, XV, Issue 40 (October 5, 1971), 1–2.
"New Peaks for Coke," *Financial World*, CXXV (March 30, 1966), 11.
"Nickel Drink Is Groggy, The," *Fortune*, January, 1951, pp. 78–79.
"Packaging Pacemarkers," *Modern Packaging*, January, 1966.
"Pageant of Coca-Cola Packaging," *Packaging Digest*, VIII, No. 8 (August, 1971), 14.
"Pants Fling for Coke, A," *Investor's Reader*, L (July 7, 1971), 28–29.
Pause for Living, Vol. X, No. 3 (Spring, 1964); Vol. XII, No. 2 (Winter, 1965–1966); Vol. XIII, No. 1 (Autumn, 1966); Vol. XIII, No. 2 (Winter, 1966–1967); Vol. XIV, No. 3 (Spring, 1968); Vol. XIV, No. 4 (Summer, 1968); Vol. XV, No. 1 (Autumn, 1968); Vol. XV, No. 4 (Summer, 1969).
Price, L. "Coke Is Most Advertised Product in the World: '57 Budgets Hit $40,000,000," *Advertising Age*, XXIX (June 9, 1958), 84.
Refresher, Magazine of The Coca-Cola Company, The (75th Anniversary Edition), 1961.
Renspie, R. G. "Coca-Cola Does Not Sell Itself; Tells Plan That Does," *Advertising Age*, XXXII (February 6, 1961), 105.
Schuyler, P. W. "Coke Bottlers Call Preprints Smash Hit," *Editor and Publisher*, XCV (June 16, 1962), 17.
Sinclair, F. "Things Go Better with Coke Is Motif of Coca-Cola's New Advertising," *Advertising Age*, XXXIV (August 26, 1963), 1.
Strout, C. K. "Investment Audit of Coca-Cola Company—Great Company That Continues to Forge Ahead Both at Home and Abroad," *Magazine of Wall Street*, CXIII (December 14, 1963), 302–305.
"Sun Never Sets on Coca-Cola, The," *Time*, LV, No. 20 (May 15, 1950), 28–32.
"Teenagers and Tastemaking; Coca-Cola Franchisers Use Radio to Round Up Market," *Broadcasting*, LVI (June 1, 1959), 85.
"This Is Coca-Cola?," *Business Week*, October 8, 1960, p. 80.
"To Pause and Be Refreshed," *Fortune*, IV, No. 1 (July, 1931), 65–67.
Toffler, A. "Competition That Refreshes," *Fortune*, LXIII (May, 1961), 124–128.

Townsend, James L. "Robert Woodruff of Coca-Cola," *Atlanta Magazine*, June, 1963, pp. 70–73.

"Use Honor Plan for Bottler Returns, Coke Ads Advise Retailers," *Advertising Age*, XXXV (January 27, 1964), 4.

Weiner, J. B. "Why Things Go Better at Coke," *Dun's Review and Modern Industry*, LXXXVIII (October, 1966), 28–30.

Wharton, Don. "Coca-Cola: Its Fame and Fortune," *The Reader's Digest*, L, No. 302 (June, 1947), 33–37.

NEWSPAPERS

Because of the specialized nature of the following references, they will be presented in chronological order instead of the more standard alphabetical order.

"Coca-Cola Company Sold to New York Interest," *The New York Times*, August 1, 1919, page 17, column 6.

"Coca-Cola of Delaware—Sold to Trust Company of Georgia," *The New York Times*, August 22, 1919, 16:2.

"Coca-Cola of Delaware—Sold to Trust Company of Georgia," *The New York Times*, August 23, 1919, 13:3.

"Coca-Cola Wins Suit to Protect COKE Trademark," *The New York Times*, December 7, 1920, 20:7.

"Coca-Cola Company—Supreme Court Petitioned by KOKE Company," *The New York Times*, January 4, 1921, 8:4.

"Coca-Cola President C. H. Candler Denies Starting Action to Dissolve Voting Trust Agreement," *The New York Times*, October 29, 1921, 21:4.

"Coca-Cola Wins Suit to Restrain Old Dominion Beverage Company from Using TAKOLA," *The New York Times*, June 14, 1922, 24:3.

"Coca-Cola of Canada Organized," *The New York Times*, December 23, 1923, 20:2.

"U. S. Government Files Income Tax Suit Against Coca-Cola," *The New York Times*, May 28, 1924, 36:2.

"Coca-Cola Company Control Rests in Open Market as Result of Coca-Cola International Corporation Listing on N.Y. Stock Exchange," *The New York Times*, April 16, 1926, 38:6.

"Coca-Cola International Corporation Merger with Canada Dry Off," *The New York Times*, May 10, 1928, 40:4.

"Coca-Cola in History," *The New York Times*, March 14, 1929, 26:3.

"Coca-Cola Company—R. W. Woodruff, President," *The New York Times*, October 3, 1929, 41:3.

"Coca-Cola Company Settles Tax Suit for $1,000,000," *The New York Times*, October 16, 1929, 48:3.

"Coca-Cola Counterfeit Ring, Which Cost Company More Than $100,000 in Past Year, Raided in Bronx," *The New York Times*, April 18, 1931, 15:8.

"Coca-Cola Stockholders Approve Domestication of Company in Georgia," *The New York Times*, November 18, 1931, 38:5.

"Coca-Cola Sues Loft, Inc., and Happiness Candy Stores, Inc., to Bar Sales of Substitute for Coca-Cola; Is Sued by Pepsi-Cola Company for $2,000,000 Damages," *The New York Times*, May 5, 1932, 30:2.

"The Mirror Files Suits Asking $1,250,000 for Alleged Interference with Sale of Pepsi-Cola," *The New York Times*, May 13, 1932, 28:7.

"Coca-Cola Company Sued by Happiness Candy Stores, Inc., for $2,500,000," *The New York Times*, May 19, 1932, 17:2.

"Court Throws Out Four Suits of Happiness, Mirror and Loft for $10,000,000; Refuses to Dismiss Three Libel Suits for $250,000 Each," *The New York Times*, July 15, 1932, 28:2.

"Court Decision That Company Must Answer Libel Suits by Loft, Inc., & Mirror," *The New York Times*, October 22, 1932, 6:6.

"Wilmington, Delaware, Court Dismisses Suit Against Happiness, Inc., & Loft, Inc.," *The New York Times*, June 7, 1933, 29:1.

"Coca-Cola Company Rehearsing for Suit Against Loft & Happiness Denied," *The New York Times*, August 10, 1933, 37:5.

"Coca-Cola Company to Change from Operating to Holding Company; Operating Subsidiary to be Formed," *The New York Times*, December 28, 1933, 30:2.

"Annual Meeting of Bottlers; $6,000,000 to Spend on Advertising in 1934," *The New York Times*, January 23, 1934, 31:2.

"Mrs. L. P. Evans Elected to Board, R. W. Woodruff Re-elected President," *The New York Times*, March 20, 1934, 41:1.

"S. F. Boykin Elected President of Atlanta Company," *The New York Times*, October 3, 1934, 36:5.

"B. Haimowitz, J. Haimowitz, L. Ash, & J. Perloff Serve Sentences for Violation of Trademark Law in Making Spurious Coca-Cola Syrup," *The New York Times*, December 29, 1934, 7:1.

"No Charge to Follow Dropping of Georgia Charter," *The New York Times*, May 8, 1935, 31:2.

"Court Upholds Denial of Injunction Against Loft & Happiness, Inc.," *The New York Times*, May 14, 1935, 36:7.

"Coca-Cola Company Sues Four Companies for Alleged Infringement of Traderights," *The New York Times*, November 28, 1935, 41:5.

"Coca-Cola Company Gives Employees One Month Extra Pay in Celebration of 50th Anniversary; and Declares Extra Dividend," *The New York Times*, November 18, 1936, 20:3.
"T. Jones Resigns as Vice-Pres. in Charge of Marketing," *The New York Times*, May 5, 1937, 45:4.
"Coca-Cola Company Rents 1st Concession & Exhibit Space at N.Y. World's Fair," *The New York Times*, January 17, 1938, 21:7.
"Coca-Cola Company Replies to Injunction Suit by Pepsi-Cola Company," *The New York Times*, September 20, 1928, 2:4.
"Pepsi-Cola Company of Canada Charged with Tradename Infringement," *The New York Times*, July 27, 1938, 13:4.
"Coke's Big with Memorabilia Buffs," Atlanta *Constitution*, December 11, 1970, 12-B.
"Coke: Atlanta's Money Tree," *The New York Times*, January 10, 1971.

INDEX

FREE PUBLIC LIBRARY UNION NEW JERSEY
3 9549 00049 4071